SALVATION

Crystal Clear

SALVATION
Crystal Clear

DR. CURTIS HUTSON

SWORD of the LORD
PUBLISHERS
P. O. BOX 1099, MURFREESBORO, TN 37133

ISBN 0-87398-806-X

SECOND PRINTING: January, 1989

PRINTED AND BOUND IN THE UNITED STATES OF AMERICA

Foreword

The most important message in the world is the Gospel. When Jesus instructed His followers to go into all the world and preach, He did not leave them on their own to choose the message. He said in Mark 16:15, "Go ye into all the world, and preach the gospel to every creature." The Gospel is the one message the Lord wants every creature in the world to hear. This wonderful message is described in I Corinthians 15 as the death, burial and resurrection of Christ. Jesus died for our sins, the sins of the whole world. He was buried, and after three days and nights God raised Him from the dead to show His satisfaction with the payment Jesus made for our sins. And one is saved simply by trusting Jesus Christ.

We have often heard preachers say of a certain town, "This place is gospel-hardened"; but in our experience of traveling throughout the country and preaching in revivals, Bible conferences and Sword of the Lord Conferences on Revival and Soul Winning, we have discovered that for the most part people are more gospel-ignorant than gospel-hardened. Many preachers confuse grace and works, teaching that one is saved by trusting Christ as Saviour plus something else—plus good works, plus baptism, plus reformation, etc.

Paul said in Galatians 1:6-8, "I marvel that ye are so soon removed from him that called you into the grace of Christ unto another gospel: Which is not another; but there be some that trouble you, and would pervert the gospel of Christ. But though we, or an angel from heaven, preach any other gospel unto you than that which we have preached unto you, let him be accursed [damned]."

The Gospel is salvation by grace through faith in Christ and His finished work. Another gospel is adding anything to the finished work of Christ on the cross such as baptism, works, reformation, etc.

An old preacher, after lecturing to a group of young ministerial students, was asked to give one word of advice. He replied, "My preacher brothers, make it plain to men how they are to be saved."

In these messages, we have worked at making salvation plain as day. The author has never preached one of these sermons without someone trusting Christ as Saviour. Literally thousands have been won to Christ with these simple, clear gospel messages. As many as 684 have trusted Christ as Saviour in a single service when one of these messages was preached.

These are sermons that win souls. It is our prayer that preachers will use them to the winning of multiplied thousands to Christ and that Christians everywhere will use the truths and illustrations in these messages to win souls.

Dr. Curtis Hutson
Editor, SWORD OF THE LORD

Introduction

The greatest preacher that I have ever heard on the subject of salvation is Dr. Curtis Hutson.

If I had an unsaved loved one who would agree to hear only one preacher preach one sermon, I would ask him to hear Dr. Curtis Hutson preach on the subject of salvation.

If the world's population would agree to view one sermon on worldwide television, I would want that sermon to be on the subject of salvation, and I would want Dr. Curtis Hutson to preach it.

If I could plan a great Bible conference and compel every preacher of the Gospel to attend, I would invite Dr. John R. Rice to preach on prayer; Dr. Bob Jones, Sr., to preach on Christian character; Brother Lester Roloff to preach on faith; Dr. G. B. Vick to preach on the church; Dr. R. G. Lee to preach on Heaven; Dr. Lee Roberson to preach on total surrender; and Dr. Curtis Hutson to preach on salvation.

When my beloved friend explains the way to Heaven, God's gift never seems so free, Jesus' price never seems so paid, assurance never seems so sure, the DO never seems so DONE, works never seem so helpless and God's offer of salvation never seems so available.

As I read this manuscript I found myself saying over and over again, "Why didn't I think of that?" With profound discernment Dr. Hutson makes simple the greatest story ever told!

This book simply HAD to be written, and Dr. Curtis Hutson HAD to write it. Preaching on salvation is to Dr. Hutson what "Payday Someday" was to Dr. R. G. Lee; what "Sinners in the Hands of an Angry God" was to Jonathan Edwards; what "The New Birth" was to George Whitefield; and what "Prayer: Asking and Receiving" was to Dr. John R. Rice.

I can remember many of the times when Dr. Rice and I would sit across the table from each other and discuss the future of THE SWORD OF THE LORD and wonder together in whose hands that future would be held. Thank God, now that that future is present, it is in the dedicated and capable hands of Curtis Hutson. He has caught the mantle and worn it well. He has used it to part many of the same "Jordans" that his predecessor parted. As editor, he has been willing to share the present with the past and has refused to quench even a little of the flow of truth that came from the lips and pen of Dr. John R. Rice.

So, here it is—salvation presented in its purity. Read it. Share it. Put it in the hands of preachers so they can make it plain. Put it in the hands of the unsaved so that they can see it plainly. Put it in the hands of God's children so that they can rejoice in the reality of God's grace while remembering that wonderful day when the Holy Spirit showed to them through human instrumentality "so great salvation."

On these pages the Holy Spirit once again uses a yielded instrument to make clear the most important thing in the world that man must see. Thank God!

Dr. Jack Hyles

Table of Contents

Chapter 1

Salvation Plain and Simple

"And that from a child thou hast known the holy scriptures, which are able to make thee wise unto salvation through faith which is in Christ Jesus." —II Tim. 3:15.

Salvation is the most important thing in the world, both now and hereafter. If you are not saved, nothing else really matters.

An old man and a little boy were out together for a boat ride. As they rode across the lake, a beautiful leaf came floating by. Taking the leaf in his hand, the old man asked, "Son, do you know anything about botany?"

"No, Sir," replied the boy.

"Why," said the old man, "you have missed twenty-five percent of your life."

After a while the boat passed some beautiful rocks along the shore. "Look at those beautiful stones," said the old man. "Do you know anything about geology, Son?"

"No, Sir, I'm afraid not," the boy replied.

"Then, you've missed twenty-five percent of your life," he said.

In the early evening stars appeared in the sky. Looking up at them the old man asked, "Son, do you know anything about astronomy?"

"No, Sir," replied the boy, "I know nothing about astronomy."

"Well," said the old man, "you have missed twenty-five percent of your life."

Now it was time to go home, and when they turned the boat for shore it flipped over in the water and sank. The young boy started swimming for shore. Looking back and noticing the old man was only splashing the water, he yelled, "Mister, do you know how to swim?"

"No!" screamed the old man.

The boy replied, "Then you've lost your life."

If you know everything else, but do not know Christ as personal Saviour, you have lost your life. The Bible says in John 3:36, "He that believeth not the Son shall not see life; but the wrath of God abideth on him."

I think many people are in Hell because they did not know how to be saved. In many cases, I think they wanted to be. The Bible seems to indicate this in Matthew 7:22, 23:

"Many will say to me in that day, Lord, Lord, have we not prophesied in thy name? and in thy name have cast out devils? and in thy name done many wonderful works? And then will I profess unto them, I never knew you: depart from me, ye that work iniquity."

These people wanted to go to Heaven and offered to God their good works as a claim for Heaven. But according to Jesus they were not saved: "Depart from me, ye that work iniquity."

In the parable of the ten virgins in Matthew 25, all ten thought they were ready to meet the bridegroom, and all ten went out to meet him. But when the bridegroom came, five found they were not ready.

It is possible to be saved and know beyond a doubt that when you die you will go to Heaven. The way of salvation is plain and simple.

In the Matter of Salvation, We Are Dealing With an Infinitely Holy God

There can be no understanding or appreciation for the plan of salvation without understanding this. This infinitely holy God has said that sin must be paid for. He said to Adam in Genesis 2:17, "In the day that thou eatest thereof thou shalt surely die." Ezekiel 18:4 tells us, "The soul that sinneth, it shall die." Romans 6:23 says, "The wages of sin is death." And we read in James 1:15,

"Sin, when it is finished, bringeth forth death." God Almighty has declared that sin must be paid for. And the payment is death.

This death is more than dying with a gunshot wound or with cancer. It is described in Revelation 20:14 as the second death: "And death and hell were cast into the lake of fire. This is the second death."

If I had to pay what I owe as a sinner, then I must die, go into Hell and stay there forever and ever. That's the price that God demands for my sins.

The Bible does not say the wages of sin is joining the church. Joining every church in town would not pay what I owe as a sinner.

The Bible does not say the wages of sin is being baptized. I could be baptized until every tadpole in the creek knew my Social Security number by memory, but that would not pay my sin debt.

The Bible does not say the wages of sin is turning over a new leaf. Reforming would not pay what I owe as a sinner.

The Bible does not say the wages of sin is performing good works. By working a thousand lifetimes, I still could never earn Heaven.

If I offered to God my works as a hope of Heaven, the motive behind the works would render them ineffective. There is only one motive that God accepts—love. We read in I Corinthians 13:3, "And though I bestow all my goods to feed the poor, and though I give my body to be burned, and have not charity, it profiteth me nothing." Good works that are not motivated by love will not be rewarded. If I worked in order to go to Heaven, the motive for my service would be fear. I would be working to stay out of Hell. The fear of Hell would be my motive, and thus render the works ineffective.

The Bible says, "The wages of sin is death." God has one payment for sin, and that is an eternal death in the lake of fire. The only thing I can do to pay my debt is die, go into Hell and stay there forever.

This Infinitely Holy God Says All Men Are Sinners

The Bible says in Isaiah 53:6, "All we like sheep have gone astray; we have turned every one to his own way." Again in Ecclesiastes 7:20, we read, "For there is not a just man upon earth, that doeth good, and sinneth not." Romans 3:10 says, "As it is written, There is none righteous, no, not one." Now verse 23 says, "For all have sinned, and come short of the glory of God." "Come short" simply means "to miss the mark." How far we miss the mark is not the important thing, but the fact that we have missed it.

When I went to high school one had to make seventy to pass. If he averaged anything less, he had to repeat the grade.

Suppose one student averaged sixty-five and another thirty-five: a thirty-point difference between their grade averages, yet both are in the same predicament. Both are below the passing mark.

When God looks down on this world He says in the words of Romans 3:22, "For there is no difference."

"Lord, what do You mean—no difference? Some folks live better than others."

"There is no difference," God says, "For all have sinned, and come short of the glory of God."

Suppose I hang a target on the wall and ask each person in the room to take a dart and do his best to hit the bull's eye. Now everybody in the room throws a dart. Some miss the bull's eye by only a quarter of an inch. Others miss it by a foot. Still others miss the whole target. Not one hits the bull's eye.

When all the darts are thrown, I say, "There is no difference."

Says someone. "What do you mean—no difference? I only missed the bull's eye by a quarter of an inch."

I say, "There is no difference because all came short of the bull's eye."

My friend, in God's sight there is no difference between sinners. We may not commit the same sins, but all men are sinners, and God says ALL sin must be paid for.

The Infinitely Holy God Says That We Are Already Condemned

The Bible says in John 3:18, "He that believeth on him is not condemned: but he that believeth not is condemned already, because he hath not believed in the name of the only begotten Son of God." Some people have an idea that we are going to die and go to a judgment. At that judgment God is going to weigh our good works against our bad works. If the good outweighs the bad, He will allow us into Heaven, but if the bad outweighs the good, He will condemn us to Hell.

That teaching is not found in the Bible. We are already condemned, says John 3:18: "He that believeth not is condemned already, because he hath not believed in the name of the only begotten Son of God." The condemned criminal is the one who has been arrested, tried, found guilty, and sentenced to die in the electric chair. He is already condemned and is on death row awaiting the date of execution.

According to what God has said, I am a sinner, my sins demand a payment, and that is death—the second death in the lake of fire. This is not a sentence that is going to be given me after a judgment; I am already under that sentence if I am not trusting Jesus Christ as my Saviour.

The person who is not trusting Jesus Christ completely for salvation is already condemned. He is living under the sentence, and the moment the heart stops beating, the soul and spirit leave the body and go immediately to Hell. The rich man in Luke 16:22, 23 "also died, and was buried; And in hell he lift up his eyes, being in torments. . . ."

God says all men are sinners. He says sin must be paid for. And God says we are already condemned.

How Can an Infinitely Holy God Forgive Sin?

The answer is, God does not forgive sin but He forgives the sinner. Sin must be paid for. Somebody must bear the burden. I have been told that "forgive" literally means "to bear the burden." If I owed someone a thousand dollars and was not able to pay, and I asked, "Would you please forgive the debt?" and the man consented, that means he bore the burden.

In order for an infinitely holy God to forgive the sinner, someone had to pay the debt, someone had to bear the burden. Praise the Lord, that is where Jesus comes in! God took every sin we have ever committed and will ever commit and laid those sins on Christ two thousand years ago at Calvary. Isaiah 53:6 says, "The Lord hath laid on him the iniquity of us all." And the Bible says in I Peter 2:24, "Who his own self bare our sins in his own body on the tree. . . ." Read also I Peter 3:18, "For Christ also hath once suffered for sins, the just for the unjust, that he might bring us to God. . . ."

The greatest truth is the truth of the substitutionary death of Jesus. Jesus Christ actually took all my sins—past, present, and future—and bore them in His own body.

Friend, God Almighty looked down through the telescope of time and saw every sin you would ever commit, put those sins in one big package and laid them on Christ, "The Lord hath laid on him the iniquity of us all."

While Jesus was bearing our sins in His body, God punished Him in our place to pay a debt that we owe, so that when we die we won't have to pay it.

Somebody says, "The Jews killed Christ." Another says, "It was the Roman soldiers." But the Bible says, "For God so loved the world, that he gave his only begotten Son, that whosoever believeth in him should not perish, but have everlasting life." God let Jesus die in our place. He actually punished Jesus in our place so we could escape the punishment. Romans 8:32 declares, "He that spared not his own Son, but delivered him up for us all. . . ."

Jesus uttered seven things while hanging on the cross. The sixth utterance was, "It is finished." Among other things, the statement meant that our sins were completely paid for.

How Can I Be Sure That God Was Satisfied With the Payment Jesus Made?

I can answer that in three words—an empty tomb! When the prisoner is set free, it means his debt to society has been paid. So when God Almighty raised Jesus from the dead, He was saying to the whole world, "I am satisfied with the payment My Son made for your sins."

In certain parts of the world, a merchant selling his goods simply displays them on a counter or table without a price tag attached. When someone comes along wishing to buy an item, he lays down some money. The merchant looks at it, and if he is not satisfied with the payment, he leaves it lying on the table. Then the man wishing to buy the item adds to the money. If the merchant is still not satisfied with the price offered, he again leaves the money on the table. When enough is put down to satisfy the merchant, and he reaches down and takes it up, he is saying in essence, "I am satisfied with the payment."

When God raised Jesus Christ from the dead and took Him back to Heaven, He said to the whole world, "I am satisfied with the payment My Son made for your sins."

That's what Isaiah 53:10 says, "It pleased the Lord to bruise him. . . ." That expression does not mean that God got certain joy or glee out of seeing Jesus die on the cross. The word "pleased" literally means "satisfied." Isaiah 53:11 says, "He shall see of the travail of his soul, and shall be satisfied. . . ." The death of Jesus Christ on the cross fully satisfied the just demands of a holy God. Now we must accept the satisfaction that Jesus made to God for our sins, or satisfy God ourselves. Dear friend, if we satisfy God ourselves we must die, go into Hell, and stay there forever and ever. That's the payment He demands.

What Can You Do to Let God Know You Are Satisfied With the Payment?

If you try to add anything to what Jesus has done, no matter how good the addition may be, you are saying by your actions, "I am not really satisfied with the payment Jesus made."

It is not the death of Jesus Christ on the cross–plus my baptism that saves. It is Jesus alone. Acts 4:12 says, "Neither is there salvation in any other: for there is none other name under heaven given among men, whereby we must be saved." If I am trusting Christ–plus baptism, then I am not really satisfied with the payment Jesus made for my sins.

To show that we are fully satisfied with the payment, we must cease to trust any and everything else and trust Jesus alone. I must cease to trust my good works, no matter how good they may be. I must cease to trust my church membership, no matter how good my church may be. I must cease to trust my baptism, no matter how beautiful the ordinance. I must cease to trust my good life, no matter how pure and noble. To trust anything other than what He did at Calvary for salvation is to say to God, "I am not fully satisfied with the payment Your Son made for my sins. I feel I must have something else."

In order to show God that I am satisfied with the payment made, I must trust Jesus Christ completely. The Bible says in John 3:36,

"He that believeth on the Son hath everlasting life. . . ." Now, dear friend, there is no promise in the Bible to those who partially believe on Christ. The promise is to those who believe on Christ. If I trust Jesus Christ ninety percent and something else ten percent, the ten percent destroys the ninety. The ten percent says I am not fully trusting Christ, and the Bible says in John 3:18, "He that believeth not is condemned already, because he hath not believed in the name of the only begotten Son of God." The rest of John 3:36 reads, ". . . and he that believeth not the Son shall not see life; but the wrath of God abideth on him."

Dear friend, have you let God know that you are satisfied with the payment Jesus made for your sins by trusting Jesus and Him alone for your salvation?

How Can You Know That if You Trust Jesus Christ as Your Saviour, You Will Go to Heaven?

The answer is simple. You have the promise of God Himself. And keep in mind that God is too wise to be mistaken and too honest to deceive us. If God said it, it is guaranteed! When He prescribes a cure, He is bound by His honor to put potency into it.

What does He say? John 3:36, "He that believeth on the Son hath everlasting life. . . ." If you are trusting Jesus Christ completely for your salvation, then God says you have everlasting life not someday but now. God says in John 3:18, "He that believeth on him is not condemned. . . ." Here He promises that the one trusting Jesus Christ completely for salvation is no longer under the sentence. The sentence has been lifted. He is not condemned. He does not have to pay the sin debt since it has been paid for him.

I had rather have the Word of God than to have every angel in Heaven come down to earth and say to me, "Curtis, you have everlasting life. You will never perish. You are going to Heaven."

If the angels were to come down, I would say, "I'm glad you came, but you really didn't help me. I have Word from a greater authority—God Himself."

God says to me in John 6:37, "Him that cometh to me I will in no wise cast out." I understand that in the Greek there are five negatives in this verse. Preaching in an old country church, a Greek professor said that verse in the Greek means, "Him that cometh to me I will never, no never, no never, no never, no never cast out."

After the service an old lady came to him and said, "He may have to say it five times for you professors, but one time is enough for me."

I certainly agree. If God said one time that I had everlasting life, I will stake my eternity on it. What better assurance can one have than God's own Word? Hebrews 6:18 says it is impossible for God to lie. Titus 1:2 says God cannot lie.

The worst sin is not trusting Jesus Christ as Saviour and it is the only sin for which a man will go to Hell. Mark 16:16 says, "He that believeth not shall be damned."

Do It Without Delay

This is the way of salvation plain and simple. Now will you do something about it? Will you trust Jesus Christ today as your Saviour? If you will trust Him as your Saviour, please write and tell me the good news:

Dr. Curtis Hutson
Sword of the Lord Foundation
Box 1099
Murfreesboro, Tennessee 37133

You can say something like this:

"I have read your sermon, 'Salvation Plain and Simple.' I know that I am a sinner, and that as a sinner I owe the sin debt. I also believe that Jesus Christ died on the cross in my place, and that His death paid in full what I owe as a sinner. Here and now I do trust Him as my Saviour. From this minute on, I am fully depending on Him for my salvation."

"Please send me some free literature that will help me as I set out to live the Christian life."

And be sure to give your name and address.

God bless you!

Chapter 2

The Text That Made Salvation Plain to Charles Spurgeon

"Look unto me, and be ye saved, all the ends of the earth: for I am God, and there is none else."—Isa. 45:22.

This year I read an old biography of Charles Haddon Spurgeon, the famous pastor of the Metropolitan Baptist Tabernacle in London who lived about a hundred years ago.

When Spurgeon was only seven, he could read very well. His grandfather was pastor of a church that had had only four different pastors in two hundred years. Spurgeon would sometimes spend time with him, and an aunt who never married looked after him while he was in his grandfather's home.

Charles Spurgeon during the day would read his grandfather's books. Occasionally church members would meet in his grandfather's home to discuss the Bible. He would allow the members to suggest a topic for discussion. Charles, at age seven, would often suggest the topic—a topic he had been reading about that day. When discussing it, the people were amazed that he knew more about the topic than his grandfather. When he was yet a teenager, he was pastoring a church and preaching to thousands.

They thought: *Well, this will blow by. He is a teenager and a novelty, and this attraction will not last.* But it did last. I have read that when Spurgeon was pastor of the Metropolitan Baptist

Tabernacle, people had to get tickets two and three weeks early in order to get into the building to hear him preach. He sometimes asked the church members to stay at home so visitors could find room in the church services.

Many of the sermons we use in THE SWORD OF THE LORD are by Charles Haddon Spurgeon. In my library I have eighty large volumes of his sermons. As far as I know, he has more sermons in print than any man who has ever lived—thousands and thousands of them. Newspapers in London carried his sermons every week; and, I guess, for that reason the sermons were kept and later put into book form.

In the book, *Life and Works of Spurgeon,* published in 1890, Mr. Spurgeon gives the following account of his conversion.

> I will tell you how I myself was brought to the knowledge of the truth. It may happen the telling of that will bring someone else to Christ.
>
> It pleased God in my childhood to convince me of sin. I lived a miserable creature, finding no hope, no comfort, thinking that surely God would never save me. At last the worst came to the worst—I was miserable; I could do scarcely anything. My heart was broken in pieces. Six months did I pray—prayed agonizingly with all my heart, and never had an answer. I resolved that, in the town where I lived, I would visit every place of worship in order to find out the way of salvation. I felt I was willing to do anything and be anything if God would only forgive me.
>
> I set off, determined to go round to all the chapels; and I went to all the places of worship; and though I dearly venerate the men that occupy those pulpits now, and did so then, I am bound to say that I never heard them once fully preach the Gospel. I mean by that, they preached truth, great truths, many good truths that were fitting to many of their congregation—spiritually-minded people; but what I wanted to know was, How can I get my sins forgiven? And they never once told me that. I wanted to hear how a poor sinner, under a sense of sin, might find peace with God; and when I went I heard a sermon on "Be not deceived: God is not mocked," which cut me up worse, but did not say how I might escape.
>
> I went again another day, and the text was something about the glories of the righteous: nothing for poor me. I was something like a dog under the table, not allowed to eat of the children's food. I went time after time; and I can honestly say, I don't know that I ever went without prayer to God;

> and I am sure there was not a more attentive hearer in all the place than myself, for I panted and longed to understand how I might be saved.
>
> At last, one snowy day—it snowed so much I could not go to the place I had determined to go to, and I was obliged to stop on the road, and it was a blessed stop to me—I found rather an obscure street, and turned down a court, and there was a little chapel. I wanted to go somewhere, but I did not know this place. It was the Primitive Methodists' chapel. I had heard of these people from many, and how they sang so loudly that they made people's heads ache; but that did not matter. I wanted to know how I might be saved, and if they made my head ache ever so much I did not care. So, sitting down, the service went on, but no minister came. At last a very thin-looking man came into the pulpit and opened his Bible and read these words: "Look unto me, and be ye saved, all the ends of the earth." Just setting his eyes upon me, as if he knew me all by heart, he said, "Young man, you are in trouble." Well, I was, sure enough. Says he, "You will never get out of it unless you look to Christ."
>
> And then, lifting up his hands, he cried out, as only, I think, a Primitive Methodist could do, "Look, look, look! It is only look!" I saw at once the way of salvation. Oh, how I did leap for joy at that moment! I know not what else he said; I did not take much notice of it—I was so possessed with that one thought. Like as when the brazen serpent was lifted up, they only looked and were healed. I had been waiting to do fifty things, but when I heard this word "Look!" what a charming word it seemed to me! Oh, I looked until I could almost have looked my eyes away! And in Heaven I will look on still in my joy unutterable.
>
> I now think I am bound never to preach a sermon without preaching to sinners. I do think that a minister who can preach a sermon without addressing sinners does not know how to preach.

When I read those words about Spurgeon's conversion, I thought about my own experience as a young boy. I don't remember the first time I went to church, but I remember hearing the preacher say something like this: "You must be born again." I got the idea that if I were not born again, I would not go to Heaven but to Hell. I heard what he said, but I didn't understand what he meant.

I remember his saying, "Jesus Christ died for you." And as a young boy I used to wonder how the death of Jesus on a cross could get me to Heaven. I did not understand the substitutionary death of Jesus, the vicarious sufferings of Jesus, that He was actually suffering in my place and in your place, and He was paying everything we owe as sinners and satisfying the just demands of a holy God!

In later years when I began to study the Bible and understood the Gospel, I wondered why no one ever made it plain to me how to be saved.

Now if I were to ask you individually about your experiences, I believe most in this congregation would say you had a similar experience as that of Mr. Spurgeon and myself. The majority of people who attend church for years never fully understand how to be saved, never get a good mental grasp of the Gospel. For that reason, I want to preach a clear salvation message this morning, using the text that Charles Haddon Spurgeon heard the day he was saved:

"Look unto me, and be ye saved, all the ends of the earth: for I am God, and there is none else."—Isa. 45:22.

Notice first in the text

I. THE SOURCE OF SALVATION

The text says, "Look unto *ME,* and be ye saved." I emphasize the word "me," meaning Jesus, the Lord, Christ. Absolutely futile is any plan of salvation that includes anything other than Jesus Christ. He will not share the privilege of saving someone with a church, with an individual, or with an organization. He is not a partial Saviour; He is *the* complete Saviour, the only Saviour; and no one else helps Him save. If we added anything to it, it would take away from what He did at Calvary.

Jesus is the source of salvation, says John 1:13: "Which were born, not of blood, nor of the will of the flesh, nor of the will of man, but of God."

Now I'm a Baptist, but the Baptist church is not the source of salvation. I joined a church, but being a church member is not the source of salvation. The text does not say, "Look unto the church," or, "Look unto your good life," or, "Look unto your baptism," or, "Look unto your reformation," or, "Look unto the ordinances," or, "Look unto the sacraments." The text says, "Look unto *me,* and be ye saved, all the ends of the earth."

Ladies and gentlemen, the Man who divided history into BC and AD is either the world's greatest con artist or the Saviour. Jesus Christ is either the most fantastic liar that ever walked on this earth or He is what He claimed to be—the Son of God. And what He said is absolutely true.

Now you must decide that for yourself. I have decided He was not a con artist, that He is the Saviour. I have decided that He wasn't a liar, that He did tell the truth. But you decide for yourself.

If He did tell the truth, then we must face what He said. And He plainly said in John 14:6, "I am *THE* way, *THE* truth, and *THE* life: no man cometh unto the Father, but by me." That needs no interpretation; it just needs to be read and accepted.

Acts 4:12 declares, "Neither is there salvation in any other: for there is none other name under heaven given among men, whereby we must be saved." Over and over and over again the Bible makes it plain that Jesus is the Saviour.

John 3:16—the best known verse in the Bible—says, "For God so loved the world, that he gave his only begotten Son, that whosoever believeth *in him* should not perish, but have everlasting life."

John 3:18 says, "He that believeth *on him* [the Son] is not condemned [not under sentence]: but he that believeth not is condemned already, because he hath not believed in the name of the only begotten Son of God." Jesus is the Saviour. The Bible says in I John 5:12, "He that hath the Son hath life; and he that hath not the Son of God hath not life." That is as plain as it can be. It doesn't say, "He that hath the church hath life." It doesn't say, "He that hath the Baptist label hath life." It doesn't say, "He that hath baptism hath life." It doesn't say, "He that hath a good moral life hath life." It doesn't say, "He that is honest hath life." It says, "He that hath the Son hath life; and he that hath not the Son of God hath not life." That word "hath" is an important word. Don't forget it.

One is a Christian because of what he *has,* not because of what he does. What must one have in order to be a millionaire? You say money, and you are right. But to be a millionaire, one must have a specific amount of money—a million dollars. Very simple, isn't it? Everybody understands that. It is not what one does nor how one lives that makes him a millionaire; it is not what one promises to do in the future that makes him a millionaire; it is what one *has* that makes him a millionaire. The key word, the hinge, is *have, have, have;* not *do.*

Now let me ask you a simple question, so simple that many well-meaning people stumble over it. What must one have to be a Christian? Christ. "He that *hath* the Son hath life." Jesus Christ is the source of salvation.

I accepted Christ when I was eleven years old. I was baptized shortly thereafter. I have tried to live good since then. But if I had to die right now and stand at Heaven's gate and an angel were to come to the gate and ask, "Why should we let you into Heaven?" I would not say, "I'm a preacher," nor, "I preach five or six times a week," nor, "I edit a religious paper that goes into 120 foreign countries." I wouldn't say, "I have lived good," nor, "I have been baptized," nor, "I have turned over a new leaf and made great promises about how I would live." I would simply say, "My only hope of Heaven is that Jesus Christ died for me, and I am looking to Him for salvation."

My hope is built on nothing less
Than Jesus' blood and righteousness;
I dare not trust the sweetest frame,
But wholly [completely, without reservation] **lean on Jesus' name.**

The source of salvation is Jesus. The text says, "Look unto *me,* and be ye saved, all the ends of the earth: for I am God, and there is none else."

One of the saddest things is that many well-meaning people are looking to something other than Jesus Christ for salvation. Some are looking to their good, moral life; others, to church rituals, church membership, or church ordinances. Some are looking to their baptism and depending on that to get them to Heaven. But there is no promise to those who look unto anything other than Jesus Christ.

Oh, why doesn't the world see it! Why don't religious leaders understand it! "Look unto *me,* and be ye saved, all the ends of the earth: for I am God, and there is none else." Christ is the only source of salvation.

We not only have the source of salvation in the text; we also have

II. THE SCOPE OF SALVATION

"Look unto me, and be ye saved, *all the ends of the earth.*" Don't miss this. I love preaching for several reasons, but the main reason is because everybody is a prospect, everybody needs what I have to offer through the Bible—forgiveness.

If I am selling refrigerators, I know everybody doesn't need a refrigerator. If I am selling automobiles, I know everybody doesn't need an automobile. But there is nobody alive who doesn't need forgiveness, because everybody has sinned. Romans 3:23 says, "All have sinned, and come short of the glory of God."

The scope of salvation—"all the ends of the earth."

I have no patience with those who teach a limited atonement. If anything in the Bible is made clear, it is the fact that Christ died for all men.

Hebrews 2:9 says, "But we see Jesus, who was made a little lower than the angels for the suffering of death, crowned with glory and honour; that he by the grace of God should taste death for *every* man."

First John 2:2 says, "And he is the propitiation [atoning sacrifice] for our sins: and not for our's only, but also for the sins of the *whole world.*"

John 3:16 makes it clear that salvation is for the whole world: "For God so loved *the world,* that he gave his only begotten Son, that whosoever believeth in him should not perish, but have everlasting life." Jesus can save the worst sinner just as easily as He can save the most moral man.

"Look unto me, and be ye saved, *all the ends of the earth.*" Salvation is for *all* men.

Second Peter 3:9 tells us, "The Lord is not slack concerning his promise, as some men count slackness; but is longsuffering to us-ward, not willing that any should perish, but that *all* should come to repentance."

Again the Bible says in I Timothy 2:4, "Who will have *all* men to be saved, and to come unto the knowledge of the truth."

Not only did Jesus die on the cross for all men and make salvation possible for "all the ends of the earth," but He invites all men to come to Him.

In Matthew 11:28 Jesus invites all, "Come unto me, *all* ye that labour and are heavy laden, and I will give you rest."

The last invitation in the Bible opens the door as wide as God could possibly open it and offers salvation to all. "And the Spirit and the bride say, Come." Then God opens the door a little wider and says, "And let him that heareth say, Come." And then He opens the door even wider and adds, "And let him that is athirst come." Then to make sure that everyone is included in the invitation, He opens the door as wide as possible and says, "And whosoever will, let him take the water of life freely" (Rev. 22:17).

The scope of salvation is found in the words of the text, "all the ends of the earth."

Two thousand years ago God took every sin you ever have committed and every sin you ever will commit if you live to be a thousand years old; and He laid those sins on Jesus, just like I lay this Bible on my hand. Now that is not just preacher talk; that is in the Bible, in Isaiah 53:6: "The Lord hath [past tense] laid on him [Jesus] the iniquity of us all."

The greatest truth that ever coursed through my brain is what I am telling you right now—that all the sins I ever have committed (even the ones I forgot about and the ones I hope nobody finds out about) were laid on Jesus Christ two thousand years ago. And that is not a figure of speech but an actual fact.

First Peter 2:24 says, "Who his own self bare our sins in his own body on the tree." That is a fact! Second Corinthians 5:21 says, "For he hath made him to be sin for us, who knew no sin; that we might be made the righteousness of God in him."

"Look unto me, and be ye saved, all the ends of the earth." Salvation is for everybody. The death of Jesus Christ on the cross is sufficient for all, but it is efficient only to those who believe. That word "believe" is found 99 times in the Gospel of John alone!

The scope of salvation is "all the ends of the earth."

We have in the text not only the source of salvation and the scope of salvation, we also have

III. THE SIMPLICITY OF SALVATION

This is where most people stumble. We feel that something so wonderful cannot be obtained so easily. All one has to do to be saved is look to Jesus. In the words of the text, "Look unto me, and be ye saved."

I've a message from the Lord, hallelujah!
The message unto you I'll give;
'Tis recorded in His Word, hallelujah!
It is only that you "look and live."

Look and live, my brother, live!
Look to Jesus now and live;
'Tis recorded in His Word, hallelujah!
It is only that you "look and live."

The text does not say, "Look unto me, turn over a new leaf, live right, keep the Ten Commandments, and promise you will never sin again, and be ye saved." No—a thousand times no! It simply says, "Look unto me, and be ye saved."

If one had to promise never to sin again in order to be saved, then I would never be saved. Now don't get me wrong. Christians ought to live as good as they possibly can; but the text doesn't say, "Look unto me and promise never to sin again."

I try to live good. There are many sinful things that I have never done, but I would not get on my knees this morning and tell God that I will never sin again, because I know I would be lying. I will sin again before the sun goes down. And don't look too surprised; so will you.

The Bible says in James 4:17, "Therefore to him that knoweth to do good, and doeth it not, to him it is sin." I don't know anyone who doesn't leave undone every day some good thing that ought to be done. If my salvation depended on my never sinning again, I would be hopelessly lost.

I have never cursed. It is a waste of breath. Cursing is the one sin we get nothing for. If a man steals, he at least gets what he steals. If one commits immorality, he has at least satisfied his fleshly desires. But when one curses, he gets nothing for it. Though I have never cursed, there have been a few times when I came close.

I was driving behind a fellow not too long ago here in town. We had stopped at a stop light. He had all the windows rolled up, and his radio was going so loud that he couldn't hear my horn blow when the light turned green. The light turned red. When it turned green again, I blew the horn again. By this time four or five people behind me were blowing their horns at me, while I was blowing my horn at him. But he didn't hear a thing. He sat there through three red lights! Now I have never cursed, but if someone had written some curse words on a piece of paper, I would have signed it! I mean I was so mad I could have killed the guy in Christian love!

Salvation is not promising God I will never sin again. That is ridiculous. You will sin, because many little things you think are not sin are sin. The Bible says your very best is sin. Isaiah 64:6 makes it clear that "all our righteousnesses are as filthy rags"—not our worst but our best. God is so much holier than we that when we put our best before Him, it looks like filth in His sight. If we had to save ourselves by our good living, nobody would ever be saved. There is no way you can live a perfect, sinless life. You are going to mess up. Folks are going to do things that are not right, going to promise things they can't fulfill. You are going to become angry and say things you shouldn't say, and maybe do things you shouldn't do.

Salvation does not depend upon our living but upon our looking. The text says, "Look unto me, and be ye saved, all the ends of the earth." The simplicity of salvation is "look."

There's light for a look at the Saviour,
And life more abundant and free!

"Look" does not mean simply to admit the historical Personage of Jesus as a fact. Everybody does that. Every time you date a check, you do that. But to look unto Jesus means to depend on Jesus.

Let me illustrate. Suppose the preacher cosigned for me to borrow money. When the due date came and the bank called and said, "The money is due," I said, "I don't have a dime. I can't pay for it."

So I call the preacher and say, "Preacher, they are going to lock me up in the morning if I don't pay that bill."

The preacher says, "Brother Curtis, don't worry about it. Just look to me," and hangs up the phone. What he meant by "look to me" is, "I've got it covered. I'll take care of it. You depend on me."

And when the Bible says, "Look unto me, and be ye saved," it means, "Depend on Me. I've got it covered." It means, "Trust Me." It means, "Rely on Me." There is a similar expression in the New Testament, in Hebrews 12:2, "Looking unto Jesus the author and finisher of our faith."

Martin Luther, the great reformer in Germany, translated the verse "off looking unto Jesus," which means turning the head away from everything else and looking only to Jesus. It means looking away from my good life, looking away from ritual, looking away from ceremony, looking away from church membership, looking away from baptism—looking away from everything else and looking *only* to Jesus.

There is absolutely no promise in anybody's Bible for those who partially look unto Jesus and partially look unto something else.

I got on a plane last week and flew out to Austin, Texas. I had to get completely on the plane, not halfway on the plane and halfway in the car. I couldn't say to my wife, "Let me put one foot in the plane and keep one foot in the car, just in case the plane doesn't make it." Had I done that, when the plane took off, I would have been in a mess!

And the person who has one foot on Jesus Christ and one on something else, no matter what the something else is, is going to be in a mess when he dies. Salvation is not partially trusting Jesus, not partially looking unto Jesus; but salvation is wholly, completely looking unto Jesus.

I can't save myself. The world can't save me. The preacher can't save me. The church can't save me. Either Jesus saves me or I won't be saved.

Looking unto Jesus means trusting Him completely. It means putting both feet on Jesus and having no claim and no hope of Heaven except the fact that Jesus Christ died for you and paid your sin debt in full.

Oh, the simplicity of salvation! "*Look* unto me, and be ye saved, all the ends of the earth."

Now I have one more thought before I close. The text not only gives us the source of salvation, the scope of salvation, and the simplicity of salvation, but it also gives us

IV. THE SECURITY OF SALVATION

"Look unto me, and be ye *saved.*" We use that word all the time. What does it mean? If somebody is saved, he is saved from something.

If a man is swimming, gets leg cramps and begins to sink in the water and you go out in a boat and save him, that means you saved him from drowning, you saved him from death. If a building is on fire and you rush up into a room and bring a man down and say, "I saved him," you mean you saved him from the fire.

The Bible word "saved" means you are saved from something. We don't like to hear about it, but I must tell you there is a real Hell. It is literal. It is a place of fire and everlasting punishment. If the Bible is true and Jesus is not a con artist or the most fantastic liar who ever lived, then there is a real Hell, and it is an awful place. In Jesus' solemn warning of Hell, He said in Mark 9:43-48,

"And if thy hand offend thee, cut it off: it is better for thee to enter into life maimed, than having two hands to go into hell, into the fire that never shall be quenched: Where their worm dieth not, and the fire is not quenched. And if thy foot offend thee, cut it off: it is better for thee to enter halt into life, than having two feet to be cast into hell, into the fire that never shall be quenched: Where their worm dieth not, and the fire is not quenched. And if thine eye offend thee, pluck it out: it is better for thee to enter into the kingdom of God with one eye, than having two eyes to be cast into hell fire: Where their worm dieth not, and the fire is not quenched."

Now consider the importance of these words. Jesus said Hell is so bad that it is better for a man to cut his hand off and enter into life maimed than have two hands and go into Hell. He went on to say that Hell is so bad that if a man's foot causes him to go to Hell, he would be better off to cut off his foot and enter into life having one foot than to go into Hell having both feet. Jesus said if a man's eye offends him, he is better off to pluck out his eye and go into life having one eye than to go into Hellfire having both eyes. Hell must be awful since this kind of physical suffering is to be preferred before Hell.

Now some argue that these words of Jesus were only an illustration. Of course we disagree; but even if it is an illustration of a place, then the place has to be worse than the illustration, because no illustration fully describes the event or the thing itself.

"Look unto me, and be ye saved." The person who looks to Jesus is saved from Hell.

Most religions do not teach that a person is saved by looking unto Jesus or trusting Jesus. They teach that he is put into a position to be saved provided he does certain other things. But the text says, "Look unto me, and be ye saved." It does not say, "Look unto me, and I will put you in a position to be saved provided you endure to the end, provided you don't sin again, provided you get baptized, provided you join the church, and provided you keep the Ten Commandments." The text plainly says, "Look unto me, and be ye saved." A man is not saved as long as he is in danger of being lost.

Suppose a man is drowning in a lake and I swim out to save him. If I bring him within ten yards of the shoreline, is he saved? Absolutely not! He is not saved until I pull him completely out of the water and rescue him from the danger of drowning. When we look to Jesus, we are not put in a position to be saved; we are saved, we are rescued from the danger of being lost.

"Look unto me, and be ye saved." Saved from what? Hell. If I trust Jesus as my Saviour, I won't have to go to Hell when I die. I'll go to Heaven and be there forever and ever and ever and ever. To look to Christ means to have faith in Christ, to depend on Christ, to rely on Christ the same way you rely on your family doctor, the same way you rely on your dentist, the same way you rely on an airplane pilot. It means you have confidence in Him that He is all He offers Himself to be.

Your doctor says, "I have studied medicine. I can diagnose your case. I can tell you what is wrong. I can prescribe something that will cure you." So you take him at his word. You trust him.

It is the same way with Jesus. You take Him at His word. He says, "I'm your Saviour. I am the only way to get to Heaven. I am life. He that hath the Son hath life. He that believes on Me has everlasting life. If you will trust Me, you will never go to Hell, but you will live in Heaven forever." We must accept what He says, believe that He is all He offers Himself to be and trust Him completely for salvation.

I am not asking you to change religions. I am not asking you to join a church. I am simply asking you to make dead sure you are trusting Christ and nothing else for salvation, that you are looking unto Him. Anybody in the world who looks unto Him is saved.

"Look unto me, and be ye saved, all the ends of the earth: for I am God, and there is none else."

I URGE YOU TO TRUST CHRIST TODAY

You have read the sermon, "The Text That Made Salvation Plain to Charles Spurgeon." When it was preached, scores came to trust Christ as Saviour. There is absolutely no way to be saved other than looking unto Jesus. Won't you look unto Him today? Won't you trust Him completely for your salvation?

If I were in your home, talking with you personally, I would ask you to pray a simple prayer telling Jesus you were fully trusting Him for salvation. Since I am not in your home or office, let me ask you who are reading these lines to trust Christ today. If you will, then tell Him in your own words,

> Dear Lord Jesus, I know that I'm a sinner. I do believe the promise that if I look to You, I will be saved. Here and now I am completely trusting You for salvation. I am totally depending on You to take me to Heaven when I die. Amen.

If you prayed that simple prayer or one similar telling Christ you would trust Him as Saviour, then I have some free literature I want to send that will help you as you set out to live the Christian life. All you need do to receive your free literature is write to me:

Dr. Curtis Hutson
Sword of the Lord Foundation
P. O. Box 1099
Murfreesboro, Tennessee 37133

Tell me, "I have read your sermon, 'The Text That Made Salvation Plain to Charles Spurgeon.' Knowing that I'm a sinner and that I cannot save myself, I here and now look to Christ for my salvation. I am totally depending on Him to take me to Heaven when I die. Please send me the free literature that will help me as I set out to live the Christian life." Include your name and full address.

Chapter 3

The Whole Gospel in a Single Verse
I Timothy 1:15

Occasionally in reading through the Bible you read a verse that seems to have in it the entire Gospel.

Martin Luther said of these verses. "They are little Bibles or Bibles in miniature." First Timothy 1:15, my text this morning, is such a verse:

"This is a faithful saying, and worthy of all acceptation, that Christ Jesus came into the world to save sinners; of whom I am chief."

In reading condensed notes, one usually misses the soul and marrow of a sermon. Sermon outlines usually have a few thoughts, but you yourself must put the meat on the bones. I have never been able to use another's condensed notes. To me they just do not convey the thought of the writer.

But in my text there is nothing left out. It is as if you had taken the great truths of the Gospel and pressed them together with a hydraulic ram. "This is a faithful saying, and worthy of all acceptation, that Christ Jesus came. . . to save sinners; of whom I am chief."

Here is:

I. OUR NAME, OR A BROAD WORD OF DESCRIPTION

I suppose one of the most important questions that could be

asked would be, "For whom is salvation meant?" In this text the Holy Spirit gives the answer: "This is a faithful saying, and worthy of all acceptation, that Christ Jesus came. . . TO SAVE SINNERS."

Jesus Christ came to save sinners of all sorts, not certain kinds of sinners but just sinners; not respectable sinners but sinners; not proud sinners but sinners—drunkards, thieves, adulterers, liars, murderers, whoremongers—He came to save them all.

It matters not what form your sin may have taken, you are still a sinner. I trust I am speaking to a congregation that recognizes you are sinners. If there be any here who do not feel that you are sinners, then I have no message for you. Furthermore, if there be any here who feel that you are not a sinner, *then the Bible has no message for you,* because "Christ Jesus came. . . to save *sinners."*

Jesus said, "I am not come to call the righteous, but sinners to repentance" (Matt. 9:13). "The Son of man is come to seek and to save that which was lost" (Luke 19:10).

A man had been in prison for a crime he supposedly had committed. After serving some time, it was discovered that he was innocent. And the Queen insulted him by giving him a free pardon. A pardon for what? He wasn't guilty.

If Jesus Christ offered pardon and mercy to a man who thought he was innocent, it would be an insult to that man. Pardon and mercy are not for the innocent but for the guilty. Salvation is for sinners. "This is a faithful saying, and worthy of all acceptation, that Christ Jesus came. . . to save sinners."

If the word "*sinner*" fits you, then you are included. If it does not fit you, then you are excluded by the fact that you have failed to admit that you are a sinner. No one goes to Heaven except he who recognizes that he fits in this category—sinner. Your sin may have taken a different form than the other fellow's, and you may not be as vile as some, but you are a sinner nonetheless. He came to save moral sinners, immoral sinners, respectable sinners—all kinds of sinners.

You will notice that **Jesus came to save sinners without qualification.** There is no adjective before the noun. "This is a faithful saying, and worthy of all acceptation, that Christ Jesus came. . . to save **sinners.**"

Much of our doctrine and some of our beliefs come from songs we sing or hear. Some songwriters have done an injustice by qualifying sinners. For instance, some speak of "humble sinners," "trembling sinners," "sorrowing sinners." The songs put a qualifying word before sinners, but the Bible does not.

I used to think that before I could be saved I had to be a sorrowing sinner. The problem was, I didn't know how much I had to sorrow to be the kind of sinner that Jesus came to save. I worked long trying to make myself feel sorry for my sin. I would feel sorry, but I often wondered, *Am I sorry enough?* Others wept; and because I didn't, I thought, *Perhaps I am not feeling sorry enough for my sins.*

I find comfort in this verse. There is no qualifying word before sinners. Jesus Christ came to save sinners—period. Trying to earn salvation through our goodness is like one drop of perfume in an ocean of filth. The truth is, we don't have one drop of goodness in us.

Read our description in Romans, chapter 3. Here Paul describes us from the crown of our head to the sole of our feet. He says our mouth is an open sepulcher, our feet are swift to run to mischief and shed innocent blood—God's description of the sinner. We are all sinners. God Almighty sees all of us the same—respectable and disreputable sinners, but sinners nonetheless.

He not only came to save sinners without qualification, and not only to save all sorts of sinners; but, shocking as this may sound, **He came to save sinners in their pollution.**

I have heard preachers say such things as, "Now you clean up, straighten up, and fly right! If you don't straighten out your life, you are going to Hell."

That is like telling a dog to stop barking. That is like walking up beside the casket of a dead man and saying, "Get up and start walking." He cannot walk. He is dead. And the man without Jesus Christ is a dead sinner. Jesus doesn't ask the sinner to get better to get saved; He saves him so he can get better.

Do we read, "Prodigal son, before you come home, get a razor and shave, cut your hair, brush your teeth, put on some clean clothes and a nice tie, get some decent shoes on your feet, then come home and the father will receive you"? No! It says, "Prodigal son, come home with your rags, your shaggy hair and unshaven face, your vile character. Come home as you are, and the father will clothe you when you get here."

Jesus came to save sinners in their pollution. He mixed with sinners. He ate with sinners. He lived with sinners. He died for sinners. He made His grave with the wicked. And He went to Paradise with a sinning thief. I am not encouraging sin; I am showing that reformation is not an instrument of salvation.

What would you think if you went to admit yourself at the hospital and the attendant said, "Now go home and get well. And when you are completely well, we will receive you." You would say, "Man, you must be crazy! If I were well, I wouldn't need the hospital."

Jesus said, "They that are whole need not a physician." He will clean you up after you come to Him, but He will save you in your pollution.

Jesus came to save sinners without strength. "This is a faithful saying, and worthy of all acceptation, that Christ Jesus came. . . to save sinners." Sinners without strength. Romans 5:6 says, "For when we were yet without strength, in due time Christ died for the ungodly." The truth is, the sinner has no desire to be saved. Oh, he may have a desire to miss Hell; but he has no desire to be saved. We are without strength to feel or desire to be better and without strength to do better if we had the desire. "This is a faithful saying, and worthy of all acceptation, that Christ Jesus came. . . to save sinners."

I wish I had the ability to pry the gate of salvation as wide as it should be opened, but I am incapable of presenting it as open as it really is. Jesus Christ came to save sinners.

I want you to notice not only our name but:

II. OUR NEED, OR A BRIGHT WORD OF SALVATION

Jesus Christ came to s-a-v-e sinners. You might think He came to condemn. In the book of Genesis, when the people sinned and started to build the tower of Babel, God didn't come down to save but to condemn; and He scattered them across the face of the earth. Since God has given man every opportunity to do right, and man still turns his back on God, you would think He came to condemn man; but that is not true. He came to save man.

Jesus said in John 3:17,18, "For God sent not his Son into the world to condemn the world [us]; but that the world through him might be saved. He that believeth on him is not condemned: but he that believeth not is condemned already." He didn't come to condemn us but to save us.

Notice something else. **He didn't come to show us how to save ourselves.** Most religions of the world don't understand this. He didn't come to show you how to save yourself; He came to save you. This is a faithful saying, and worthy of all acceptation, that Christ Jesus came to save, not to show. He didn't lay out certain things and say, "In the doing of these things you will save yourself." No. He came to save you. He didn't come to point out the way and say, "Now if you will get on that way and stay on that way and never err, you will make it." No. He came *as* the way. In John 14:6 He said, "I am the way," not the one who points out the way. He didn't say, "Follow some prescribed way and Heaven will be your home." Wait a minute. That is the unauthorized translation. What He said was, "No man cometh unto the Father, but by me."

Religion says, "Study the Bible and make sure you live up to this, and live up to that, and do this, and do that, and you may go to Heaven when you die." Friends, Jesus Christ didn't come to show the sinner how to save himself; He came to save him. Bless His name!

In salvation, Jesus is not an instructor, but a Saviour. He didn't come to condemn but to save. He didn't come to show us how to save ourselves; He came to save. **Furthermore, He didn't come to help us save ourselves; He came to save us.**

A lot of people teach that Jesus is necessary but that He is not enough. They say, "I know Jesus' death on the cross was necessary; but if you are not baptized, you are not saved." He didn't come to help you save yourself; He came to save sinners. He didn't make the downpayment and say, "All right, here is the installment book. Make sure you keep up the payments." No. He paid it.

Jesus paid it all,
All to Him I owe;
Sin had left a crimson stain,
He washed it white as snow.

In spinning a robe of your own righteousness, before the sun goes down you will find it all unraveled. Yet being ignorant of the righteousness of God, man goes about to establish his own righteousness and refuses to submit himself to the righteousness of Christ. "For Christ is the end of the law for righteousness to every one that believeth" (Rom. 10:4).

I am glad He didn't say, "All right, Curtis, I will be responsible for 90% of your salvation and you for the other 10%." I am glad He didn't say, "I will do 99% and leave you 1%." I would have messed up my 1%!

He didn't come to show me how to save myself; He came to save me. He didn't come to help me save myself; He came to save me. Every false religion in the world says, "Do and live"; but Jesus says, "Live and do."

Take your hands off it. Don't touch it. Accept it like it is. Receive it as a free gift from God Almighty and be saved! The dirtiest thieves this side of Hell are religious thieves who try to go to Heaven some other way and will not accept the clear plan of salvation.

He didn't come to make us content to be unsaved. I have heard people say, "I have no desire to be saved. I am content like I am." Christ didn't make you that way.

The crippled man at the pool of Bethesda had been there for years waiting for something to happen. He had been waiting for the moving of the water. At the moving of the water, whoever got in was healed. Jesus didn't say, "Let's wait here until the water moves again, then you get in." No. He said, "Rise, take up thy bed, and walk."

You don't have to wait for the water to move. You don't have to wait for lightning to strike. You don't have to be knocked down in a church aisle. You only have to believe on the Lord Jesus Christ, come to Him, trust Him, and put your case in His hands. "Believe on the Lord Jesus Christ, and thou **shalt** be saved!" That is all you need.

He didn't come to put us in a position to be saved providing we never sin again. He came to save us. He doesn't take us so far down the road, then leave us to go the rest of the way alone. He, like the shepherd, puts the lost sheep on His shoulders and delivers it safely home. The Bible says, "Jesus Christ came to **save** sinners." And you are not saved as long as you are in a position to be lost again. He came to **save** sinners. And when the sinner is saved, he is saved!

> **Yes, I to the end shall endure,**
> **As sure as the earnest is given;**
> **More happy, but not more secure,**
> **The glorified saints in Heaven!**

I am as saved as any saint already in Heaven! I am as sure to go to Heaven as any saint who is in Heaven now. They may be more happy than I, but they are no more secure. Jesus didn't come to put us in a position to be saved; He came to **save** us. "This is a faithful saying, and worthy of all acceptation, that Christ Jesus came. . .to save sinners."

Are you saved? You say, "I hope I am." What do you mean, "I hope I am"? If you ask me if I am saved, I will answer before you finish the question, "I am saved!" You could sing that song this morning, "Saved, Saved, Saved," because you are saved. You couldn't sing it if you were only in a position to be saved provided you held on and didn't sin again. Jesus came to save.

Notice next in the text:

III. HIS NAME, OR A GLORIOUS WORD OF HONOR

"This is a faithful saying, and worthy of all acceptation, that CHRIST JESUS. . . ." Christ Jesus. We saw our name or a broad word of description; now we see His name or a glorious word of honor. He didn't send an angel on this errand—Gabriel or Michael. He didn't pick out the best man and send him on this errand. Christ Jesus came!

"Christ" means "anointed." Christ, the Anointed One. Anointed and commissioned by God Almighty to go on an errand. "Jesus" means "Saviour." "Thou shalt call his name JESUS: for he shall save his people from their sins" (Matt. 1:21). The Anointed One, the One commissioned to go into the world and be the Saviour! God said, "Jesus, You are to go into the world. I will anoint You, commission You to be the Saviour of sinners."

It didn't say the independent Baptists came into the world to save sinners, nor that the Baptist preachers came into the world to save sinners. It didn't say the Virgin Mary came into the world to save sinners, nor that the Pope came into the world to save sinners. No. A thousand times no! "This is a faithful saying, and worthy of all acceptation, that Christ Jesus came into the world to save sinners." If you don't go to Heaven by Jesus Christ, you will not go. "Neither is there salvation in any other" (Acts 4:12).

Notice another thing:

IV. HIS DEED, OR A SURE WORD OF FACT

"This is a faithful saying, and worthy of all acceptation, that Christ Jesus CAME. . . ." Came. It has already happened! He came. If He came, that means **He existed before He came here.** He didn't begin at Bethlehem.

"In the beginning was the Word, and the Word was with God, and the Word was God. The same was in the beginning with God. All things were made by him; and without him was not any thing made that was made."—John 1:1-3.

He came. He had existed long before.

Wait a minute! This world had a distinguished Visitor a couple of thousand years ago. God Almighty came down to this earth wrapped in human flesh and walked along the sandy seashore of Galilee—God Almighty who made the stars, the moon, and the planets; God Almighty who holds His hands up to the sea and says, "Come this far and no farther." He came!—a sure word of fact.

So-called mainline denominations have departed from the Faith and teach another plan of salvation. But no matter how far you get away from it, it is still a fact that He came. If everybody in the world were to turn their noses up at Him and form their own religion, it is still a fact that He came.

Down from His glory,
Ever living story,
My God and Saviour came,
And Jesus was His name.
Born in a manger,
To His own a stranger,
A Man of sorrows, tears and agony.

He not only existed before, but **He willingly came.** It wasn't like the man on his first parachute jump who had to be pushed out of the plane. Jesus came willingly. It will take several thousand years to thank Him for it. He wasn't One who came to the earth not knowing what He would face, but He came knowing when He left Heaven everything that He would suffer.

Even when He was here, He knew when He was going to die; and He knew exactly how. Long before it happened, He said, talking to Nicodemus in John 3:14, "As Moses lifted up the serpent in the wilderness, even so must the Son of man be lifted up." He said, "I am going to die on the cross."

Some of us have gone on errands. Had we known what would be involved, we would not have gone. But Jesus Christ left Heaven knowing *all* the consequences, *all* the agony, *all* the suffering; yet He willingly came. A sure word of fact—He came—and no one will ever change it.

Notice the next thing in the text:

V. OUR ACCEPTANCE, OR A WORD OF PERSONALITY

"This is a faithful saying, and worthy of all acceptation, that Christ Jesus came. . . to save sinners; OF WHOM I AM CHIEF." "Of whom I am chief."

Some may argue with Paul. I, too, would contest his statement, because I feel that I am the "chief." I have never met a sinner who didn't feel the same way after he was saved! When you consider the infinite cost of your salvation, there is only one conclusion you can reach: *I must have been an awfully, awfully, awfully bad sinner. I must have undoubtedly been the chief of sinners for God Almighty to allow them to pluck His beard, spit in His face, and smite Him with a reed. I must have been a horrible sinner for God Almighty to rob Heaven and send Jesus to die in my place, to suffer indescribable agony and be clothed in His own blood and have them strip Him naked before His followers to get me saved.*

Say, Paul, wait a minute! If I can't be first in line, then surely I am second.

Here is a word of personality, ". . . of whom I am chief." Appropriation of the sinner's Saviour begins by confession. He is the sinner's Saviour. But if you want to appropriate the sinner's Saviour, you must start with confession: "I am a sinner." You then may not feel you are the chief—not many sinners do. But after you are saved and understand the price paid for your redemption, you will know you are.

I have had people say to me, "I know I am bad, but I am not

as bad as So-and-So." That is all right. That is enough confession if you just know that you are a sinner. Appropriation starts by confessing, "Lord, I'm a sinner."

Then confession flowers into faith. "This is a faithful saying, and worthy of all acceptation, that Christ Jesus came . . . to save sinners," and I am one of them. That is faith. Paul is really saying He came to save me. He used a general statement, "Jesus came into the world to save sinners"; but he added, "I am a sinner."

In this room this morning isn't there some man, woman, boy, or girl who would be willing to come down this aisle during the invitation and not only say, "I am a sinner," but say, "Jesus Christ came to save sinners, and I am one of them." You won't be saved until you are willing to say, 'Of whom I am one." He came to save sinners. "Lord, here is a sinner whom You came to save. You died on the cross for me. You paid my sin debt. You suffered my Hell. You died in my stead. I am one of them."

There is confession, but confession that flowers into faith. And, of course, confession that flowers into faith should bloom in a public profession. If you not only see yourself as a sinner but see Christ Jesus as your Saviour, then you ought to make a public declaration of your faith in Him as your Saviour.

If you have been saved, then you are not ashamed of Jesus Christ. The palms of your hands may perspire a little, and you may be nervous, but you won't be ashamed. You may get a little tense, but you won't be ashamed. "Whosoever believeth on him shall not be ashamed" (Rom. 10:11).

"This is a faithful saying, and worthy of **all** acceptation." It is worthy for the little boy to accept. It is worthy for the little girl to accept. It is worthy for the old man to accept. It is worthy for the elderly woman to accept. It is worthy for respectable sinners to accept. It is worthy for sinners with no reputation to accept. It is worthy for liars and whoremongers and sinners of all kinds to accept.

Do you fit the general description of "sinners"? Then He died for you. He paid what you owe, and He suffered your Hell.

TRUST HIM: HE HAS NEVER TURNED ONE DOWN

Dear friend, Jesus Christ has been saving sinners the same way for years. He has never turned one down. The wonderful promise in John 6:37 is, "Him that cometh to me I will in no wise cast out." Won't you trust Him today as your Saviour? He came to save sinners. Are you a sinner? Don't you want to go to Heaven when you die? Then trust Him now. Tell Him in your own words:

> Dear Lord Jesus, I know that I am a sinner. I do believe that You died for me, so here and now I trust You as my Saviour. From this moment on I am fully depending on You for my salvation. Now help me to live for You and to be a good Christian. Amen.

If you will pray that simple prayer and write to tell me so, I have some free literature I want to send that will help as you set out to live the Christian life. All you need do to receive your free literature is mail a letter to me:

Dr. Curtis Hutson
Sword of the Lord Foundation
P. O. Box 1099
Murfreesboro, Tennessee 37133

In your letter say, "I have read your sermon, 'The Whole Gospel in a Single Verse.' I believe that Jesus Christ came to save sinners. I also know that I am a sinner and believe He came to save me. Knowing that I am a sinner and believing that Jesus Christ died on the cross for my sins, I now trust Him as my personal Saviour. I promise to tell others of my decision. Please send me the free literature that will help me as I set out to live the Christian life." Then give your name and full address.

Chapter 4

"So Great Salvation"

"How shall we escape, if we neglect so great salvation."—Heb. 2:3.

No one who understands the doctrine of salvation would deny that salvation is the greatest thing in the world. If a person is not saved, nothing else really matters. When we say "great," we do not always mean what God means when He uses the word.

I have often heard "great" used to describe many things and events. As a matter of fact, the expression, "That is a great man," has almost become a habit with some people.

This text states the greatness of salvation and warns of the danger of neglecting it. In this message I want to give four reasons why salvation is so great.

I. SALVATION IS GREAT BECAUSE OF WHAT IT INCLUDES

When I was eleven years old, I trusted Jesus Christ as my Saviour, though I did not understand then everything that was included in my salvation. I knew that if I were to die after that moment, I would go to Heaven and miss Hell; but that was about all I knew about salvation. Most people, in thinking about salvation, think only of escaping Hell. To be sure, salvation means being saved from the penalty of sin, which is Hell; but salvation includes much more.

1. Salvation Includes Deliverance From the Reign of Sin

Romans 5:21 states, "That as sin hath reigned unto death, even so might grace reign through righteousness." Here the Bible is not speaking about the acts of sin but the sinful nature. When we were born, we inherited a sinful nature.

In Psalm 51:5 David said, "Behold, I was shapen in iniquity; and in sin did my mother conceive me." We were born with what the Bible calls sin, which constantly pulls us in the wrong direction. Before salvation, one is a slave to that nature. Everything you do before salvation is motivated by the sin nature. You have no other motivating power.

Men start drinking. They take a social drink, then another, then another, until finally they get the habit; then after a while they become drunkards. They spend thousands of dollars trying to break the habit because sin gets a hold and reigns in their lives.

Men have said to me in tears, "I would give ten thousand worlds if I could quit drinking," or, "if I could break a certain habit." And they mean it. Before salvation, sin reigns as a king in our lives; but salvation included deliverance from the reign of sin.

Jesus said, "If the Son therefore shall make you free, ye shall be free indeed" (John 8:36). Paul said, "Where the Spirit of the Lord is, there is liberty" (II Cor. 3:17). When the Holy Spirit comes into our hearts, He gives liberty and we no longer have to be slaves of Satan. That alone is enough to make every man want to be saved.

But salvation is not only great because it includes deliverance from the reign of sin;

2. Salvation Is Great Because It Includes Peace With God

In Romans 5:1 the apostle said, "Therefore being justified by faith, we have peace with God through our Lord Jesus Christ."

The word "peace" means to reconcile two who have been enemies. In Romans 5:1 the word "peace" does not mean a change in your feelings but a change in God's feelings toward you. Before being saved you are God's enemy. Jesus said, "He that is not with me is against me; and he that gathereth not with me scattereth abroad" (Matt. 12:30). There is no neutral ground.

People have said to me, "I'm not anti-religious, I'm not anti-Christ, I'm not anti-church. I am not for Him, but I am certainly not against Him." I know they were sincere, but Jesus said, 'If you are not for me, you are against me.' There are only two positions: for Him or against Him. If you are without the Saviour, God regards you as His enemy, not His friend. James 4:4 says, "Whosoever therefore will be a friend of the world is the enemy of God."

However, the moment you put your faith in the Lord Jesus Christ, Paul says you are justified by faith and you have peace with God. God puts His arm around you, and He no longer regards you as an enemy but a friend.

Say, if there were no Hell, if there were no Heaven, I still would want to be saved so I could be the friend of God while I live on earth. I would want to be saved just for the sake of being for Him and not against Him.

"So great salvation." It is great because it includes deliverance from the reign of sin and peace with God; but it is great, too, because

3. It Includes Deliverance From the Penalty of Sin

That is the main thing, "The wages of sin is death" (Rom. 6:23). Ezekiel 18:4 states, "The soul that sinneth, it shall die." God said to Adam in Genesis 2:17, "For in the day that thou eatest thereof thou shalt surely die."

There is a penalty for sin, and you can't get around it. The sinner owes a penalty, and God does not sacrifice His justice on the altar of His love. The penalty has to be paid for the sinner to go to Heaven. The penalty is Hell—the second death, the lake of fire. If I go on without salvation, without trusting Jesus as Saviour, then I must pay the penalty I owe. And the only way I can pay what I owe as a sinner is to die, go into Hell and stay there forever and ever and ever—paying on it but never getting it paid.

John 3:36 warns, "He that believeth not the Son shall not see life; but the wrath of God abideth on him." It stays there. Ten million years—and the wrath of God is still abiding. When the sinner has been in Hell a billion years, the wrath of God will still be abiding on him; he will still be suffering the torments of Hell, which are the penalty of sin.

But wait a minute. Two thousands years ago Jesus came to earth. He lived a sinless life. He went to the cross. God put our sin upon Him, and He died in our place to pay the penalty we owe. When we trust Jesus Christ as Saviour, the sentence is lifted and we are saved from the penalty of sin. John 3:18 states, "He that believeth on him is not condemned." The sentence has been lifted! The believing sinner is no longer under sentence; he is not condemned.

Romans 8:33 asks, "Who shall lay any thing to the charge of God's elect? It is God that justifieth." God is the One who justifies, and no one can lay anything to our charge. The sentence is gone, and we will never again be under the penalty of sin.

We read in Romans 8:1, "There is therefore now [n-o-w, not after awhile] no condemnation [no judgment] to them which are in Christ Jesus." It doesn't say, "There is no condemnation to those which are in the baptistry, or to those which are in the church, or to those which are in the 4-H Club." But, "There is therefore now no condemnation to them which are in Christ Jesus."

The person who is trusting Christ as Saviour is in a safe place. He is in Jesus Christ. Salvation is great because it includes being saved from the penalty of sin. No Hell for the believer. Jesus took his Hell 2,000 years ago.

But wait a minute. It is also great because

4. It Includes Having Your Own Attorney

I have often wondered how it would feel to have your own attorney. We had several attorneys in our church, but they were not as good as the One I am talking about. The One I speak of has never lost a case. When you trust Jesus Christ as Saviour, you get your own Lawyer.

The Bible says in I John 2:1, "My little children, these things write I unto you, that ye sin not. And if any man sin, we have an advocate" — an Attorney, a Counselor, One who pleads our case with God—our own private Attorney. He knows when I am in trouble before I do, and He pleads my case. Isn't that wonderful! He is my Advocate in Heaven.

5. It Is a Great Salvation Because It Includes the Abiding Presence of the Holy Spirit

When a person receives Christ as Saviour, the Holy Spirit comes in to take up permanent residence. Galatians 4:6 says, "And because ye are sons, God hath sent forth the Spirit of his Son into your hearts, crying, Abba, Father."

The day I became a son of God by faith in Jesus Christ, God gave the Holy Spirit to abide in me forever. No matter how dark the night, nor how severe the pain, nor how much the persecution, the Holy Spirit will never leave me. Jesus said, "And I will pray the Father, and he shall give you another Comforter, that he may abide with you for ever" (John 14:16).

Sometimes we who teach salvation by grace through faith are accused of giving a license to sin. Those who object say, "It will cause people to go out and live like the Devil." I disagree. Which is a better deterrent: a speed sign beside the highway that says, "Thou shalt not exceed 55 miles per hour," or the presence of a state patrolman with the blue lights on top of his car?

One of the men in our church, a policeman, stopped me one night. When he saw who it was he said, "O Pastor!"

I said, "Oh."

"You know, this is a 25 mph speed limit through here."

I answered, "Man, you can't go into all the world and preach the Gospel at 25 mph!"

"Go ahead," he said, "but don't do it again!"

I drove within the speed limit the rest of the way home. What the signs failed to accomplish, the presence of the policeman did.

When you are born again, the Holy Spirit comes in to take up His permanent residence; and His presence in your life will cause you to live more like you ought to live than ten thousand rules and regulations.

6. So Great Salvation Includes a Perfect Standing Before God

When you trust Jesus Christ as Saviour, God looks at you as if you had never committed a sin. He gives you a perfect standing. Your state may not always be perfect, but your standing is. God sees you as clean and pure and just as Jesus Himself. "Therefore being justified by faith, we have peace with God through our Lord Jesus Christ" (Rom. 5:1). It is great salvation!

II. SALVATION IS GREAT BECAUSE OF WHAT WAS REQUIRED TO ACCOMPLISH IT

When God created the worlds, He did it with His word: Psalm 33:6, "By the word of the Lord were the heavens made; and all the host of them by the breath of his mouth." Second Peter 3:5 says, ". . . by the word of God the heavens were of old." Hebrews 1:3 states, "Who being the brightness of his glory, and the express image of his person, and upholding all things by the word of his power. . . ."

God Almighty spoke and the worlds came into existence. But God could not save sinners by His word alone. He could not say, "Let sinners be saved," and have every sinner saved. It took more than His word.

The point I am trying to make is this: it took more for salvation of sinners than it did to create all the worlds, all the planets, and all the universe. God only had to speak and they came into existence. But when God wanted to save sinners, He had to come into the world Himself, take upon Himself a human body, live a perfect, sinless life in that body thirty-three years, bear in that body our sins and suffer on a cross everything we would have to suffer if we died without Him and went to Hell. He had to be raised from the dead for our justification.

I am saying that when He was ready to save sinners, it took more than speaking a word. He had to take the sinner's place and suffer the sinner's Hell in order for the sinner to be saved. Salvation is very expensive. Jesus paid it all two thousand years ago at Calvary. He could form the world by the word of His mouth, but He could only save sinners as He Himself took on the human body, went to Calvary, suffered Hell, was buried and rose again on the third day. It took much more to save sinners than it did to create worlds.

Salvation is great because of what was required to accomplish it.

III. SALVATION IS GREAT BECAUSE OF ITS AVAILABILITY

Most people in America can get a good education, but this is not true in some countries. All men cannot have riches. Their opportunities are not as good as others. All men may not have health. Some are born sickly. There are many things that are not available to all men. But regardless of what the hyper-Calvinists teach, salvation is available to any and every man.

When Mr. Moody was preaching on "whosoever will, let him come," a hyper-Calvinist said, "Mr. Moody, don't you know that some are elected to be saved and others are elected to be lost and just 'whosoever' cannot be saved?"

D. L. Moody answered, "I preach the Gospel to 'whosoever'; and if I happen to get one saved who was elected to be lost, I believe God will forgive me."

That was a good answer. It is a "whosoever" salvation.

"And the Spirit and the bride say, Come. And let him that heareth say, Come. And let him that is athirst come. And whosoever will, let him take the water of life freely."—Rev. 22:17.

"For God so loved the world, that he gave his only begotten Son."—John 3:16.

"But we see Jesus, who was made a little lower than the angels for the suffering of death, crowned with glory and honour; that he by the grace of God should taste death for every man."—Heb. 2:9.

"And he is the propitiation for our sins: and not for our's only, but also for the sins of the whole world."—I John 2:2.

Not one sinner ever lived whom Jesus didn't die for. There is not a sinner on the top side of God's earth who cannot be saved if he wills to be saved.

In John 5:40 Jesus says, "And ye will not come to me, that ye might have life."

Jesus says in John 12:32, "And I, if I be lifted up from the earth, will draw all [a-l-l, not the elect; you don't spell elect 'a-l-l'] men unto me."

Romans 5:18, "Even so by the righteousness of one the free gift came upon all [that is not elect, that is 'a-l-l'] men unto justification of life."

Second Corinthians 5:19, "God was in Christ, reconciling the world unto himself."

First Timothy 2:4, "Who will have *a-l-l* men to be saved, and to come unto the knowledge of the truth."

First Timothy 2:6, "Who gave himself a ransom for *a-l-l.*"

First Timothy 4:10, "We trust, in the living God, who is the Saviour of *a-l-l* men, specially of those that believe."

Titus 2:11, "For the grace of God that bringeth salvation hath appeared to *a-l-l* men."

Over and over again the Bible says that Jesus Christ was sent to be the Saviour of the world. First John 4:14 says, "The Father sent the Son to be the Saviour of the world." Salvation is great because of its availability.

Then too:

IV. SALVATION IS GREAT BECAUSE OF ITS SIMPLICITY

Dr. Bob Jones, Sr., once said, "Simplicity is truth's most becoming garment." Paul said, "But I fear, lest by any means, as the serpent beguiled Eve through his subtilty, so your minds should be corrupted from the simplicity that is in Christ" (II Cor. 11:3). It sounds so simple that most men reject it. But let me tell you, salvation can be had by all men simply by believing.

Some of you are thinking, "That is too easy. You mean to tell me that if I just believe on the Lord Jesus Christ, I will be saved?" That's what the Bible says: "Believe on the Lord Jesus Christ, and thou shalt be saved" (Acts 16:31). Ninety-nine times the Gospel of John says believe, believe, believe.

The Bible word "believe" means to trust, to depend, to rely upon. It is one thing to say, "I believe in my head that the automobile will run," and another thing to trust it to carry you to your destination.

It is said that a tight-wire walker stretched a long rope across Niagara Falls. He would go across that wire rope and come back. Then he got on a bicycle and rode it across and back. After that he pushed a wheelbarrow across and back. When he got back to the other side, he looked down at a boy and said, "Do you believe I can take you across in that wheelbarrow?"

"Oh, I sure do," the boy replied. "I have seen you go back and forth on the bicycle and with the wheelbarrow."

"Well, get in."

But the boy refused. There is a difference in believing in your head that the man can do it and trusting him to do it.

The Bible word "believe" means to trust Him to do it. It means that you say in your head, "I know I'm a sinner. I know that sinners owe a penalty and the penalty is the second death in the lake of fire. I know that Jesus Christ died on the cross two thousand years ago for sinners. I know He died for me. I know when He died He paid what I owe. I know that. I believe that."

You are very close to being saved when you accept that. But you must not only believe Jesus did die for you and that His death paid your sin debt; you must come to the place where you say and sincerely mean it, "From this moment on, I will completely depend on Jesus and trust Him for my salvation." You must get in the wheelbarrow. You can die and go to Hell believing that Jesus is a good Man, that He died for sinners and that He will carry sinners to Heaven. That is not enough; you must trust Him completely for your salvation. You must trust Him and nothing else.

I am not going to Heaven because I go to church regularly. I am not going to Heaven because I read the Bible. I am not going to Heaven because I pray. I am not going to Heaven because I live good. I am not going to Heaven because of my denominational affiliation. I am going to Heaven for one reason and one reason only: Jesus Christ took my place 2,000 years ago and died for me to pay what I owed. He suffered my Hell, and I am going to Heaven on a free pass.

I was in a little country church a few months ago. After the service was over, I noticed a man walking back and forth, up and down the aisle. I introduced myself and said, "Sir, I believe you raised your hand that you were not sure you were saved."

"Yes," he said.

"You stayed behind. Evidently you are concerned."

He said, "I am."

Taking the Bible I told him the gospel story that I have told thousands and thousands of times. I explained that he was a sinner. He said, "I know." I showed him what he owed as a sinner and how Jesus paid what he owed when He died at Calvary. He listened very attentively, then said, "Yes, I know."

We bowed our heads, I prayed, and then asked, "Will you trust Him?" I explained what trusting is.

"Yes, I will," and he trusted Christ.

After leading him to Christ, I asked, "Now, if you died today, would you go to Heaven?"

"I hope so," he said.

"I can't leave you like that, Sir. I don't want to leave you with a 'hope so,' I want to leave you with assurance."

I took the Bible and showed him where it says, "Whosoever believeth [trusteth] in him should not perish, but have everlasting life."

"Has what?" I asked.

He replied, "Everlasting life."

I continued, "I don't suppose God meant that."

"Oh, yes, He meant it."

"If He meant it, do you have everlasting life?"

"If I'm trusting Him."

"Well, are you trusting Him completely to get you to Heaven?"

"Yes, I am."

Then I said, "He that believeth on the Son hath what?"

Again he said, "Everlasting life."

I gave him this illustration: "Sir, if you don't go to Heaven, I won't go to Heaven."

He said, "Oh, but you're a preacher! You are conducting this revival meeting!"

"I know. But, you see, I'm not trusting the fact that I'm a preacher to get me to Heaven. I am not trusting the fact that I am holding a revival meeting to get me there. I am trusting the same thing to get me to Heaven that you are trusting to get you to Heaven.

"Suppose you and I get in a boat and start across a lake. You say, 'I hope I make it.' And I say, 'Well, I hope I do, too.' But you say, 'I know you are going to make it. You are a preacher. You are holding a revival meeting.' Then I say, 'Wait a minute, Sir, if you don't make it, neither will I. We are both in the same boat. We are trusting the same vessel to get across the lake. If this thing springs a leak, we are both going down.' "

He began to smile and said, "I see."

I assured him, "I am trusting the same thing to get me to

Heaven that you are trusting to get you to Heaven."

What are you trusting for your salvation? The Bible says, "Believe on the Lord Jesus Christ, and thou shalt be saved."

SO GREAT SALVATION

So great salvation has won my heart,
From the Creator it had its start;
First He made man to live a life complete,
He then the choice did give His will to meet.
Since that sad moment when man did fail,
God in His mercy still does prevail;
For our redemption a plan He gave—
So great salvation, our souls to save.

So great salvation has changed my heart,
My life's ambition He did impart;
A new desire to live, His will, not mine,
His righteousness He gives, He is divine.
Now all around I see sin's poverty,
God in His goodness can make us free;
For our redemption a plan He gave—
So great salvation, our souls to save.

—Gloria Roe

I URGE YOU TO TRUST CHRIST NOW

You have read my message, "'So Great Salvation.'" The Bible warns, "How shall we escape, if we neglect so great salvation." If you refuse to take advantage of this great salvation by trusting Jesus Christ as Saviour, then it is impossible for you to escape the penalty of sin. The penalty of sin is Hell, the second death, the lake of fire. Revelation 20:14 states, "And death and hell were cast into the lake of fire. This is the second death."

I urge you now to trust Christ as your own personal Saviour. Will you pray this prayer?

> Dear Lord Jesus, I know I'm a sinner. I do believe that You died for me. Realizing the greatness of salvation, I now accept You as my Saviour. From this moment on, I am fully depending upon You to get me to Heaven. Now, help me to live for You and to be a good Christian. Amen.

Then will you write to tell me you have trusted Christ? I have some free literature I want to send that will help you as you set out to live the Christian life. All you need do to receive your free literature is write me:

Dr. Curtis Hutson
Sword of the Lord Foundation
P. O. Box 1099
Murfreesboro, Tennessee 37133

and say, "I have read your message, 'So Great Salvation.' I know I am a sinner and do believe that Jesus Christ died for me. The best I know how I do trust Him as my Saviour. From this moment on I am fully depending on Him to get me to Heaven. Please send me the free literature that will help me as I set out to live the Christian life."

Chapter 5

Lessons From Calvary

"And they that passed by reviled him, wagging their heads, And saying, Thou that destroyest the temple, and buildest it in three days, save thyself. If thou be the Son of God, come down from the cross. Likewise also the chief priests mocking him, with the scribes and elders, said, He saved others; himself he cannot save. If he be the King of Israel, let him now come down from the cross, and we will believe him. He trusted in God; let him deliver him now, if he will have him: for he said, I am the Son of God. The thieves also, which were crucified with him, cast the same in his teeth. Now from the sixth hour there was darkness over all the land unto the ninth hour. And about the ninth hour Jesus cried with a loud voice, saying, Eli, Eli, lama sabachthani? that is to say, My God, my God, why hast thou forsaken me?"—Matt. 27:39-46.

"And one of the malefactors which were hanged railed on him, saying, If thou be Christ, save thyself and us. But the other answering rebuked him, saying, Dost not thou fear God, seeing thou art in the same condemnation? And we indeed justly; for we received the due reward of our deeds: but this man hath done nothing amiss. And he said unto Jesus, Lord, remember me when thou comest into thy kingdom. And Jesus said unto him, Verily I say unto thee, To day shalt thou be with me in paradise."—Luke 23:39-43.

The Bible is a most amazing Book. It is the inspired, inerrant

Word of God. Not only were the truths in the Bible revealed to Bible writers, but the words to convey those truths are God-chosen. That is what we mean by "verbal inspiration."

Not long ago *Reader's Digest* condensed the Bible. But what they did not know was that the Bible had already been condensed to its minimum.

We must remember that the Bible is not a revelation of what God knows but a revelation of what God wants men to know. If it were a revelation of what God knew, the world could not contain the books that would have been written; because there is absolutely nothing that God doesn't know. This is proven by John 21:25: "And there are also many other things which Jesus did, the which, if they should be written every one, I suppose that even the world itself could not contain the books that should be written."

As the Bible is a condensed Book, then every word is important and filled with meaning. There is nothing accidental in the Bible record of what took place on Calvary. God planned every detail, and every part has tremendous meaning and significance. Christ's death on the cross was no afterthought with God. It was not an emergency measure. Concerning Jesus Christ, the Bible says that He was "the Lamb slain from the foundation of the world" (Rev. 13:8).

Since God is omniscient, He knew beforehand that man would sin and so, before man was created, He planned a way of escape, a way of salvation.

The cross has many important lessons.

First, we have the lesson of the

Crown of Thorns

Matthew 27:29 says, "And when they had platted a crown of thorns, they put it upon his head. . ." to mock Jesus because He claimed to be a King.

I have read that those thorns had points as sharp as a needle and as poisonous and painful as the sting of a wasp. When they pressed that crown upon His head, the poison caused His face and head to swell, bringing agonizing pain.

Men placed the crown of thorns on His head to mock Him, to cause additional pain. But God had another reason for that thorny crown. Thorns are a symbol of the curse. After Adam and Eve sinned, God pronounced a curse upon man and the entire earth. We read in Genesis 3:17,18:

"And unto Adam he said, Because thou hast hearkened unto the voice of thy wife, and hast eaten of the tree, of which I commanded thee, saying, Thou shalt not eat of it: cursed is the ground for thy sake; in sorrow shalt thou eat of it all the days of thy life; Thorns also and thistles shall it bring forth to thee; and thou shalt eat the herb of the field."

Whenever we see a thorn, it is God's reminder that sin brings a curse. The death of Jesus Christ on the cross was payment for our sins, and all who trust Him are saved from the curse of sin. Galatians 3:13 tells us the good news: "Christ hath redeemed us from the curse of the law, being made a curse for us: for it is written, Cursed is every one that hangeth on a tree."

The crown of thorns teaches that sin brings a curse but that the death of Christ saves us from the curse of the law.

Then there is the lesson of the

Three Hours of Darkness

While Jesus was on the cross, it became as black as an Egyptian midnight from 12:00 until 3:00 in the afternoon. "And it was about the sixth hour, and there was a darkness over all the earth until the ninth hour" (Luke 23:44).

Several years ago I preached a sermon entitled "Calvary, the Sinner's Hell in Review." I read the account of the crucifixion and the story of the rich man in Hell from Luke 16. I went from one to the other, showing that Jesus suffered on the cross everything the rich man in Hell suffered.

The rich man suffered the agony of thirst, for he said, "Father Abraham, have mercy on me, and send Lazarus, that he may dip the tip of his finger in water, and cool my tongue; for I am tormented in this flame." On the cross Jesus cried out, "I thirst."

The rich man suffered the agony of separation. He was told by Abraham, "Between us and you there is a great gulf fixed: so that they which would pass from hence to you cannot; neither can they pass to us, that would come from thence." On the cross Jesus was separated from the Father. He cried, "My God, my God, why hast thou forsaken me?"

Concerning the lost, Matthew 22:13 tells us, "Bind him hand and foot, and take him away, and cast him into outer darkness; there shall be weeping and gnashing of teeth." According to this verse, part of the suffering of the lost will be darkness.

Concerning fallen angels, Jude 6 says that they are "reserved in everlasting chains under darkness unto the judgment of the great day." On the cross Jesus was suffering the sinner's Hell and part of that Hell is darkness.

When we sing, "Jesus Paid It All," we can rest assured that it is more than sentiment; it is a solid fact. Jesus paid our sin debt, and He paid it in full.

Next is the lesson of the

Cry During the Darkness

Jesus uttered seven things while suspended between Heaven and earth—as if rejected by both. Three utterances came before the darkness, one during the darkness, and three after the darkness. The cry that came during the darkness is found in Matthew 27:46, "My God, my God, why hast thou forsaken me?" This is the only time in the earthly life of Jesus that He addressed God other than "Father." He spoke of Him to the people as God; but when He spoke to Him, He always addressed Him as "Father." Now it is different. He is crying, "My God, my God. . . ." What does it mean?

The Bible says in II Corinthians 5:21, "For he hath made him to be sin for us, who knew no sin; that we might be made the righteousness of God in him." On the cross Jesus has taken the sinner's place, and the sinner does not know God as his Father. The cry of Jesus, "My God, my God, why hast thou forsaken me?" is the cry of an abandoned soul without a Saviour.

Jesus was forsaken by the Father that He might suffer the agony of separation so that those who believe on Christ will never have to suffer such agony. He was separated from the Father for a few hours that we might live with the Father forever and ever.

It is difficult to see how anyone who understands the substitutionary death of Jesus on the cross can reject such a Saviour.

Then there is the lesson of the

Fifth Cross Utterance

The fifth utterance from the cross is found in John 19:28: "After this, Jesus knowing that all things were accomplished, that the scripture might be fulfilled, saith, I thirst."

I mentioned earlier that Jesus suffered on the cross everything lost people suffer in Hell. If He didn't, then our sin debt has not been fully paid. In Hell the rich man said, "Send Lazarus, that he may dip the tip of his finger in water, and cool my tongue; for I am tormented in this flame." The rich man suffered the agony of thirst; but on the cross Jesus suffered the same agony in order to fully pay what we owe as sinners.

Why did they nail Him to Calvary's Tree?
Why? tell me, why was He there?
Jesus the Helper, the Healer, the Friend,
Why, tell me, why was He there?

All my iniquities on Him were laid,
He nail'd them all to the Tree;
Jesus the debt of my sin fully paid,
He paid the ransom for me.

Next is the lesson of the

Impenitent Thief

There were three crosses on Calvary—a thief on either side and Jesus in the middle. History tells us that the Roman government reserved execution by crucifixion for the worst of criminals. Those crucified were so low, vile and base that they were not considered worthy of a decent or respectable burial.

Not only were they nailed to the cross, but I have read that at the foot of the cross a ditch was dug and when the man died, he was rolled into it like a dead dog, covered up and left there. That was their plan for Jesus, but Joseph of Arimathaea came and begged His body and buried Him in a borrowed tomb. The Lord was crucified between two thieves because man wanted to brand Him forever as that kind of character. But God had those two thieves there for another purpose.

At first both thieves joined with the crowd in railing on Christ. "The thieves also, which were crucified with him, cast the same in his teeth," says Matthew 27:44. But as the hours went by, one thief saw something in Jesus that made him change his mind. In Luke 23:40,41, he said to the other thief:

"Dost not thou fear God, seeing thou art in the same condemnation? And we indeed justly; for we receive the due reward of our deeds: but this man hath done nothing amiss."

But the other thief, whom we call the impenitent one, was not affected in the least. Rather he continued railing at Christ to the bitter end, showing how hard and calloused the human heart can become. It is difficult to believe that he could be crucified next to the very Son of God, yet continue his railing, knowing that there was absolutely nothing to gain by it.

Every time a person rejects Christ as Saviour, his heart becomes more and more hardened, lessening his chances of ever being saved.

One of the Devil's best tricks is to say to men, "Wait until you feel more like it." That sounds reasonable, but the Devil knows that every time a person says no to Christ, he feels less and less like it.

Several years ago someone made a study of this by counting the crowd and asking at what age people were saved. This person came up with this answer:

If one isn't saved by the time he is 21, the chances are 5,000 to 1 that he will ever be saved.

If he isn't saved by the time he is 30, the chances then are 15,000 to 1 that he will ever be saved.

If he isn't saved by the time he is 40, the chances then are 30,000 to 1.

And if he isn't saved by the time he is 50, the chances are 150,000 to 1 that he will ever trust Christ as Saviour.

Every time a person says no to Jesus Christ, it is easier to say no the next time.

The impenitent thief shows how hard the human heart can become through its continual rejection of Jesus Christ. If someone reading these lines has the least desire to trust Christ, I urge you not to wait another moment. Every time you reject Him, you feel less and less like accepting Him as Saviour.

Finally, the lesson of the

Penitent Thief

The thief on the other side of Jesus cried out, "Lord, remember me when thou comest into thy kingdom" (Luke 23:42). And in verse 43 Jesus said to him, "Verily I say unto thee, To day shalt thou be with me in paradise." My, what wonderful lessons in these words!

This thief teaches us that even the most wicked sinner can be saved if he will only call on Christ and trust Him as Saviour. This thief teaches us that none is beyond redemption, that none has waited too late.

The dying thief rejoiced to see
That fountain in his day;
And there may I, though vile as he,
Wash all my sins away.

An old preacher once said, "There was one such case recorded in the Scriptures that none need despair, but only one that none might presume."

We know this thief was saved because Jesus said, "To day shalt thou be with me in paradise." In other words, "I am going to take you to Heaven with Me today."

Now note several important lessons.

He wasn't saved because he was good. This man had no goodness to offer Christ. He was a thief and the worst kind of criminal. The very fact that he was being crucified indicated that.

Many religions teach that man is saved by his own good life. But we are reminded in Titus 3:5, "Not by works of righteousness which we have done, but according to his mercy he saved us." And in Ephesians 2:8, 9, "For by grace are ye saved through faith; and that not of yourselves: it is the gift of God: Not of works, lest any man should boast."

People say that you must be good to go to Heaven. But no man goes to Heaven on his own goodness; he goes on the goodness of God. The Bible says in Romans 10:4, "For Christ is the end of the law for righteousness to every one that believeth." You don't get better to get saved; you get saved to get better. Jesus did not come to save good people; He came to save sinners.

Paul said in I Timothy 1:15, "This is a faithful saying, and worthy of all acceptation, that Christ Jesus came into the world to save sinners; of whom I am chief." No man qualifies for sonship until he recognizes his sinnership.

This thief was saved despite the fact that he wasn't good. And his salvation teaches that one is saved by grace alone through faith alone.

He wasn't saved because he was a member of the church. This poor thief never had time to join a church. When he died, they took him down from the cross, rolled him into a ditch that had been prepared for his burial, and covered him with dirt.

Thousands of religious people say that you must belong to a church in order to be saved. In fact, some go so far as to teach that if you don't belong to their particular denomination, then you are not saved. They claim that their church is The Church and anyone who dies outside of it goes to Hell. How sad that men should put a church up as the Saviour!

Now everyone who trusts Christ as Saviour should join a good Bible-believing church and attend it faithfully. But you don't join a church to get saved; you join a church because you are already saved.

Dear friend, Jesus Christ is the Saviour, and He doesn't share it with anything or anyone. Many who have joined a church will not go to Heaven. Jesus said in Matthew 7:22, 23,

"Many will say to me in that day, Lord, Lord, have we not prophesied in thy name? and in thy name have cast out devils? and in thy name done many wonderful works? And then will I profess unto them, I never knew you: depart from me, ye that work iniquity."

Religion has never taken anybody to Heaven, but it has taken multitudes to Hell.

A man might have good character; he may have good works; he may have membership in a good church; but if he doesn't have Jesus Christ, he doesn't have life according to I John 5:11, 12:

"And this is the record, that God hath given to us eternal life, and this life is in his Son. He that hath the Son hath life; and he that hath not the Son of God hath not life."

He wasn't saved because he was baptized. Jesus said to him, "To day shalt thou be with me in paradise." In other words, "I am going to take you to Heaven with Me today." Now let's face the facts. This thief was never baptized. If baptism were essential to salvation, Jesus would have said, "I'm sorry but I cannot take you to Paradise unless we can get down off these crosses and I can baptize you."

Now every believer should be baptized. But you don't get baptized to get saved; you get baptized because you are already saved. The Bible order is always, "believe and be baptized."

Baptism is like putting the wedding band on the finger after one is married. Placing the band on the finger does not marry the person; it is only a symbol to show others that he is married. And baptism is an outward symbol showing that one has trusted Jesus Christ as Saviour, that he believes in the death, burial and resurrection of the Son of God.

God puts no condition or requirement on salvation that could possibly shut anyone out. There is no condition in the Bible that any sinner on earth could not comply with and be saved instantly. The only condition is found in Acts 16:31, *"Believe* on the Lord Jesus Christ, and thou shalt be saved."

He was saved because he saw himself as a sinner. In Luke 23:41, this penitent thief said, "And we indeed justly; for we receive the due reward of our deeds: but this man hath done nothing amiss." With these words, this poor thief admitted that he was a sinner, that he was getting what he justly deserved.

I once heard a preacher say, "I used to ask people, 'Are you saved?' Now I ask, 'Have you ever been lost?' " The dear man meant that men must see themselves as sinners before they can be saved. Jesus said, "I came not to call the righteous, but sinners to repentance" (Luke 5:32). Paul said, "Christ Jesus came into the world to save sinners; of whom I am chief." And Luke 19:10 says, "For the Son of man is come to seek and to save that which was lost."

I heard a Presbyterian preacher say that if we went to Heaven and wrote across Heaven's door, "For sinners only," God would come out and smile. Heaven is for sinners who have trusted Jesus Christ as Saviour.

One of the most difficult things to do is to get men to see they are sinners in need of a Saviour. Some will say, "I live a good life." Others, "I pay my just and honest debts." Still others, "I'm a good father and a good husband." When I asked one man if he were sure he would go to Heaven when he died, he replied, "Well, I'm not so bad." But Romans 3:10 tells us, "There is none righteous, no, not one."

He was saved because he trusted Jesus Christ for salvation. This poor thief knew that he could not save himself, that Jesus Christ was his only hope of salvation, so he cried, "Lord, remember me when thou comest into thy kingdom."

No way could he promise to do better, for his life was coming to an end. No way could he be baptized; he would be dead before they could get him to a baptistry. His only hope was Jesus. And, by the way, that was all he needed. Jesus is tailor-made for sinners!

Someone gave this acrostic:

Jesus
Exactly
Suits
Us
Sinners

It took great faith for that thief to believe that Jesus was God. Remember both were hanging on a cross, and this poor thief was looking at a dying Jesus. But he trusted Him anyway. If this penitent thief could trust Christ, then how much easier it is for us to trust Him today!

We are living nearly 2,000 years this side of any empty tomb. The world has had almost 2,000 years in which to witness and experience the saving power of a risen Christ. God saved this thief to show the world that Jesus will save anybody who will trust Him. One never gets too low nor too deep in sin. God means it when He says in Isaiah 1:18, "Though your sins be as scarlet, they shall be as white as snow; though they be red like crimson, they shall be as wool."

But remember—two thieves were crucified with Christ. One died rejecting Christ, and the other died trusting Him for salvation.

While preaching on the urgency of salvation, the preacher said, "You ought to be saved now. Tomorrow may be too late."

A man in the balcony stood and shouted down to the preacher, "But what about the dying thief?"

The preacher looked up and said, "Which thief?"
You see, two thieves died that day.

I Urge You to Trust Christ Today

You have seen from the story of the crucifixion that Jesus Christ died to pay man's sin debt, that His death on the cross fully paid what we sinners owe. You have also seen that Jesus is willing to save the worst of sinners and that no one need despair.

If you have never trusted Jesus Christ as Saviour, won't you call on Him today? In your own words tell Him that you know you're a sinner, that you believe He died for you, and that you are fully trusting Him to take you to Heaven when you die. If you will trust Him and write to tell me so, I have some free literature I want to send that will help you as you set out to live the Christian life. All you need do to receive your free literature is fill out the decision form below and mail it to me.

My Decision

Dr. Curtis Hutson
Sword of the Lord Foundation
P. O. Box 1099
Murfreesboro, Tennessee 37133

Dear Dr. Hutson:

I have read your sermon, "Lessons From Calvary." Knowing that I'm a sinner and believing that Jesus Christ died for me, I here and now trust Him as my Saviour. I believe He fully paid my sin debt, and I am completely depending on Him to take me to Heaven when I die.

Please send me the free literature that will help me as I set out to live the Christian life.

Date ______________________________

Name ____

Address ______________________________________

____

Chapter 6

Four Truths About Salvation

"If we say that we have no sin, we deceive ourselves, and the truth is not in us."—I John 1:8,9.

"My little children, these things write I unto you, that ye sin not. And if any man sin, we have an advocate with the Father, Jesus Christ the righteous: And he is the propitiation for our sins: and not for our's only, but also for the sins of the whole world."—I John 2:1, 2.

"He that committeth sin is of the devil; for the devil sinneth from the beginning. . . . Whosoever is born of God doth not commit sin; for his seed remaineth in him: and he cannot sin, because he is born of God. In this the children of God are manifest, and the children of the devil: whosoever doeth not righteousness is not of God, neither he that loveth not his brother."—I John 3:8-10.

"Whosoever believeth that Jesus is the Christ is born of God: and every one that loveth him that begat loveth him also that is begotten of him."—I John 5:1.

"These things have I written unto you that believe on the name of the Son of God; that ye may know that ye have eternal life, and that ye may believe on the name of the Son of God."—I John 5:13.

There are five chapters and 105 verses in the First Epistle of

John. The word "truth" or "know" is found thirty-six times.

From these five chapters I call attention to four truths about salvation.

Everyone Needs to Be Saved

First John 1, verses 8 and 9, says, "If we say that we have no sin, we deceive ourselves, and the truth is not in us. If we confess our sins, he is faithful and just to forgive us our sins, and to cleanse us from all unrighteousness." Notice the word "sin" in verse 8.

Sin is what we are—that's our nature. David said in Psalm 51:5, "Behold, I was shapen in iniquity; and in sin did my mother conceive me." Something inside all of us pulls us in the wrong direction.

Every little baby is born with a sin nature. Little ones come into the world with their fists clenched as if to say, "Mine!" No child automatically says, "Yes, Sir" or "Yes, Ma'am" or "Thank you very much." They have to be taught these courtesies. (By the way, anything you have to be taught to do is not part of your nature, and anything you do without being taught is part of your nature.)

A child doesn't have to be taught to be selfish. A little fellow can be in the living room playing with twenty-five toys, and if a neighbor child comes over and picks up one of them, he will yell, "That's mine! That's mine! Give it to me; it's mine!" A child must be taught to share.

He also must be taught to say, "Thank you." If I had said it once, I've said it a thousand times to my children, "Now what do you say?" And I've had to say it over and over again until they said, "Thank you."

When a little boy was given a piece of cake and he said, "Thank you, Ma'am," the lady was so startled that she turned and said, "Oh! I like to hear little boys say, 'Thank you.' " The little fellow grinned and said, "Put some ice cream on it and I'll say it again."

We were born with a sin nature. And everyone needs to be saved. Psalm 58:3 tells us, "The wicked are estranged from the womb: they go astray as soon as they be born, speaking lies." When I first saw that verse, I thought, *Now wait a minute! How can a child start telling lies from his mother's womb when he can't yet talk?*

However, our first baby had not been home very long before I learned how the wicked go astray as soon as they are born, speaking lies.

My wife and I were sound asleep. In the middle of the night the most blood-curdling, spine-tingling scream came out of that baby's bedroom. "WHAAH! WHAAH!"

I nudged Gerri: "Go see about your baby!" When she got to the bedroom, that little one looked up and said, "Goo, goo!" She had cried like she was hurting, but she wasn't. She couldn't spell lie and she couldn't say lie, but she lied. And she really lied nearly every night for months. Any time she wanted attention, she screamed like she was really hurting. But when we got to her little crib, she would look up and say, "Goo, goo!"

The Bible is right—the wicked so go astray as soon as they are born, speaking lies.

I have a red-headed boy who lied after he was able to talk. I remember catching him one day with both hands in a jar of strawberry jam. Slipping up behind him, I loudly said, "Tony!" He looked around. I said, "Look me in the eyes, Boy, and don't you lie to me! Have you had your hands in that strawberry jam?"

That little fellow looked up with the most innocent expression and said, "No, Thir! No, Thir!"

I was so angry! I said, "Son, look at me. Daddies have a way of knowing when boys put their hands in strawberry jam. And I want you to know that I know whether or not you have had your hands in that jam jar. If you will tell me the truth, I won't whip you. Now look me in the eyes and tell me. Have you had your hands in that jam jar?"

Again he said, "No, Thir! No, Thir!" He said that with jam all over both hands, arms and face!

I said, "Son, if you haven't had your hands in that jam jar, what is that all over your arms?"

He looked down, paused, then said, "I don't know. What is that?"

You laugh because yours did the same thing. Why do they do it? Something inside called sin pulls them in the wrong direction.

Everyone needs to be saved because everyone has a *sin nature.* Then everyone needs to be saved because everyone has committed sins. Verse 9 says, "If we confess our *sins,* he is faithful and just to forgive us. . . ." *Sin* in verse 8 is what we are. *Sins* in verse 9 are the things we do because we are what we are.

Not every person has committed the same sins, but we read in Romans 3:23, "For all have sinned, and come short of the glory of God." I've never been drunk. I don't know what whiskey or beer taste like. I don't know the taste of cigarettes. There are a lot of sins that I have not committed. But I know I have sinned.

I used to think a man was a sinner because he sinned. But that's not necessarily true. The sins don't make the sinner. The sinner makes the sins. A dog is not a dog because he barks. He barks because he is a dog. And I might say not all dogs bark the same. Some dogs bark more than others, yet all dogs are dogs.

Now, I've said that to say this: Not all men sin the same. Some sin more than others, but all men are sinners. You don't have to commit every sin in the catalog to be lost.

Dr. Joe Henry Hankins once asked his doctor, "Doc, what is the strongest poison known to man?"

The doctor replied, "Potassium cyanide."

Brother Hankins said, "Doc, how much potassium cyanide would a man have to drink in order for it to kill him?"

The doctor's answer was, "Brother Hankins, it is so strong that if a man took the stopper out of a bottle of potassium cyanide and touched underneath his tongue where the blood vessels are nearest the surface, he wouldn't live to get the stopper back into the bottle."

Brother Hankins continued: "What difference would it make if he were to drink the whole bottle?"

The doctor replied, "I don't see what you're getting at, Brother Hankins. It wouldn't make any difference. The man would be dead either way."

Then Brother Hankins explained, "Doc, a lot of people in this country think they have to commit every sin in the catalog to be lost. The truth is, they are lost whether they ever commit another sin or not."

Everyone needs to be saved because everyone has a sin nature. And everyone has committed sins. "All have sinned, and come short of the glory of God." There are no perfect people.

Everyone Can Be Saved

Look at I John 2:1,2, "My little children, these things write I unto you, that ye sin not. And if any man sin, we have an advocate with the Father, Jesus Christ the righteous: And he is the propitiation [or atoning sacrifice] for our sins: and not for our's only, but also for the sins of the whole world."

The greatest truth is the truth of the substitutionary death of Jesus. Two thousand years ago God took every sin I had ever committed and all the sins I will ever commit and laid them on Christ, for Isaiah 53:6 says, ". . . the Lord hath laid on him the iniquity of us all." And I Peter 2:24 says, "Who his own self bare our sins in his own body on the tree. . . ."

When I once told a lady that Jesus Christ died for all her sins—past, present and future, she said, "I can understand how He died for my past sins that I've already committed, but I don't understand how He died for my future sins that I haven't even committed yet."

I smiled as I said, "Lady, when Jesus Christ died, all your sins were future. You were not even born." She nodded in agreement.

If I had to remember every sin I have ever committed and confess it to go to Heaven, then I would be lost forever. I can't remember all the sins I've ever committed, but even the sins I've forgotten about, Christ bore them in His own body. Every lie I've ever told, every act of disobedience, every evil thought, every sin I've ever committed, was laid on Christ. And while Jesus Christ was bearing my sins in His own body, God punished Him in my place to pay the debt that I owe.

The Bible says in Romans 6:23 that "the wages of sin is death." And Ezekiel 18:4 tells us, ". . . the soul that sinneth, it shall die." God's payment for sin is death, which is described as the second death, the lake of fire, in Revelation 20:14: "And death and hell were cast into the lake of fire. This is the second death." If we had to pay what we owe as sinners, we would have to go into Hell forever and ever.

Since God is immutable, His payment for sin never changes. But two thousand years ago God placed all our sins on Christ and punished Him in our place to pay the debt we owe. That's what I John 2:2 means: ". . . he is the propitiation for our sins: and not for our's only, but also for the sins of the whole world."

Oh, why was He there as the Bearer of sin if on Jesus
my guilt was not laid;
And why did He shed His life-giving blood if His dying
my debt has not paid?

Now if Jesus Christ died for the whole world, if He is the propitiation or atoning sacrifice for the whole world, then it sounds like the whole world is saved. But all the people in the world are not. The whole world is potentially saved, but no one is actually saved until he trusts Jesus Christ as his Saviour. The death of Christ on the cross is sufficient for all, but it is efficient only to those who believe.

Nobody will ever look out of Hell and say to Jesus, "I wanted to be saved, but You didn't die for me," since Christ died for the whole world. Hebrews 2:9 says that He tasted death for every man.

Since Jesus Christ is the propitiation for our sins and not for ours only but also for the sins of the whole world, then everyone who needs to be saved can be saved.

Everyone Is Saved the Same Way

First John 5:1, "Whosoever believeth that Jesus is the Christ is born of God. . . ." Note the word "believeth" here. "Believe" is found at least ninety times in the Gospel of John. And in John 3:36 Jesus divides the whole world into two groups: "He that believeth on the Son hath everlasting life: and he that believeth not the Son shall not see life. . . ." The Bible "believe" means "to trust, to depend on, to rely on."

There is only one way to be saved—Acts 16:31: "Believe on the Lord Jesus Christ, and thou shalt be saved."

When I worked at the post office, a lady came in one day and said, "Now, Preacher, here's the way I can see religion. We all came to the post office this morning. But we all came a different route. You came one way, I came another. Others in the post office came still other ways. None came the same way, but we all arrived at the post office. Now, that's the way it is with religion. Each of us has our own religion, and as long as we are sincere in what we believe, we will end up in Heaven. What do you think about that?"

I answered her, "There's only one thing wrong with that. When we die we're not going to the post office! There may be forty-seven ways to the post office, but there's only one way to Heaven."

Everyone is saved the same way. All are saved by trusting Jesus Christ as Saviour. And by the way, there is no promise to those who partially believe on Christ. You must trust Jesus Christ and Him alone. It is not Jesus—plus church membership, or Jesus—plus baptism, or Jesus—plus turning over a new leaf. It is Jesus and Him alone.

Everyone is saved the same way—by trusting Jesus Christ as Saviour; First John 5:1, "Whosoever believeth that Jesus is the Christ is born of God. . . ."

Everyone Can Know It

Says I John 5:13, "These things have I written unto you that believe on the name of the Son of God; that ye may know that ye have eternal life." Several times in this First Epistle of John we find the expression, "we know," "we know," "we know." Here it says you can know you have eternal life. You don't have to hope so or think so. This verse and others say the written Word is the basis of our assurance.

Some people doubt their salvation because they base their assurance on feelings. When feelings change, they begin to doubt. I feel good, but I don't know I'm saved because I feel good. I know I'm saved because the Bible says so, and I feel good because I know I'm saved. Why trust your changing feelings when you can trust the unchanging Word of God?

Others doubt their salvation because they don't remember the exact day and hour they trusted Christ as Saviour. When I was saved I was eleven years old. At that time I had no watch, and I very seldom, if ever, looked at a calendar. I don't remember the day and hour I was saved, but I do know I'm trusting Christ as Saviour.

The Bible does not say, "This excellent memory have I given you that you may know you have everlasting life." Rather, it says, "These things have I written unto you. . . that ye may know. . . ." Jesus gave the written Word as the basis of our assurance.

The Bible says in John 3:36, "He that believeth on the Son hath everlasting life." If I'm trusting Jesus Christ as my Saviour, then I know I have everlasting life because God said so, and He cannot lie.

Somebody said, "God said it. I believe it, and that settles it." That's wrong. God said it, and that settles it, whether anybody believes it or not.

Everybody who is saved can know it by taking God at His Word, and He said, "He that believeth. . . hath everlasting life." He said, "These things have I written unto you that believe on the name of the Son of God; that ye may know that ye have eternal life." If you are trusting Jesus Christ as Saviour, then according to God's Word you have everlasting life. Believe it.

Salvation Can Be Yours Today

You have read the sermon, "Four Truths About Salvation." You can be saved today and know you have everlasting life. If you will trust Jesus Christ as your Saviour, write to me so that I may rejoice with you. I have some free literature I would like to send you that will help you in your Christian life. All you need do to receive it is to write me:

Dr. Curtis Hutson
Sword of the Lord Foundation
P. O. Box 1099
Murfreesboro, Tennessee 37133

and say, "I know that I need to be saved. I know that I'm a sinner. I do believe that Jesus Christ died for me like the Bible says. And here and now I do trust Him as my Saviour. Please send me the free literature that will help me in my Christian life."

And be sure to give your name and address plainly.

God bless you!

Chapter 7

The Touch of Faith

Her Condition; Her Consultants; Her Cure; Her Confession

"And when Jesus was passed over again by ship unto the other side, much people gathered unto him: and he was nigh unto the sea. And, behold, there cometh one of the rulers of the synagogue, Jairus by name; and when he saw him, he fell at his feet, And besought him greatly, saying, My little daughter lieth at the point of death: I pray thee, come and lay thy hands on her, that she may be healed; and she shall live. And Jesus went with him; and much people followed him, and thronged him. And a certain woman, which had an issue of blood twelve years, And had suffered many things of many physicians, and had spent all that she had, and was nothing bettered, but rather grew worse, When she had heard of Jesus, came in the press behind, and touched his garment. For she said, If I may touch but his clothes, I shall be whole. And straightway the fountain of her blood was dried up; and she felt in her body that she was healed of that plague. And Jesus, immediately knowing in himself that virtue had gone out of him, turned him about in the press, and said, Who touched my clothes? And his disciples said unto him, Thou seest the multitude thronging thee, and sayest thou, Who touched me? And he looked round about to see her that had done this thing. But the woman fearing and trembling, knowing what was done in her, came and fell down

before him, and told him all the truth. And he said unto her, Daughter, thy faith hath made thee whole; go in peace, and be whole of thy plague."—Mark 5:21-34.

I call your attention to verse 28, "For she said, If I may touch but his clothes, I shall be whole."

In this chapter, Jesus conquered demons, disease and death. He cast the demons out of the maniac of Gadara, healed the woman with the issue of blood and raised Jairus' daughter from the dead. This miracle of the healing of the woman with an issue of blood occurred while Jesus was on the road to the house of Jairus to raise his daughter from the dead. It is not meant to stand alone but had a relation to the raising of Jairus' daughter. In order to build Jairus' faith, our Lord allowed him to see this special miracle.

We sometimes speak of killing two birds with one stone. Our Lord knows how to bless two souls with one touch. There have been occasions when I have led souls to Christ, not so much for the sake of winning souls but to motivate, inspire and encourage someone who was with me to win souls. Our Lord wrought this miracle while moving on to work another. He is so wonderful that what He does incidentally is marvelous!

Four things I call to your attention regarding the healing of the woman with an issue of blood.

Her Condition

Verse 25 states, "And a certain woman, which had an issue of blood twelve years." This was a real condition. It was not imaginary. Our Christian Science friends, who are neither Christian nor scientific, say it is all in the mind; but this woman's condition was real. She had an issue of blood for twelve years.

Sin is real. The Bible says in I John 1:8, "If we say that we have no sin, we deceive ourselves, and the truth is not in us." When children are born, they are born with a sin nature. David said in Psalm 51:5, "Behold, I was shapen in iniquity; and in sin did my mother conceive me." Every child is born with a sin nature; something inside is pulling him in the wrong direction.

My father spent his time teaching me what was right; but I

learned more wrong accidentally than I did right on purpose. Why? Because I have a sin nature inside. Jeremiah 17:9 states, "The heart is deceitful above all things, and desperately wicked: who can know it?"

An old preacher brought a wonderful sermon on the depravity of the human heart. When he had finished, a young modernist came up to him and said, "I can't swallow that depraved heart you preached about tonight." The wise preacher responded, "You don't have to swallow it. It is already in you."

All men are sinners. All have depraved hearts. "All we like sheep have gone astray." And like the woman in our story, our condition is real, not imaginary. Our social ills are not social at all but sinful ills, and the more we feed and cultivate this sin nature with alcohol, pornography, X-rated movies and TV programs that make sinful living appear acceptable, the more sinful (or so-called social) ills we will have.

This woman's condition was real. Every person born into the world has a real condition called sin. We inherited this condition from our parents and they from their parents—all the way back to the first man Adam. So the Bible says in Romans 5:12, "Wherefore, as by one man sin [a real condition] entered into the world, and death by sin; and so death passed upon all men, for that all have sinned."

What your children are taught in the public schools is contrary to this Bible truth. In the public schools, they are taught the theory of evolution. If man is the product of evolution, then where, when and how did sin enter into the world? The Bible teaches that the first man created, Adam, was given one prohibition:

> *"Of every tree of the garden thou mayest freely eat: But of the tree of the knowledge of good and evil, thou shalt not eat of it: for in the day that thou eatest thereof thou shalt surely die."*—Gen. 2:16,17.

That first man Adam disobeyed God, became a sinner and plunged the entire human race into sin, for we are told in Romans 5:19, "For as by one man's disobedience many were made sinners." If the evolutionists are right, then the story of Adam is untrue. And if the story of Adam is untrue, then you have no place for sin to enter the world.

Now, if you believe in evolution, don't come arguing with me about it after the service. You know more about your kinfolks than I do. Some of mine may have hung by the neck, but none ever hung by the tail, I'll guarantee you.

The woman's condition was real, not imaginary; and the sinner's condition is real. He has a sin nature inside that pulls him in the wrong direction.

Not only was her condition real, but it was leading to her death. She had an issue of blood for twelve years. Leviticus 17:11 states, "The life of the flesh is in the blood." This continual loss of blood would eventually result in her death.

The man without Christ also has a condition that is leading to death. "The soul that sinneth, it shall die" (Ezek. 18:4). "The wages of sin is death" (Rom. 6:23). "Sin, when it is finished, bringeth forth death" (Jas. 1:15). Sin may be fun, it may have its pleasures; but it always leads to death. God said to Adam, ". . . for in the day that thou eatest thereof thou shalt surely die."

Sin not only leads to physical death, it leads to the second death—the lake of fire. The person who dies without trusting Jesus Christ as Saviour will eventually be cast into the lake of fire to spend eternity. Revelation 20:14 states, "And death and hell were cast into the lake of fire. This is the second death." The second death is eternal separation from God in a lake of fire.

Her condition was real, and it was a condition leading to death. The sinner's condition, too, is real and eventually leads to death—the second death in the lake of fire.

Her Consultants

Next I call your attention to her consultants. Verse 26 states, "And had suffered many things of many physicians." I would hate to suffer many things of one physician. You must remember that they did not have hospitals then like we have today. They had no anesthesia. Words cannot describe the pain and agony she experienced for twelve years. She had suffered many things of many physicians. No doubt she had drunk many gallons of sickening drugs. But, as Job 13:4 says, they were "all physicians of no value."

The man without Christ has many consultants. There are those who advise, "Be sincere. It makes no difference what you believe as long as you are sincere."

Sincerity is not the saviour. If one is trusting anything other than Jesus Christ for salvation, he is lost, no matter how sincere he is.

I am thinking of a young man, a member of the church where I served as pastor for twenty-one years. He loved deer hunting. He had a new deer rifle with a telescopic sight. He also had a new television set with the largest screen available.

One Sunday afternoon he was watching television and cleaning his deer rifle. A big game show was on TV and a large buck appeared on the television screen. The man aimed at the deer. He sincerely thought the gun wasn't loaded. He sincerely pulled the trigger and he sincerely destroyed that television set! The fact that he was sincere did not help at all. The television was blown to bits.

If a person is not trusting Jesus Christ as Saviour, no matter how sincere he is, he will be sincerely lost.

Other consultants advise, "Live the best you can." But the Bible says in Isaiah 64:6, "All our righteousnesses are as filthy rags." The best one can do is not good enough. "All have sinned, and come short of the glory of God" (Rom. 3:23).

Other consultants advise, "Join the church." But church membership is not salvation. Getting into the church doesn't make one a Christian any more than getting into the oven makes one a biscuit.

Still others advise, "All man needs is a good environment. You change the man by changing his environment." Adam had the best environment. He was in the Garden of Eden. He had the most beautiful woman. I guess he did; he had the only one! Talk about good environment—he didn't even have a mother-in-law! But a perfect environment didn't prevent Adam from sinning.

Man needs more than a good environment; he needs to be born again. You don't change man by changing his environment. You change the environment by changing the man.

The lady in our story had suffered many things of many physicians and "had spent all that she had, and was nothing bettered, but rather grew worse." It is sad but sometimes true that the man without Christ spends all he has before turning to Jesus for salvation. I have known men to spend their family, respect, fortune, health and nearly everything else before finally turning to Christ and trusting Him as Saviour.

Dear friends, when you have tried everything else, trust Jesus. We have tried education and social reform, but salvation doesn't come wrapped in a diploma. You don't go to Heaven head first but heart first. Like the woman in the story, the person without Christ will only get worse until he comes to Jesus Christ and trusts Him as Saviour.

Her Cure

Next I call your attention to her cure. "When she had heard of Jesus, came in the press behind, and touched his garment. For she said, If I may touch but his clothes, I shall be whole. And straightway the fountain of her blood was dried up."

"When she had heard of Jesus. . . ." Faith comes by hearing. Romans 10:17 tells us, "So then faith cometh by hearing, and hearing by the word of God." She heard of Jesus and therefore had faith to trust Him for the cure.

If after you tell someone about Christ and he does not accept Him as Saviour immediately, don't be discouraged. Tell him again and again and again, for "faith cometh by hearing."

Let me give you an example. I was in my office the day President John Kennedy was assassinated. There was no telephone in the church so no one could reach me to tell what had happened. Several hours after his death I left the office to go home. When I stopped at a nearby service station, someone asked, "Did you hear that the President was shot?"

"Oh, no," I said, "that couldn't be!"

"Yes, it happened earlier today."

I did not believe it. I stopped to make a visit before I went home and the person I visited asked, "Wasn't that bad about the President being shot!" I still didn't believe it. It was hard for me to believe that the President of the United States was dead.

When I arrived at home, I was met with the news, "The President has been shot. The President is dead!" It was still hard to believe. I watched the news on television for several minutes before I finally accepted the fact that the President had been assassinated.

The first time I heard it I did not believe it, nor did I believe it the second and third times I heard it. But after my wife told me and I saw it on national news, I believed it. Faith came by hearing. "When she had heard of Jesus. . . ."

In verse 28 she said, "If I may touch but his clothes, I shall be whole." She did not say, "If I could hold Him," or, "If I could have Him put His hands on me and pray for me." She said, 'If I may touch but his clothes, if I could make the slightest contact with him, I shall be whole!'

Some have said to me, "But I don't have enough faith to be saved." Dear friends, faith is not the Saviour. Faith is an attitude of the soul through which Jesus saves. It is not the measure but the object of faith that saves. You can take a very small faith and get a mighty big Saviour! The slightest faith in Jesus Christ will bring everlasting life to the believer.

If you will admit you are a sinner, that you owe a sin debt, that Jesus Christ died on the cross to pay your sin debt, and if you will completely depend on Him to get you to Heaven, then God says you have everlasting life. John 3:36 promises, "He that believeth on the Son hath everlasting life."

Notice, too, that her cure was instant: "And straightway the fountain of her blood was dried up." Salvation is not a long, drawn-out process but instantaneous. "Believe on the Lord Jesus Christ, and thou shalt be saved" (Acts 16:31). There is no step between death and life. You are either in or out, guilty or pardoned, dead or alive, saved or lost. One moment Noah was outside the ark; the next moment he was inside. The moment you trust Jesus Christ as Saviour you have everlasting life instantaneously. "And straightway the fountain of her blood was dried up."

Notice, too, that her touch was intentional and voluntary. God never burglarizes the human will. Every person must come to Christ and trust Him of his own free choice. The only thing that stands between salvation and the sinner is the sinner's will. Jesus said in John 5:40, "And ye will not come to me, that ye might have life."

If you have never trusted Jesus Christ as your personal Saviour, will you trust Him now? It is your decision. Will you admit you are a sinner and, believing that Jesus Christ died for you, will you trust Him as your personal Saviour? It is a decision that only you can make. It must be intentional and voluntary.

Notice, too, that her cure was complete. The fountain of blood was dried up. She did not gradually get better and better and better until she was finally well. The death of Jesus Christ on the cross is complete payment for your sins. Trusting Jesus is not one of many steps to salvation; it is the step, and the moment one trusts Christ as Saviour, he is no longer condemned. He has everlasting life. He is passed from death unto life. "Verily, verily, I say unto you, He that heareth my word, and believeth on him that sent me, hath everlasting life, and shall not come into condemnation; but is passed from death unto life" (John 5:24).

Her Confession

Finally, I call your attention to her confession. In verse 30 Jesus asked, "Who touched my clothes?" Jesus is omniscient. He knows everything. He knew who touched Him. He wasn't asking for information but giving the woman an opportunity to come out and confess Him publicly. And, thank God, she came out.

Verse 33 says, "But the woman fearing and trembling, knowing what was done in her, came and fell down before him, and told him all the truth." Every person who has trusted Jesus Christ as personal Saviour should make a public confession. The Bible says in Romans 10:10, "For with the heart man believeth unto righteousness; and with the mouth confession is made unto salvation." Too many Christians are like Arctic rivers—frozen at the mouth. Jesus said, "Whosoever therefore shall confess me before men, him will I confess also before my Father which is in heaven. But whosoever shall deny me before men, him will I also deny before my Father which is in heaven" (Matt. 10:32,33).

If you have trusted Jesus Christ as your Saviour, you should go forward in a church service and publicly confess Him before men; let it be known you are trusting Him for salvation.

"Oh," someone says, "I don't want to be a fanatic!"

Suppose you married and the new husband said to you, "I don't want to be a fanatic about this marriage business. I'll tell you what you do. You ride in the back seat. As a matter of fact, ride on the floorboard so no one can see you! Now, don't misunderstand, I love you; I just don't want to be a fanatic about this marriage business. After you have ridden on the floorboard for several months, then you can sit on the back seat. And after a year or so, you can start riding in the front seat with me. Let's not be fanatical about being married."

If your mate made such a suggestion, you would think he didn't love you or maybe was ashamed of you.

Well, what must Jesus think when those who trust Him will not confess Him openly and publicly and will not identify with Him and His church by being baptized!

Friend, if you have trusted Jesus Christ as your Saviour, unfurl your flag. Come out into the open. Don't be a secret believer. When Jesus asked, "Who touched my clothes?" He wanted to bring her out of the crowd; and He wants everyone who is trusting Him as Saviour to come out of the crowd, to make a public profession and receive believer's baptism.

If you have trusted Jesus Christ as your Saviour but have never made a public confession of your faith, I urge you to go forward in the next service and make your public profession. If you have not been baptized since you have been saved, I urge you to find the right preacher and the right church and be baptized as soon as possible.

"And his disciples said unto him, Thou seest the multitude thronging thee, and sayest thou, Who touched me?" Many are thronging Christ today, and some are touching Him. Have you touched Him?

Have You Touched Him?

Are you trusting Him as your Saviour? If not, will you trust Him now? Put in your own words:

Dear Lord Jesus, I know I'm a sinner. I do believe You died for me and the best I know how I trust You as my Saviour. From this moment on I am depending on You for my salvation.

If you will pray such a prayer and write to tell me so, I have some free literature I want to send to help you as you set out to live the Christian life. All you need do to receive your free literature is send a letter to me,

Dr. Curtis Hutson
Sword of the Lord Foundation
P. O. Box 1099
Murfreesboro, Tennessee 37133

and say, "I have read your sermon, 'The Touch of Faith.' I know I am a sinner and do believe that Jesus Christ died on the cross to pay my sin debt. Here and now I do trust Him as my Saviour. From this moment on I am depending on Him to get me to Heaven. Please send me the free literature that will help me as I set out to live the Christian life."

Give your name and address plainly.

Chapter 8

The Unbelievable Gospel

"Who hath believed our report? and to whom is the arm of the Lord revealed? For he [Christ] *shall grow up before him as a tender plant, and as a root out of a dry ground: he hath no form nor comeliness; and when we shall see him, there is no beauty that we should desire him. He is despised and rejected of men; a man of sorrows, and acquainted with grief: and we hid as it were our faces from him; he was despised, and we esteemed him not. Surely he hath borne our griefs, and carried our sorrows: yet we did esteem him stricken, smitten of God, and afflicted. But he was wounded for our transgressions, he was bruised for our iniquities: the chastisement of our peace was upon him; and with his stripes we are healed. All we like sheep have gone astray; we have turned every one to his own way; and the Lord hath laid on him the iniquity of us all. He was oppressed, and he was afflicted, yet he opened not his mouth: he is brought as a lamb to the slaughter, and as a sheep before her shearers is dumb, so he openeth not his mouth. He was taken from prison and from judgment: and who shall declare his generation? for he was cut off out of the land of the living: for the transgression of my people was he stricken. And he made his grave with the wicked, and with the rich in his death; because he had done no violence, neither was any deceit in his mouth. Yet it pleased the Lord to bruise him; he hath put him to*

grief: when thou shalt make his soul an offering for sin, he shall see his seed, he shall prolong his days, and the pleasure of the Lord shall prosper in his hand. He shall see of the travail of his soul, and shall be satisfied: by his knowledge shall my righteous servant justify many; for he shall bear their iniquities. Therefore will I divide him a portion with the great, and he shall divide the spoil with the strong; because he hath poured out his soul unto death: and he was numbered with the transgressors; and he bare the sin of many, and made intercession for the transgressors."—Isa. 53:1-12.

Someone has suggested that the book of Isaiah is the Bible in miniature. There are 66 books in the Bible: 39 in the Old Testament and 27 in the New. And there are 66 chapters in the book of Isaiah. If we divide the chapters in Isaiah into 39 and 27, we discover that the first 39 chapters—representing the Old Testament—deal with justice and judgment, while the last 27 chapters—representing the New Testament—deal with grace, pardon and forgiveness.

As a matter of fact, the 40th chapter, which begins the last 27 chapters, opens, "Comfort ye, comfort ye my people, saith your God. Speak ye comfortably to Jerusalem, and cry unto her, that her warfare is accomplished, that her iniquity is pardoned." Isaiah 53 has to be the outstanding chapter in the book. There are twelve verses in Isaiah 53, and twelve mentions of the substitutionary death of Jesus.

For instance, verse 5 says: "But he was wounded for our transgressions"—substitution. "He was bruised for our iniquities"—substitution. "The chastisement of our peace was upon him"—substitution, taking our place. Verse 6 says: "All we like sheep have gone astray; we have turned every one to his own way; and the LORD [capital letters, signifying it is translated "Jehovah," the personal name of God] hath laid on him [Jesus] the iniquity of us all"—again, substitution.

Martin Luther said Isaiah 53 is so precious it should be written on parchment of gold and lettered with diamonds.

There are at least 85 references in quotes from Isaiah, chapter 53, in the New Testament; there may be more.

The chapter opens with a question: "Who hath believed our

report? and to whom is the arm of the Lord revealed?" Then the next verse says, "For he shall grow up before him as a tender plant, and as a root out of a dry ground: he hath no form nor comeliness; and when we shall see him, there is no beauty that we should desire him." The question is: "Who hath believed our report?"

I speak this morning on "The Unbelievable Gospel." Not many things cause me concern, but here is one thing that troubles me, one thing I have not figured out and cannot get hold of: Whenever the Gospel is presented clearly, with no possible misunderstanding, why doesn't every person come immediately to trust Jesus Christ as Saviour? I can't figure that out. Can you?

I was sitting at my dining table when I understood it the first time. I had read in Isaiah 53:6, "The Lord hath laid on him the iniquity of us all." I stood and puffed and blew. I marched across the floor and back again. My wife said, "Curtis, what's wrong?"

I said, "This verse."

"What verse?"

"Isaiah 53:6."

"What does it say?"

"The Lord hath [past tense] laid on him the iniquity of us all."

She said, "What about it?"

I said, "Honey, do you realize that God Almighty took every sin you have ever committed or will ever commit if you live a thousand years, and laid those sins on Jesus!" I took my notebook and explained further: "Just like I lay this paper on the the Bible, just like I lay down this envelope, just so God laid on Jesus the iniquity of us all." I said to her, "Imagine, every sin you have ever committed—the ones you think nobody knows about, the ones you have tried to hide, and the little sins you have forgotten about—or ever will commit, the Lord laid them all on Christ!"

My sin—oh, the bliss of this glorious tho't—
My sin—not in part, but the whole—
Is nailed to the cross and I bear it no more,
Praise the Lord, praise the Lord, O my soul!

When I saw that for the first time and understood it I could see in my mind's eye Jesus on the cross. I could see all my sins bundled up in one concentrated capsule and laid on Christ. I could see God punishing Christ in my place. When I saw, "He was wounded for *my* transgressions, he was bruised for *my* iniquities," I literally shouted! I thought, *I've never seen anything like it! That's beautiful! Why didn't I understand it before? Why didn't some preacher explain it to me and make me understand it?*

Once I grasped the truth, I set out to give Him my life to tell that truth to others, making it as simple as I could. And the thing I don't understand is, when I give the invitation and ask men to come and trust Christ, why they don't come immediately.

I feel like the little girl I heard about. When the invitation was given and many went to trust Christ, she nudged her mother and asked, "Where are all these people going?"

Her mother answered, "Darling, they are going to the Saviour."

In a few moments the little girl nudged her mother again, and said, "Why don't we all go?"

I have often thought that if I could buy all the television time I wanted for one night, on ABC, CBS, NBC, on all the independent channels, and on all the foreign channels, say from 10:00 to 10:30, and in those thirty minutes tell the whole world how to be saved, I have thought the whole world would surely trust Christ if I made it plain.

But if I had all the prime time on television to preach, multitudes would probably be saved, but not everyone. Some would watch the telecast; they would listen just like you are listening to me right now; but when I urged them to trust Christ, some would say, "No," just like some of you are going to say, "No," this morning.

The Bible says, "Strait is the gate, and narrow is the way, which leadeth unto life, and few there be that find it. . . for wide is the gate, and broad is the way that leadeth to destruction, and many there be which go in thereat" (Matt. 7:14,13).

Isaiah said, "Who hath believed our report?"

Then in verse 2 he begins to tell why it is so unbelievable.

First, the Gospel is unbelievable because

I. IT CONCERNS AN UNBELIEVABLE PERSON

I am logical; I am reasonable; I am sensible. I don't accept things without investigation. I am like R. A. Torrey, who said there was a time when he was not sure the Bible was the Word of God; but after many hours of prayer and investigation, he came out of the darkness of scepticism into the broad daylight of certainty that the Bible is the Word of God from beginning to end.

I have a logical mind and I ask questions. I don't just swallow things. If I did not believe the Bible was the Word of God, I would have difficulty believing the Gospel. It concerns an unbelievable Person—Christ.

Speaking of Christ seven hundred years before His birth, verse 2 says, "He shall grow up. . . as a tender plant, and as a root out of a dry ground. . . ."

Did you see our space shuttle land on that hard, barren desert? Did you see a blade of grass spring up? Did you see any green trees? No, it landed on hard, parched ground. And when you saw a close-up on your TV screen, you saw hard, parched, cracked ground. No one expects to see a tender plant growing up out of dry ground.

When Jesus came into the world, He was like a tender plant out of dry ground. He was born of a virgin with no earthly father. That is unbelievable! If I didn't believe the Bible, I wouldn't believe this biological impossibility. But I believe it because the Bible says it happened. And I believe the Bible because there are fifty-seven reasons that I cannot reject with my logical mind.

When Jesus came, it was hard to believe He was born of a virgin who had never known a man; but that is truly the way He came. He came into the world by way of a borrowed womb, and went out by way of a borrowed tomb. He is the only Man who ever borrowed a grave. You may borrow a cup of sugar, or a loaf of bread, or a pound of butter, but you don't borrow a grave! However, Jesus did because He knew He would only need it for three days and nights. He knew when the owner died, the tomb would be empty and ready for his burial.

Not only did He have an unbelievable entrance, but he also had an *unbelievable appearance.* Verse 2 continues, "He hath no form nor comeliness; and when we shall see him, there is no beauty that we should desire him."

In Israel I met Jews every day on the street. Jesus Christ was an ordinary-looking Jew. You think had you been living when Jesus was here, you could have spotted Him a mile away. You think He would have had a halo about His head, enshrouded in light. You think He would have stood out in the crowd. No. He had no form nor comeliness, and if you had seen Him, there was no beauty that you would have desired Him.

Judas betrayed Christ. When the enemy was ready to take Jesus Christ and nail Him to the cross and crucify Him, Judas had to mark Him so they would know which one He was. This traitor said, "The One I kiss will be Him, so grab Him and hold Him fast." If Judas had not marked Jesus Christ with a kiss, they might have taken Peter, James or John or any of the others, because they looked no different from Jesus.

Were Jesus to come into this church this morning, sit down next to you, open His Bible and listen to me preach, you would not recognize Him.

Even when He walked with His disciples on the road to Emmaus after His resurrection, they didn't recognize Him. He was a common, ordinary-looking Jew. Most of our ideas about Jesus we have gotten from songs or from artists' conceptions, and most artists give Him a Gentile profile. But Jesus was a Jew.

He is an *unbelievable Person,* He had an *unbelievable entrance* into the world, and He had an *unbelievable appearance.*

That is not all. He lived an *unbelievable life.* Thirty-three years on the earth, tempted in all points as we are, "yet without sin." He committed not one single, solitary sin in His whole life. He never uttered a word that He had to retract. He said nothing that caused Him to have to say to His friends on His way home, "I wish I hadn't said that."

How many times have I said to my wife, "I wish I hadn't done that," or, "I wish I hadn't said that." Jesus never had those feelings because He never made a mistake. He never prayed, "Father, forgive *Me.*" But He did pray on the cross, "Father forgive *them*; for they know not what they do." He never made one single mistake!

When Pilate turned Him over to the angry mob, he said, "I find no fault in him." Pilate's wife said to her husband, "Have thou nothing to do with that just man: for I have suffered many things this day in a dream because of him" (Matt. 27:19).

Two thieves were crucified, one on either side of Jesus. One railed at Jesus while the other spoke up: "You and I are getting what we deserve, but this Man has done nothing amiss"—wrong or faulty. Even the thief on the cross recognized His sinlessness.

He also did *unbelievable things.* In John 6 there were five thousand men plus women and children; if every man was married—ten thousand; if they had two children—twenty thousand. It was nearing sundown. The people were getting hungry. And His disciples urged, "Lord, send these people away. We have nothing to feed them. There's shortly going to be a panic here, so let's get the crowd out. They are hungry, the babies will be crying. Let's send these twenty thousand people away."

Jesus said, "They need not depart; give ye them to eat."

Still the disciples complained, "But we have nothing to give them."

Jesus asked, "What do you have?"

"Well, there is a little boy here with a lunch of five loaves and two fishes."

Jesus said, "Bring them hither to me."

Ladies and gentlemen, God Almighty in human flesh took five loaves and two fishes and sat the people down in companies of fifty and began to break that bread and fish. He gave it to the disciples, who gave it to the companies, and Jesus fed over twenty thousand people!

You say, "Impossible!" I know it. It was a miracle. And according to John chapter 6, they "ate as much as they w-o-u-l-d." It didn't say as much as they *could.* Everybody ate until they couldn't eat any more. When they were full, they took up twelve baskets of the fragments that remained.

Jesus Christ is an unbelievable Person.

I remember my first funeral. A lady had died and the family asked if I would conduct her funeral. I was just a kid preacher and had never conducted a funeral. But, since I was the pastor, I had to do it.

Not knowing what else to do, I thought I'd get the Bible and learn how Jesus conducted funerals. But I had a problem. I couldn't find where Jesus buried anyone. Oh, He was called on when someone had died. Jairus' daughter died, but instead of taking her out to the graveyard and lowering her down into the grave and saying, "Ashes to ashes and dust to dust," He touched her and said, "Young lady, arise."

A young man was in the casket in that funeral procession in

Nain. Jesus walked over, touched the casket and the young boy got out, leaving the bearers with the empty box!

This Man didn't conduct funerals; He broke up funerals!

He went to the graveyard with Martha and Mary. Lazarus was already buried in a tomb. They rolled the stone away and Jesus cried with a loud voice, "Lazarus, come forth," and Lazarus came out of the grave wrapped in graveclothes.

Jesus never had a funeral. He had resurrections!

I am saying, the Gospel is unbelievable because it concerns an unbelievable Person.

Then it is unbelievable because

II. IT DEMANDS AN UNBELIEVABLE PRICE

Take any little ten-year-old boy in this building. He may be pure and clean. He may say, "Yes, ma'am," and "Yes, sir." But if he hasn't trusted Christ as his Saviour, when he dies he will go into Hell to burn forever and ever and ever.

I can almost feel you cringe when I say that. To think, even a sweet little kid who had never gotten drunk, never committed adultery, never murdered anybody—a little ten-year-old boy couldn't have done too much wrong. You mean he burns in Hell forever? Yes. God has but one payment for sin. "He was wounded for our transgressions, he was bruised for our iniquities: the chastisement of our peace was upon him; and *with his stripes we are healed."*

Now watch this: Two thousand years ago they nailed Jesus to the cross. He could have come down. He could have prayed and the Father would have sent twelve legions of angels. He could have gotten off the cross. But Christ suffered that cross because He wanted to. It wasn't the nails that held Him there; it was love—His love for a sinner. He wanted you to go to Heaven. The Bible says He was "wounded," which means "pierced," like sticking a knife—"pierced for my transgressions." "Transgress" means to cross over the line. He was pierced for every time I crossed the line. Every time I deliberately sinned—Jesus was pierced for that. "He was bruised," or crushed, like you bruise or crush an orange or tomato—crushed for our iniquities, or our crookedness.

David said, "Behold, I was shapen in iniquity; and in sin did my mother conceive me" (Ps. 51:5). I was shaped crooked. I don't believe in the theory of evolution, because man is born with something wrong in the inside, pulling him in the wrong direction. And if man is not born again, he will keep going in the wrong direction.

He was crushed for my iniquities. On the cross Jesus Christ suffered everything that I would have to suffer if I died and went into Hell and stayed there forever and ever. He paid our sin debt at Calvary.

I have a sermon I sometimes preach entitled "Calvary, the Sinner's Hell in Review." In the sermon I read the crucifixion account, then I read the story in Luke 16 of the rich man in Hell. I go from Calvary to Hell; from Hell to Calvary. And down in Hell I hear the rich man cry, "Send Lazarus and let him dip his finger in water and cool my tongue." Then I go to Calvary and I hear Jesus scream out from the cross, "I thirst." They gave Him vinegar and gall to drink. The rich man was thirsty; Jesus was thirsty.

I hear the rich man talking to Abraham from Hell: "Send Lazarus over here." But Abraham speaks back: "There is a great gulf fixed between us and we can't pass back and forth. We are separated."

I leave Hell and go back to Calvary and I see Jesus hanging there. I hear Him scream out during the darkness, "My God, my God, why hast thou forsaken me?" He is separated from God. The rich man is separated from God.

I read where the wicked shall be turned into Hell, into outer darkness where there is weeping and gnashing of teeth. I then go back to Calvary and read that from twelve noon until three in the afternoon, God Almighty pulled the shades of Heaven and it became as black as an Egyptian midnight, so black that you could feel it—the blackness of Hell.

And I see that on the cross Jesus suffered everything men suffer if they die and go to Hell, because on the cross Jesus was paying what we owe as sinners. And if He did not suffer what we would have to suffer, then He has not paid what we owe.

The songwriter said,

None of the ransomed ever knew
How deep were the waters crossed;
Nor how dark was the night that the Lord passed thro'
Ere He found His sheep that was lost.

I once thought, *Nobody will ever know how much Jesus suffered on the cross, except those who die and go to Hell.* But I was wrong. Even those who die and go to Hell won't know how much He suffered! They will be paying on the sin debt forever, but never getting it paid. John 3:36 says, "...he that believeth not the Son shall not see life; but the wrath of God *abideth* on him." He will be in Hell forever and ever and ever, paying the debt. He will never get it paid in full! He will never get out! The only way out of Hell is to stay out.

But on the cross Jesus paid the sin debt in full. He didn't have to stay on the cross forever. He suffered enough in a few hours to compensate for all the suffering you would have to do for an eternity.

Now I can't understand that. That is unbelievable! That is more than my finite mind can comprehend. I can only explain it by saying that since He was infinite, He could suffer infinitely. And He suffered enough on the cross to pay in full our sin debt. Then He cried out, "It is finished. It is paid in full!" Thank God, it was—paid in full!

The greatest truth that ever coursed through my brain was the fact that I was a sinner and that Jesus Christ took my place, suffered my Hell, paid what I should have paid, and let me go to Heaven on a free pass. "The gift of God is eternal life."

The Gospel is unbelievable because it concerns an unbelievable Person and demands an unbelievable price. But listen, ladies and gentlemen, the price has been paid.

Jesus paid it all,
All to Him I owe;
Sin had left a crimson stain,
He washed it white as snow.

And

Oh why was He there as the Bearer of sin, if on Jesus my guilt was not laid?
And why did He shed His life-giving blood, if His dying my debt has not paid?

III. IT ACCOMPLISHES AN UNBELIEVABLE PURPOSE

The Gospel is unbelievable because it accomplishes an unbelievable purpose. First, justice is satisfied. Let me show you what I mean, then I will read the verse.

Before anybody ever sinned, God said to Adam in Genesis 2:17, "...for in the day that thou eatest thereof thou shalt surely die." He was saying, "You sin, and the penalty is death."

Now when Adam disobeyed God, he became a sinner and was under the penalty, which was death. Ezekiel 18:4 says, "...the soul that sinneth, it shall die." And Romans 6:23 says, "The wages of sin is death." God said that sin demands a penalty, and the penalty is death. The Bible teaches that death is more than dying with a gunshot wound or cancer. It is the second death—eternal separation from God in a lake of fire. "And death and hell were cast into the lake of fire. This is the second death" (Rev. 20:14).

Now follow me. A just God said, "You have sinned. The penalty is death. That death is eternal separation from Me in the lake of fire."

Now wait. If God lets us go to Heaven, He will sacrifice His justice and cease to be a just God. Yet He loves us. He does not want us to go to Hell.

But God planned a way so His justice could be satisfied and His love demonstrated. He took our guilt and placed it over on Jesus. And the penalty He demanded from us was collected from Jesus. So the debt has been paid by Another; we don't have to pay it. And when Jesus died on the cross, that satisfied the just demand of a Holy God who said that sin must be paid for. Justice was satisfied.

Look at verse 10: "Yet it pleased the LORD to bruise him; he hath put him to grief." What? It pleased God to bruise Jesus? God up in Heaven is looking down; He sees Jesus on the cross, and is He getting pleasure out of it? Is He laughing? Smiling? Saying, "Oh, I am enjoying seeing My Son suffer Hell on the cross. This is really making Me happy"? Is God really enjoying it as He watches them pluck the beard from His Son's face and spit on Him; as He watches the weight of the body pull all the bones out of joint; as He sees them beat Him with a scourge until He had 195 furrows across His back, like you had taken a pocketknife and cut it, until He was so swollen He didn't look like a human being hanging on a cross? Do you think God is enjoying it?

Listen, my neighbor's expensive horse was struck by lightning the other day. Both the front shoulder and leg were broken and he had to be put to sleep. As the horse lay there on the ground waiting for the veterinarian to come and put him to sleep, I saw my neighbor was crying. He brushed that horse as if he were grooming him for another show. As tears coursed down his cheeks he said, "You are going to die in a few minutes, but you are going to be beautiful." I walked away. I couldn't bear to watch.

But God looked down from Heaven and watched Jesus Christ die. Not just a quick death, but a long, drawn-out, agonizing death on the cross. And it pleased God! Now that does not mean God got pleasure from it; it means He was satisfied. Look at verse 11: "He shall see of the travail of his soul, and shall be *satisfied.*"

God said sin demands a penalty. You sin, then you must pay, and the payment is Hell, the second death, the lake of fire. God cannot retract His statement and still be God; He cannot sacrifice His justice; so He put our sins on Jesus. When Jesus died on the cross and suffered our Hell, God looked down and said, "Jesus just satisfied Me for the payment Curtis Hutson owed Me. Jesus, My Son, just satisfied Me for the payment every individual owes for his sins. That is what I demanded, but My Son has paid it. Now I am satisfied."

Now up in Heaven those saints run up and down the streets shouting because every person saved before Jesus died was saved on credit!

Abraham went to Heaven on a promise that Jesus would die on the cross to pay the sin debt. And I am sure that day when Jesus died, Abraham and others must have thought as they looked over Heaven's battlements, *They are burning the mortgage on my soul! No more debt! It is paid! There is no more wondering if He will do it. He did it! It's paid! He died today!*

It accomplished an unbelievable purpose because justice was satisfied. Nothing else except the death of Jesus on the cross ever satisfied God in regards to what He demanded for your sins.

You say, "Well, I'll go to church." He didn't say going to church satisfied. You say, "I'll be baptized." He didn't say being baptized would satisfy. You say, "I'll give some money." That won't satisfy either. You can go to church, be baptized, give money, read the Bible and pray, but the only thing that satisfied the payment is the death of Jesus on the cross.

And let me say this. You must either accept the satisfaction that

Jesus made to God for your sins, or you yourself must satisfy God when you die. And for you to satisfy God, you have to go to Hell forever and ever.

Not only was justice satisfied; thank God, sinners were justified! Look at verse 11. "He shall see of the travail of his soul, and shall be satisfied: by his knowledge shall my righteous servant *justify* many."

"Justify" means more than forgiveness. If you run over my little girl and kill her in a drunken stupor, I could forgive you, but I could dead-sure never justify you. As long as you lived you would be guilty of her death. No way could you undo the guilt unless you could resurrect her.

When you come to Him by faith, He goes beyond forgiveness and justifies you, meaning that He has wiped your slate clean and that the sins you committed no longer exist. You are not just forgiven, pardoned, but the sin itself is gone. Hallelujah!

If I were unsaved, I would come this morning and trust Christ as my Saviour. Even if I knew there were no Heaven and no Hell, I would still trust Christ just to have my slate wiped clean and know I was justified, and know that in God's sight I never made one mistake.

If I were to die right now and go to Heaven, and say, "God, I am so sorry about a certain sin I committed back yonder, a sin which has bugged me all my life—a terrible thing. I am sorry about that sin," God would look at me and say, "Curtis, I don't know what you are talking about."

You say, "Is God absent-minded?" No. But He has a divine forgetter. Look at Isaiah 43:25. God speaks: "I, even I, am he that blotteth out thy transgressions for mine own sake, AND WILL NOT REMEMBER THY SINS."

The Gospel is unbelievable because it concerns an unbelievable Person, it demands an unbelievable price, and it accomplishes an unbelievable purpose. Justice is satisfied and sinners are justified. And someday, when it is all over and the believers are in Heaven, God will be glorified; because verse 12 says they divide the spoil.

Calvary was a battle. Jesus was not a victim but a Victor. When He said, "It is finished," that was the cry of a Victor. He had accomplished what He intended. The battle was over. Satan's destiny was sealed. Jesus had bruised his head. It was settled forever at Calvary. The prince of this world is already judged. The sentence is passed. It is over. Calvary settled it.

The saved in Heaven will be the spoils of that battle. We will be there only because Jesus died on the cross. And we will be the spoils of the Lord's victory on the cross. When they divide the spoils, God will be glorified with our presence in Heaven. God will say, "You are here because My Son died for you, and because I devised the plan and sent My virgin-born Son to live a sinless life, to die a substitutionary death, to bear your sins, to pay your price." Then will God be glorified, because it was God's plan, God's program and God's Son.

The Gospel is unbelievable, but you will believe the unbelievable Gospel, or you will bear an unbearable Hell. The choice is yours.

Sinner, Decide Today

You have read the sermon, "The Unbelievable Gospel," preached at Reimer Road Baptist Church in Wadsworth, Ohio. Many came to trust Christ as Saviour when this sermon was preached; and I urge you, if you have not yet trusted Christ as your own Saviour, to do so now. Admit that you are a sinner, believe that Jesus Christ died to pay all your sin debt, and then trust Him completely for your salvation.

If you will trust Him and write to tell me, I have some free literature I want to send that will help you as you set out to live the Christian life. All you need do to receive your free literature is write to:

Dr. Curtis Hutson
Sword of the Lord Foundation
P. O. Box 1099
Murfreesboro, Tennessee 37133

Tell me, "I have read your sermon, 'The Unbelievable Gospel.' I want to be saved and know for sure that when I die I am going to Heaven. I know I am a sinner and do believe that Jesus Christ died on the cross to pay my sin debt. Here and now I do trust Him as my personal Saviour. From this moment on I am completely depending on Him for my salvation and trusting Him to take me to Heaven when I die. Please send me the free literature that will help me as I set out to live the Christian life."

Be sure you write plainly your name and address.

Chapter 9

Noah's Ark—A Type of Salvation

"And God said unto Noah, The end of all flesh is come before me; for the earth is filled with violence through them; and, behold, I will destroy them with the earth. Make thee an ark of gopher wood; rooms shalt thou make in the ark, and shalt pitch it within and without with pitch. And this is the fashion which thou shalt make it of: The length of the ark shall be three hundred cubits, the breadth of it fifty cubits, and the height of it thirty cubits. A window shalt thou make to the ark, and in a cubit shalt thou finish it above; and the door of the ark shalt thou set in the side thereof; with lower, second, and third stories shalt thou make it. And, behold, I, even I, do bring a flood of waters upon the earth, to destroy all flesh, wherein is the breath of life, from under heaven; and every thing that is in the earth shall die. But with thee will I establish my covenant; and thou shalt come into the ark, thou, and thy sons, and thy wife, and thy sons' wives with thee. And of every living thing of all flesh, two of every sort shalt thou bring into the ark, to keep them alive with thee; they shall be male and female. Of fowls after their kind, and of cattle after their kind, of every creeping thing of the earth after his kind, two of every sort shall come unto thee, to keep them alive. And take thou unto thee of all food that is eaten, and thou shalt gather it to thee; and it shall be for food for thee, and for them. Thus did Noah; according to all that God com-

manded him, so did he. And the Lord said unto Noah, Come thou and all thy house into the ark."—Gen. 6:13-7:1.

The ark Noah prepared for the saving of his house is one of the most beautiful and complete types of salvation to be found in all the Bible.

I call your attention to six things regarding this ark.

I. IT WAS A DIVINE PROVISION

The ark was not Noah's idea. God said to Noah, "Make thee an ark of gopher wood" (Gen. 6:14). God gave Noah specific instructions as to how to build it, the kind of wood to use, the size it should be, and where the door and window should be placed.

Salvation, like the ark, is a divine provision. It is not an afterthought with God. Long before man sinned God provided a plan of salvation.

Revelation 13:8 says Jesus Christ was "the Lamb slain from the foundation of the world."

I once heard of a train that was destined for an awful accident. Before the days of communication as we have today, it was learned that two trains on the same track headed in opposite directions were sure to collide since there was no way to get word to the engineers.

Those who knew the accident would occur prepared a hospital train, loading it with medicine, doctors, and nurses. This was put on the track behind one train that was headed for the accident. As soon as the accident occurred this equipped train would be there to help the wounded.

So it is with salvation. Knowing that man was going to sin, God put a hospital train on the track in the Person of Jesus Christ. And as early as Genesis 3:15 He promised a Redeemer, "And I will put enmity between thee and the woman, and between thy seed and her seed. . . ." The Seed of the woman refers to the virgin birth of Christ.

The ark was a divine provision. Salvation is also a divine provision. Salvation is not man reaching up to God but God reaching down to man. Religion, on the other hand, is man reaching up to God. You don't spell salvation "do"; you spell it "done."

A little boy came to an old preacher and asked, "What can I do to be saved?"

The preacher answered, "Son, you're too late."

"What!" exclaimed the boy. "Too late to be saved?"

"Oh, no," said the preacher, "not too late to be saved, but too late to do anything. Jesus did it all two thousand years ago."

The Bible states in John 1:13, ". . . which were born, not of blood, nor of the will of the flesh, nor of the will of man, but of God." And according to Titus 3:5, it is "not by works of righteousness which we have done, but according to his mercy he saved us."

Not only was the ark a divine provision, but

II. THE ARK WAS A SHELTER FROM GOD'S JUDGMENT

God's judgment came on the world in the form of rain. It rained forty days and nights, flooding the whole earth. The rain fell but those inside the ark felt not a single drop, for they were protected by its shelter.

Two thousand years ago at Calvary the judgment of God fell, not in the form of a rain, but in the form of separation from God. When God turned His back on Jesus, He cried out from the cross, "My God, my God, why hast thou forsaken me?" (Matt. 27:46). God turned His back on Jesus Christ as the judgment of God fell on Jesus. While Jesus hung on the cross, God treated Him in exactly the same way He will have to treat every unbelieving sinner.

I have a sermon entitled "Calvary, the Sinner's Hell in Review." In it I read both the story of the crucifixion and the story of the rich man in Hell. And going from one to the other I show that on the cross Jesus suffered everything the rich man in Hell suffered.

The rich man said, "Send Lazarus, that he may dip the tip of his finger in water, and cool my tongue." On the cross Jesus cried out, "I thirst."

You see, on the cross Jesus was suffering the sinner's judgment for sin. I was judged in Christ as a sinner two thousand years ago at Calvary, and God treated Jesus Christ like He would have to treat me if I did not trust Jesus Christ as my personal Saviour. When I trust Him, I am justified, cleared from all guilt. Jesus Christ bore my guilt: He suffered my Hell; He paid my debt.

Now, those inside the ark were sheltered from God's judgment. The judgment fell on the ark, not on those inside. The person trusting Jesus Christ as personal Saviour is in a place of shelter from God's judgment, because the judgment fell on Jesus Christ at Calvary.

The Bible says, "There is therefore now no condemnation [no judgment] to them which are in Christ Jesus" (Rom. 8:1). The only safe place to hide when the woods are on fire is where the fire has already burned. And the man who is trusting Jesus Christ as Saviour is in a place where the fires of God's judgment have already burned and they will never burn there again.

The ark was a shelter from God's judgment.

III. NOAH AND HIS FAMILY WERE INVITED INTO THE ARK

God said to Noah in Genesis 7:1, "Come thou and all thy house into the ark." I am told that invitational word "come" is found more than 1,900 times in the Bible. The Bible's last invitation is in Revelation 22:17: "And the Spirit and the bride say, Come. And let him that heareth say, Come. And let him that is athirst come. And whosoever will, let him take the water of life freely." Jesus said in Matthew 11:28, "Come unto me, all ye that labour and are heavy laden, and I will give you rest."

Over and over again you are invited to come to Christ. God invited Noah, "Come thou and all thy house into the ark" (Gen. 7:1). He did not say, "Noah, go into the ark." God was already inside. He had given it a safety inspection.

Say, Friend, God was in Christ Jesus reconciling the world unto Himself (II Cor. 5:19). Today he invites you to come and trust Him as Saviour. And anyone may come.

When I was a pastor, a little boy in my church came to me and said, "Preacher, let me quote to you my memory verse. It is Matthew 11:28—'Come unto me, all ye that labour and are heavy laden, and I *will do the rest.*' "

I said, "Son, I never heard it like that before but I like it."

Friends, Jesus Christ is inviting you to come and He will do the rest.

Not only was Noah and his family invited into the ark, but notice:

IV. THE ARK HAD ONLY ONE ENTRANCE

The ark had only one door. Jesus said, "I am the door: by me if any man enter in, he shall be saved" (John 10:9). He said, "I am the way, the truth, and the life: no man cometh unto the Father, but by me" (John 14:6). Christ is the *only* door to Heaven, the only entrance. D. L. Moody said, "He is the open sesame to Heaven." He is the password.

My hope is built on nothing less
Than Jesus' blood and righteousness;
I dare not trust the sweetest frame,
But wholly lean on Jesus' name.

There was not one door for the housecat and another for the lion, the king of the jungle. Everything that rode the ark to safety had to go in the same door.

You cannot buy salvation like goods in a bargain basement. You may go to a different church, but salvation is the same everywhere. One is saved the same way, in one church as in another. It is by trusting Jesus Christ completely for salvation. "Believe on the Lord Jesus Christ, and thou shalt be saved" (Acts 16:31). There is only one way to Heaven. Acts 4:12 says, "Neither is there salvation in any other: for there is none other name under heaven given among men, whereby we must be saved." One must lay aside his manmade schemes of salvation and come to Jesus, the only way of salvation. He is the only door to Heaven.

V. NO ONE WAS BORN INSIDE THE ARK

There was not a single birth on board. Everyone was born outside the ark and had to go inside. The point I am making here is this: no one is born a Christian. The Bible says, "The wicked. . . go astray as soon as they be born, speaking lies" (Ps. 58:3). You are not a Christian because of your birth. John 1:13 states, "Which were born, not of blood [salvation is not inherited], nor of the will of the flesh, nor of the will of man, but of God."

Every person is born with a sin nature, so he must be born again or he cannot see the kingdom of God. Everyone had to go inside the ark. No one was born inside.

You are not born a Christian and you are not a Christian until you are born again. This is not to say that little children who die will go to Hell. The Bible indicates that the child who dies before reaching the age of knowing right from wrong does go to Heaven (Matt. 18:3). But once a child reaches the age of accountability he must by his own will come to Christ for salvation.

Jesus said in John 5:40, "And ye will not come to me, that ye might have life." The only thing that stands between the sinner and salvation is the sinner's will.

Finally:

VI. EVERYONE WHO WENT INSIDE THE ARK WAS SAFE

No one who entered the ark lost his life. The man who trusts Jesus Christ as Saviour is safe. Some who have trusted Christ are nervous, hoping to make it. They are nervous about their security. But, dear friends, if you have trusted Jesus Christ as your Saviour, you are absolutely safe.

When Noah and his family entered the ark, God shut the door, and no matter how bad the storm raged outside they were safe.

It was Fanny Crosby who wrote:

Safe in the arms of Jesus,
Safe on His gentle breast,
There by His love o'ershaded,
Sweetly my soul shall rest.

But, friends, it is not safe *in* the arms of Jesus. We are safer than that! We are safe *AS* an arm of Jesus. The Bible says in Ephesians 5:30, "For we are members of his body, of his flesh, and of his bones."

Have you trusted Jesus Christ as your Saviour? If not, you are invited to come to Him. "Come unto me, all ye that labour and heavy laden, and I will give you rest," says Jesus.

If you will admit you are a sinner and believe that Jesus Christ died for you, and if you will trust Him completely for your salvation, Jesus promises everlasting life. The Bible promises in John 3:36, "He that believeth on the Son hath everlasting life."

Today Is the Day

You have read "Noah's Ark—a Type of Salvation," a sermon preached on the nationwide radio broadcast, the VOICE OF REVIVAL. Just as the ark was a place of safety for Noah and his family, so Jesus Christ is a place of safety for all who will come and trust Him completely for salvation. When Noah and his family were invited into the ark, they had to make their own decision as to whether they would accept the invitation. Their going into the ark was a voluntary act.

Dear reader, Jesus Christ has provided salvation for you through His death at Calvary. He promises everlasting life if you will trust Him. The Bible states, "For God so loved the world, that he gave his only begotten Son, that whosoever believeth in him should not perish, but have everlasting life" (John 3:16).

If you will trust Jesus Christ as your Saviour, then pray this simple prayer:

> Dear Lord Jesus, I know I am a sinner and do believe that You died for me. Here and now I do trust You as my Saviour. From this moment on I am completely depending on You for my salvation and trusting You to take me to Heaven when I die. Now help me to live for You and be a good Christian. Amen.

If you will pray this simple prayer and write to tell me that you are trusting Jesus Christ as your personal Saviour, I have some free literature I want to send that will help you as you set out to live the Christian life. All you need do to receive your free literature is write to me:

Dr. Curtis Hutson
Sword of the Lord Foundation
P. O. Box 1099
Murfreesboro, Tennessee 37133

In your letter say, "I have read your sermon, 'Noah's Ark—a Type of Salvation.' I know I am a sinner and do believe that Jesus Christ died for me. Today I am accepting His invitation, 'Come unto me, all ye that labour and are heavy laden, and I will give you rest.' From this moment on I am fully depending on Jesus Christ to get me to Heaven. I do trust Him as my personal Saviour. Please send me the free literature that will help me as I set out to live the Christian life."

Chapter 10

God's Gift to the World

This is the season when thoughts turn to giving. Already Mrs. Hutson has purchased gifts for nearly every member of our family. Each is wrapped in beautiful Christmas paper and ready for presentation. Shoppers are everywhere looking for gifts for friends and family alike.

Christmastime is when we think of giving. It is a time when we think of Jesus, God's Gift to the world! Seven hundred years before His birth, the Prophet Isaiah declared, "Unto us a child is born, unto us a son is given. . ." (Isa. 9:6). The best known Bible verse in the world declares, "For God so loved the world, that he gave his only begotten Son, that whosoever believeth in him should not perish, but have everlasting life" (John 3:16).

Someone has suggested that in this text we have the greatest Giver—God; the greatest Gift—"his only begotten Son"; the greatest reason for giving—"God so loved"; and the greatest result of giving—"should not perish, but have everlasting life."

Says Romans 6:23, "For the wages of sin is death; but the gift of God is eternal life through Jesus Christ our Lord." And Jesus said to the woman at the well in John 4:10, "If thou knewest the gift of God, and who it is that saith to thee, Give me to drink; thou wouldest have asked of him, and he would have given thee living water." Romans 8:32 tells us, "He that spared not his own Son, but delivered him up for us all, how shall he not with him also freely give us all things?" Regarding this gift, the Apostle Paul said, "Thanks be unto God for his unspeakable gift" (II Cor. 9:15).

Let me share several thoughts about the greatest Gift ever given.

I. AN UNPARALLELED GIFT!

No gift in the world compares with God's gift of salvation through His only begotten Son! Jesus said in Mark 8:36, 37, "For what shall it profit a man, if he shall gain the whole world, and lose his own soul? Or what shall a man give in exchange for his soul?" All the gifts given since the beginning of time and all that will be given until the return of Christ do not compare with God's Gift to the world—"his only begotten Son." To have this Gift is to have eternal life.

The Bible says in I John 5:12, "He that hath the Son hath life; and he that hath not the Son of God hath not life." One may own everything else in the world; but when he dies, he leaves it all. On the other hand, one may not own one single item, yet if he has Jesus Christ when he dies, he has gained everything worth having—everlasting life in Heaven where there is no sickness, no pain, no sorrow, no death, no sighing, and no separation!

God's Gift is unparalleled! To have Christ is to have everything worth having in this life and the life to come.

Was e'er a gift like the Saviour given?
No, not one! no, not one!
Will He refuse us a home in Heaven?
No, not one! no, not one!

Jesus knows all about our struggles,
He will guide till the day is done,
There's not a friend like the lowly Jesus,
No, not one! no, not one!

While in a city the other day with a pastor, we passed a certain restaurant. He said, "Let me tell you about that place."

Then he told me this:

> It became famous for its good food. One day a very wealthy man heard about it, so he went there to eat. When he entered the restaurant, he asked for a private room, but none was available. He called the owner, bought the restaurant at a cost of $250,000, then had all the people leave and asked the

waiter to serve his meal. When he had finished, he gave the restaurant to the waiter who has now started a chain of restaurants under the same name.

My immediate thought was, *Boy, what a gift for a waiter to receive—the complete restaurant!* But that gift doesn't compare with God's Son!

The Gift is not only unparalleled; it is

II. AN UNLIMITED GIFT!

By that I mean it is for everyone. We have no patience with those who think salvation is for an elected few and that others must spend eternity in Hell without hope. The Bible says, "For God so loved THE WORLD, that he gave his only begotten Son." Any grade school child will tell you "the world" means every person.

The Scripture says in I John 2:1, 2, "My little children, these things write I unto you, that ye sin not. And if any man sin, we have an advocate with the Father, Jesus Christ the righteous: And he is the propitiation for our sins: and not for our's only, but also for the sins of the WHOLE WORLD."

Hebrews 2:9 says, "But we see Jesus, who was made a little lower than the angels for the suffering of death, crowned with glory and honour; that he by the grace of God should taste death for every man."

The Bible is filled with verses that tell us that Jesus Christ died for **all** men, that He was the sinner's Substitute, and that He atoned for the sins of the whole world.

We read in Isaiah 53:6, "All we like sheep have gone astray; we have turned every one to his own way; and the Lord hath laid on him the iniquity of us all." There are two "alls" in this text. The first has to do with the universal fact of sin, "All we like sheep have gone astray." Any theologian will tell you it means all men are sinners, that nobody is perfect. It means the same thing that the Bible means in Romans 3:23, "All have sinned, and come short of the glory of God."

But there is a second "all" in this text: "And the Lord hath laid on him the iniquity of us ALL." If the first "all" includes everyone who has ever lived or ever will live, then the second "all" includes the same crowd. No one will ever look out of Hell, up to Heaven, and say, "Dear God, I wanted to be saved, but You didn't give Your Son for me." No! No! Romans 8:32 says, "He that spared not his own Son, but delivered him up for us ALL, how shall he not with him also freely give us all things?"

The death of Jesus Christ on the cross was sufficient for all, but it is efficient only to those who believe. Men may die without the Saviour. They may miss Heaven, but it won't be because they could not be saved. Salvation is for ALL men.

Titus 2:11 says, "For the grace of God that bringeth salvation hath appeared to ALL men." And the Bible says in II Peter 3:9, "The Lord is not slack concerning his promise, as some men count slackness; but is longsuffering to us-ward, not willing that any should perish, but that ALL should come to repentance." And I Timothy 2:4 says, "Who will have ALL men to be saved, and to come to the knowledge of the truth."

At this Christmas season, some gifts are available only to the very wealthy. It is unlikely that anyone reading these lines will be given a Rolls Royce for Christmas. Now don't misunderstand me. I am not against luxury automobiles. I am just saying that everyone cannot afford them! It is likely that somewhere in the world someone will receive a beautiful, luxury automobile. Diamond rings, beautiful homes, and many other luxury items are not available to all.

But God's Gift is unlimited. It is available to the heathen in the remote part of the world who has never heard the Gospel! It is also available to the alcoholic, the dope addict, the murderer. It is available to the immoral person, the uneducated, the wealthy, and the poor. Jesus is just as willing to save the down-and-outer as He is the up-and-outer.

My heart rejoices when I read the New Testament and find that our Lord was attracted to what appears to be the worst cases. To the woman at the well who had been married five times and was living with a man who was not her husband, He said, "If thou knewest the gift of God, and who it is that saith to thee, Give me to drink; thou wouldest have asked of him, and he would have given thee living water" (John 4:10). At the pool of Bethesda He went to the man who had been lame thirty-eight years. The worse the case, seemingly the greater the attraction to Jesus!

There is one Gift that all can receive this Christmas, that is the Gift of God which is eternal life through our Lord Jesus Christ.

It is not only an unparalleled and unlimited Gift, but it is

III. AN UNMERITED GIFT!

Nothing anyone can do can earn it. Everything we have we received one of three ways: earned it, stole it, or somebody gave it to us. There is no way one can earn salvation. Says Titus 3:5, "Not by works of righteousness which we have done, but according to his mercy he saved us." And Ephesians 2:8, 9, "For by grace are ye saved through faith; and that not of yourselves: it is the gift of God: NOT OF WORKS, lest any man should boast."

I feel sorry for the poor religionist who is trying to earn his salvation either by his good life or his good works. Jesus said in Matthew 7:22, 23, "Many will say to me in that day, Lord, Lord, have we not prophesied in thy name? and in thy name have cast out devils? and in thy name done many wonderful works? And then will I profess unto them, I never knew you: depart from me, ye that work iniquity."

Works offered to God as a basis for salvation are considered by Him to be works of iniquity. I think it was D. L. Moody who said,

I would not work my soul to save,
For this my Lord hath done;
But I would work like any slave,
For love of His dear Son!

Often at a funeral service we will hear the preacher say, "So-and-So has gone on to his reward." Now that may sound good, but Heaven is not a reward; Heaven is a gift.

One night I visited in the home of a medical doctor and his wife. They were very gracious and kind people. The particular church to which they belonged taught works for salvation, that one must perform good works, make sacrificial gifts, live a good life, etc., in order to be saved. After visiting for a few minutes with these precious friends, I asked, "If you die today, do you know you will go to Heaven?" The dear gentleman replied, "No." His wife smiled and said, "I don't really know."

I presented the simple plan of salvation, showing them that all men are sinners and as sinners we owe the sin debt. Very carefully I showed them that Jesus Christ was not a sinner and that two thousand years ago He died on a cross for our sins. I explained how His death made full payment for our sins and that we are saved by trusting Him as Saviour. I went on to explain that salvation is a gift that can only be received.

When I had finished, I asked if they would trust Christ as Saviour. The man looked at his wife and said, "Honey, for many years we have worked and worked and worked; we have given hundreds of thousands of dollars to the church; we have tried to live good and keep the Golden Rule; but we are still going to Hell!" He was rather blunt with his statement, but he was telling the truth. Suddenly he realized that salvation was by grace through faith. There in the living room he and his wife bowed their heads and trusted Jesus Christ as Saviour. I later baptized them, and they are still faithful soul-winning Christians today.

One is not saved by trying, but by trusting. One is not saved by doing, but by resting in what has already been done. You don't spell salvation "D-O"; you spell it "D-O-N-E." Religion is a man reaching up to God, but salvation is God reaching down to man.

For nothing good have I
Whereby Thy grace to claim—
I'll wash my garments white
In the blood of Calv'ry's Lamb.

Jesus paid it all,
All to Him I owe;
Sin had left a crimson stain,
He washed it white as snow.

And when, before the throne,
I stand in Him complete,
"Jesus died my soul to save,"
My lips shall still repeat.

Jesus paid it all,
All to Him I owe;
Sin had left a crimson stain,
He washed it white as snow.

In the matter of salvation and Heaven, all one needs is Jesus. He said in John 14:6, "I am *the* way, *the* truth, and *the* life: no man cometh unto the Father, but by me." Many religions teach that Jesus Christ is necessary, but they add other stipulations such as being baptized, keeping the Ten Commandments, enduring to the end, keeping the Golden Rule—on and on and on.

The Bible not only teaches that Jesus Christ is necessary; it teaches that He is enough! To add anything to salvation other than the sacrificial death of Jesus on the cross is to say that His death was not sufficient payment for our sins.

My hope is built on nothing less
Than Jesus' blood and righteousness;
I dare not trust the sweetest frame,
But wholly lean on Jesus' name.

On Christ, the solid Rock, I stand;
All other ground is sinking sand,
All other ground is sinking sand.

Not only is God's Gift unparalleled, unlimited, and unmerited but it is

IV. AN UNCLAIMED GIFT!

Preachers use different expressions to state the same thought: "Trust Christ as Saviour"; "Believe on the Lord Jesus." Dr. Rice used the expression, "Risk Christ." Several years ago I heard an old preacher talk about "claiming Christ as Saviour."

They all mean the same thing. The majority of people in the world have never yet claimed this unparalleled Gift. There are some reading these lines who have not yet trusted Jesus Christ as Saviour. John 1:12 says, "As many as received him, to them gave he power to become the sons of God, even to them that believe on his name." Think how you would feel if you made great sacrifice to give a present to a loved one, then when Christmas morning came the loved one never opened the package! Christmas Day came and went, but the loved one never opened the package. Of course you would be sad. Your heart would be crushed.

I wonder how the loving heart of God must feel when so many multiplied thousands go year after year and never accept the Gift He provided two thousand years ago at Calvary! I urge you, dear reader, to trust Christ as Saviour. Before you open a single Christmas gift, make sure you receive the greatest Gift of all, the Lord Jesus Christ.

Exactly how do you claim Christ? How do you receive Him as Saviour? Let me make it as simple as I possibly can.

First, admit you are a sinner. No one ever receives Christ until he realizes his need of Him. The Bible says in Romans 3:10, "As it is written, There in none righteous, no, not one." We have not all committed the same sins, but all have sinned. Because we are sinners, we owe a penalty. Romans 6:23 says, "For the wages of sin is death." If we pay what we owe as sinners, it means we must die, go into Hell, and stay there forever and ever and ever! Revelation 20:14 says, "And death and hell were cast into the lake of fire. This is the second death." This is the penalty all men owe as sinners.

Second, believe that Jesus Christ died to pay your sin debt. We have already shown in this passage that Jesus Christ died for the sins of the whole world. Two thousand years ago God took every sin you have ever committed or ever will commit and laid those sins on Christ. The Bible says in I Peter 2:24, "Who his own self bare our sins in his own body on the tree. . . ." And II Corinthians 5:21 says, "For he hath made him to be sin for us, who knew no sin; that we might be made the righteousness of God in him." All our sins were laid on Jesus; and while He bore our sins in His own body, God punished Him in our place to pay the debt we owe so that when we die we won't have to pay it.

But you must do more than admit that you are a sinner and believe that Jesus died for you. You must trust Him. Acts 16:31 says, "Believe on the Lord Jesus Christ, and thou shalt be saved." To trust Christ is no different than trusting an airplane pilot or the family doctor. To trust means to depend on, to rely on, to have confidence in. When I get on an airplane, I am fully trusting the pilot to take me to my destination—nothing else or no one else. He is my only hope of reaching my destination. To trust Jesus means the same thing. I say:

> Dear Lord Jesus, I know that I'm a sinner. I deserve to go to Hell, but I believe You died for me and that Your death on the cross is sufficient payment for my sins. I cannot get myself to Heaven. No religion or no preacher can get me to Heaven. If I get there, You will have to take me; so here and now I fully trust You and depend on You completely for my salvation.

WON'T YOU TRUST HIM NOW?

Won't you claim this unclaimed Gift? Everlasting life and an eternal home in Heaven are yours for trusting.

Come, ev'ry soul by sin oppressed,
There's mercy with the Lord,
And He will surely give you rest
By trusting in His Word.

Only trust Him, only trust Him,
Only trust Him now.
He will save you, He will save you,
He will save you now.

If you will trust Him and write to tell me so, I have some free literature I want to send that will help you as you set out to live the Christian life. All you need do to receive your free literature is to write me:

Dr. Curtis Hutson
Sword of the Lord Foundation
P. O. Box 1099
Murfreesboro, Tennessee 37133

And in your letter say, "I have read your sermon, 'God's Gift to the World.' I know that I'm a sinner and do believe that Jesus Christ died for me. Here and now I receive Him as my personal Saviour. I am fully trusting Him to take me to Heaven when I die. Please send me the free literature that will help me as I set out to live the Christian life."

Then include your name and full address.

Chapter 11

Unpardonable Sin

"Then was brought unto him one possessed with a devil, blind, and dumb: and he healed him, insomuch that the blind and dumb both spake and saw. And all the people were amazed, and said, Is not this the son of David? But when the Pharisees heard it, they said, This fellow doth not cast out devils, but by Beelzebub the prince of the devils. And Jesus knew their thoughts, and said unto them, Every kingdom divided against itself is brought to desolation; and every city or house divided against itself shall not stand: And if Satan cast out Satan, he is divided against himself; how shall then his kingdom stand? And if I by Beelzebub cast out devils, by whom do your children cast them out? therefore they shall be your judges. But if I cast out devils by the Spirit of God, then the kingdom of God is come unto you. Or else how can one enter into a strong man's house, and spoil his goods, except he first bind the strong man? and then he will spoil his house. He that is not with me is against me; and he that gathereth not with me scattereth abroad."

I call your attention especially to the next two verses:

"Wherefore I say unto you, All manner of sin and blasphemy shall be forgiven unto men: but the blasphemy against the Holy Ghost shall not be forgiven unto men. And whosoever speaketh a word against the Son of man, it shall be forgiven him: but whosoever

speaketh against the Holy Ghost, it shall not be forgiven him, neither in this world, neither in the world to come."—Matt. 12:22-32.

I do not like the title *"The Unpardonable Sin,"* but I choose it because it is a familiar expression. Actually all sin is unpardonable. I mean by that that God never overlooks sin, never pardons sin. All sin must be paid for. God does forgive the sinner but not the sin. If sin could be forgiven, then God was foolish to put Jesus to death for our sins. So I say, all sin is unpardonable. All sin must be paid for. God can pardon the sinner because Jesus paid the sin debt. Actually, a better title would be "The One Sin That Men Commit That They Cannot Get Forgiveness Of."

It is frightening to think that there is something a man can do for which he will never get forgiveness in this world nor in the world to come.

There is only *one* sin, whatever it is, for which there is no forgiveness. Matthew 12:31 says, "ALL manner of sin and blasphemy shall be forgiven unto men." But the Bible speaks of one sin that will never be forgiven.

The book of Hebrews records *some* sin that men commit that they will never be forgiven for.

"For it is impossible for those who were once enlightened, and have tasted of the heavenly gift, and were made partakers of the Holy Ghost, And have tasted the good word of God, and the powers of the world to come, If they shall fall away, to renew them again unto repentance."—Heb. 6:4-6.

Now whatever the people did here would have to be the unpardonable sin, else you have two unpardonable sins.

I. SINS THAT ARE NOT THE UNPARDONABLE SIN

Some have suggested that murder is the unpardonable sin. They say if you kill somebody, you cannot restore the life, thus you have committed a sin that cannot be pardoned. But murder is not the unpardonable sin.

David was a man after God's own heart, yet the Old Testament records that he committed murder when he sent Bathsheba's husband out into the heat of battle and had him killed. That was deliberate, willful, premeditated murder. Yet God forgave him.

Peter had the intent of murder in his heart. When he drew his sword and swung at the high priest's servant and cut off his ear, he wasn't aiming at his ear but for his head! In his heart Peter wanted to commit murder but failed in his attempt.

The book of I John says that if we hate our brother without a cause, we are murderers. Though murder is an awful sin it is not the unpardonable sin.

In John, chapter 8, a woman was taken in the very act of adultery. When she was brought to Jesus, He looked down and wrote something in the sand with His finger, then when He looked up, her accusers were gone. Jesus said, "Woman, where are those thine accusers?" And she said, "Lord, no man accuses me." And Jesus said, "Neither do I condemn thee: go, and sin no more." The sin of adultery is an awful sin, but not the unpardonable sin.

A woman in John, chapter 4, had been married five times. I do not know that all of her five husbands died or if she just left them or they left her. But she decided she wouldn't even marry the next time: she simply started living with him. Jesus came to her at the well in Samaria and talked about living water. She asked Him for it and He gave her the living water. She was saved and went to town and led a multitude to Christ, and many followed her back to where Jesus was. They believed on Jesus when they saw Him for themselves. Jesus forgave her.

People who have been guilty of this particular sin, maybe more than once, maybe more than twice have come to me and said, "I don't believe God can forgive this awful thing. I don't think I can ever be saved."

I remember leading one such man to Christ. He was burdened over the fact that he was living with a woman he was not married to, and his children didn't know it. He shared this with me and thought he could not be forgiven. He actually thought he was doomed for Hell. When I told him of the woman at the well, he wept with joy and said, "Praise the Lord! I thought I could never be saved; now I find God will save me!" He trusted Jesus and was gloriously saved. He is now living a good Christian life. Adultery is not the unpardonable sin.

Taking God's name in vain is not the unpardonable sin. You say, "I don't know why you even mention that, Preacher." I mention it because it is an awful sin, about one of the worst sins one can commit, the one sin that makes an absolute fool out of a man.

Every other sin has some provocation. For instance, the Devil comes to you and says, "Hey! You are hungry, you don't have food. Why don't you steal some money?" There is a provocation to that kind of sin, and, in a sense, a reward for that sin.

If you steal something, you do have the benefit of the thing which you stole, whether it be money, car, food or whatever. There is sometimes some reasoning behind stealing, though I am against stealing. The Bible says, "Thou shalt not steal."

There is also some provocation for murder. I can understand how a man loses his temper when someone does him wrong and keeps on doing him wrong. He thinks, *I'll get even with you, buddy!* And there is the satisfaction of, *I got even with him. He won't ever do me wrong again. He's gone!* There is some satisfaction in murder—at least I can assume there is.

There is some provocation to drunkenness. I have never been drunk, but there must be some satisfaction to being drunk. I don't see any other reason why a man would take his hard-earned money and spend it on strong drink, go out on Saturday and get drunk again and again and get locked up, then come home to a nagging wife and hungry children, then go back the next week and do the same thing again. I am not condoning it, but there must be some provocation to drunkenness.

But there is absolutely no provocation to taking the Lord's name in vain. Here is a sin that the Devil gets people to commit without offering them any reward. So cursing has to be one of the worst sins. To use God's name in vain repeatedly when there is absolutely no provocation for it makes a fool out of a man.

Not only that, but the command, "Thou shalt not take the name of the Lord thy God in vain," comes before the commands about murder, committing adultery, stealing and coveting. Why? Because God knows the cancerous nature of sin, and God knows what sin is worse than another—and He puts that commandment above these other commandments. But as bad as the sin of cursing is, it is not the unpardonable sin.

In his notes in the Scofield Bible Dr. C. I. Scofield says the unpardonable sin is ascribing the works of the Holy Spirit to Satan.

I don't agree with that. I don't think that is the unpardonable sin. Some men in this town, good preachers, have, out of jealousy, ascribed the works of the Holy Spirit to Satan. When we registered 1,122 salvation decisions during our Neighborhood Bible Time, some well-meaning people in town said, "Well, all those kids didn't know what they were doing. They just went down the aisle because they gave them a piece of bubblegum or a yoyo or some other gimmick." No; they came because they heard a gospel presentation and were hungry to be saved. They came to trust Jesus Christ as Saviour. And when you attribute it to something other than God, then you are accrediting the works of the Holy Spirit to the Devil. That has been done by many people many times, yet those people are saved or were saved later. So the unpardonable sin is not ascribing the works of the Holy Spirit to the Devil.

The unpardonable sin is not simply rejecting Jesus Christ. I suppose most every Christian here turned down Christ several times before you finally accepted Him as Saviour.

I was saved at age eleven, but God spoke to my heart about being saved many times before I accepted Him. So simply rejecting Christ is not the unpardonable sin.

Now if you go on rejecting Christ and die without the Saviour, it could lead to your damnation. But that in itself is not the unpardonable sin. I can think of several people who rejected Christ in the last two weeks. I personally asked them to trust the Saviour but they would not. They can still possibly be saved. I think they did a dangerous thing in saying no. They may die in a car wreck. Jesus may come. They may have a heart attack. But that is not the unpardonable sin.

Murder, adultery, taking God's name in vain, ascribing the works of the Holy Spirit to Satan, and simply rejecting the Saviour—these things are not the unpardonable sin. Before I say what I think the unpardonable sin is, let me say a word about

II. WHO CAN COMMIT THE UNPARDONABLE SIN

No saved person can ever commit the unpardonable sin. I, Curtis Hutson, can never commit the unpardonable sin. Why? Because when I was eleven I put my faith in Jesus Christ. All my sin was pardoned once for all, forever, and the deal is already closed, shut, signed, sealed and delivered. I cannot go back and undo what I did. I am already justified by faith.

Romans 5:1 says, "Therefore being justified by faith. . . ." Justification is not something that can be reversed and followed with condemnation. To be justified means all guilt is gone, that God not only forgives your sin but promises not to impute unto you iniquity. "Blessed is he whose transgression is forgiven, whose sin is covered. Blessed is the man unto whom the Lord imputeth not iniquity [or sin] " (Ps. 32:1, 2). When God justifies a believing sinner, He makes a promise that He will never again impute iniquity to that sinner's charge. Christians stand before God as if they had never committed a single sin.

The sad thing is, those who worry most about the unpardonable sin are those whose sins are already pardoned.

I have had Christians say to me, "I'm afraid I may have committed the unpardonable sin. I know I went forward in the church and trusted Jesus, but the thought keeps coming to me that I had gone beyond the deadline."

Let me set your mind at ease. If you have trusted Jesus, you can *never* commit the unpardonable sin. The deal is settled. It is closed. It is done. The books are closed. Your sins are forgiven. Get that settled.

Jesus said in John 5:24, "Verily, verily, I say unto you, He that heareth my word, and believeth on him that sent me, hath everlasting life." H-A-T-H—not shall have, but h-a-t-h—present tense. You have it the moment you believe on Jesus. ". . . *hath* everlasting life, and shall not come into condemnation"—shall not be judged again, will never have the sentence of sin placed on him again. That is God's promise—shall not have the sentence of sin placed on him again, "but *is*"—not is going to be— "but *is*," present tense, "passed from death unto life." Period. That is a tremendous verse!

The Bible says in Isaiah 43:25, "I, even I, am he that blotteth out thy transgressions for mine own sake, and will not remember thy sins." Every Christian ought to memorize that verse and quote it back to Satan, when he comes dragging your sins up and shaking them before your face.

John 6:37 has this comforting word: ". . . him that cometh to me I will in no wise cast out." No way can you get God to cast out the person who came to Him and put his faith in Jesus Christ. So the saved person can never commit the unpardonable sin.

The unpardonable sin can be committed only by unsaved people.

Remember what I said earlier, that there is only one sin that is unpardonable. You have never heard a sermon on "The Two Unpardonable Sins." The Bible clearly says, "All manner of sin and blasphemy shall be forgiven unto men. . . ." He who speaks a word against Jesus or the Bible or the preacher or anyone else, shall be forgiven.

But one person won't be forgiven—and that is the person who blasphemes against the Holy Spirit. This is the only unpardonable sin. Since the sin mentioned in Hebrews, chapter 6, is an unpardonable sin, then both sins are one and the same.

Notice the people there who have committed the unpardonable sin. Verses 4 and 5 say, "For it is impossible for those who were once enlightened. . . to renew them again unto repentance." The one who can commit the unpardonable sin is **the enlightened sinner,** that is, the sinner who has heard the Word of God, who knows how to be saved, the sinner who understands salvation, but goes on continually rejecting Christ.

Now, there are those who believe Hebrews, chapter 6, is written to Christians, but it is not. Verse 9 says, "But, beloved, we are persuaded better things of you, and things that accompany salvation." The things that he just discussed did not accompany salvation. They were not saved.

You say, "But it says they had tasted the good word of God." Yes, they tasted it but did not eat it. You say, "But they were made partakers of the Holy Ghost." Yes, the Holy Spirit worked with them in His pre-salvation work but they rejected Christ, refusing to yield to the drawing of the Holy Spirit.

Who are those people in Hebrews, chapter 6? Unbelievers, sinners without Christ to whom the Word of God has been preached, sinners who have been enlightened by the Word of God. They have tasted the Word of God, they have gone along with the Holy Spirit in His *pre-salvation* work, but they continually rejected Christ.

No one can be saved apart from the Holy Spirit. The Bible says in John 6:44, "No man can come to me, except the Father which hath sent me draw him: and I will raise him up at the last day." The sinner is drawn to Christ by the Holy Spirit, and no way can he be saved apart from the Holy Spirit.

The people in Hebrews, chapter 6, were dealt with by the Holy Spirit before salvation. They were brought up to the place of conversion, brought up to the place of accepting Christ; they knew how to be saved, they were enlightened, they saw it, they understood it—but the enlightened sinner said, "No! I won't be saved!" Finally, the Bible says, "It is impossible. . . if they shall fall away, to renew them again unto repentance."

III. WHAT IS THE UNPARDONABLE SIN?

The unpardonable sin is committed by enlightened sinners. It is rejecting the Holy Spirit's plea until the rejecting sinner loses all desire to be saved.

It is important to understand that the unpardonable sin does not change a loving God. God's love is changeless. His is immutable. God loves sinners and He wants sinners to be saved. And the unpardonable sin cannot change an unchangeable God.

The terrible thing about the unpardonable sin is that it changes the sinner. He continually rejects Christ until he gets to the place where he doesn't want to be saved.

The book of Revelation describes the tribulation period, when all Hell breaks loose on earth, hailstones fall from Heaven weighing 120 pounds; there is pestilence, earthquakes, and a third of the population dies, then more die. Monsters are let out of Hell with a sting that torments men five months, scorpion-like creatures.

But after all the tribulation described in the book of Revelation, men have no desire to be saved. They never one time turn to Jesus and say, "We want to be saved." Rather, they still repented not but prayed to the rocks and mountains, "Fall on us, and hide us from the face of him that sitteth on the throne." They preferred suicide to salvation! "We'd rather have mountains to fall on us and kill us than to be saved."

What happened? They said no to the Holy Spirit so many times until their continued rebellion changed their own heart. They had no desire to be saved.

The unpardonable sin is unpardonable only because the one who commits it no longer desires pardon. That is the terrible thing about the unpardonable sin. When you reject Christ, the heart becomes harder and harder.

Do I hear somebody saying even this morning as we hear in every service, "Dr. Hutson, if only I could feel like I felt when I was a child, when first I heard a choir sing, when first I heard a preacher preach on Hell and my little young lips quivered and cold chills went up my young spine. When the choir sang, 'Just As I Am,' it felt as if something inside me would pull my heart out and just drag me down the aisle. I remember as a little boy, how tears coursed down my cheeks. If I ever have that feeling again, I'm going to trust Jesus as my Saviour."

What a fool you are to think you will ever have that feeling again! Satan says, "Wait until you feel more like it, then get saved." The dirty crook! He knows that the very first time God spoke to your heart you felt more like being saved than you will ever feel again. The Devil knows that every time you reject Christ, you feel less and less like it, until you make that final rejection and lose all desire to be saved.

I witnessed recently to a man over eighty. He knows he is at the point of death. He believes the Bible. He believes there is a Heaven. He believes there is a Hell. But this old man said, "I don't have any desire whatsoever to be saved."

What happened to him? He hasn't always felt that way. There was a time when his young heart wanted to trust the Saviour. What happened? He was enlightened, he heard the Word of God, he knew how to be saved, the Holy Spirit dealt with him—but he rejected Christ, and through his continual rejection, he lost all desire to be saved.

That is why only a fraction of one percent of people are ever saved after they reach fifty. Seventy-six percent of all people who are saved are saved before they are twelve. That means, if you are over twelve, your chances of being saved are narrowed down to twenty-four percent. It is not that God doesn't want to save you, not that God cannot save you, but the chances of your wanting to be saved have narrowed down. The hardest people to win are those who have been to church all their life but have continued to reject Christ—the enlightened sinner. "It is impossible for those who were once enlightened. . . to renew them again unto repentance."

You can reject Christ until finally there will be no feeling, no emotion, no desire. And every preacher in the world could not preach enough to cause one tear to come from your eyes. You will say, like that old man, "I don't want to be saved. I have no desire whatsoever to be saved." That is the unpardonable sin.

If you have any inkling of a feeling at all, if the Holy Spirit has tugged the least bit at your heart, if there is just a little warmth, the faintest desire to be saved, for God's sake, for your own sake, move quickly on that little desire before it is gone.

There is one sin that will not be forgiven in this world nor the world to come. It is the unpardonable sin, the sin of rejecting Christ until you lose all desire to be saved.

What can I say to you? I want you to be saved. I shudder to think that anybody who ever came to this church and heard me preach, would go to Hell. I believe I ought to remember everybody I have ever preached to. When I sit down to the marriage supper of the Lamb and look down that long table, I don't think I'll be interested in eating until I walk up and down the table and see if you are there. I want you to be there.

WE PLEAD WITH YOU TO TRUST CHRIST TODAY

You have read the sermon, "The Unpardonable Sin," which was preached to my beloved congregation at Forrest Hills Baptist Church where I served as their pastor for more than 20 years. We shudder to think that anyone would read this and die without the Saviour. Please, if you have the least desire to be saved, do something about it immediately.

Every time you say "no" to Christ, the desire becomes more faint until finally you lose all desire to be saved. Then you have committed the unpardonable sin. As I said to the congregation at Forrest Hills Baptist Church, the unpardonable sin is unpardonable only because the one who commits it has no desire to be pardoned. If you have the least desire to know that you are going to Heaven when you die, then I plead with you to trust Christ today. To trust Christ simply means to depend on Him, to rely on Him for salvation. Simply tell Him in your own words,

> Dear Lord Jesus, I know that I am a sinner and that I cannot save myself. I believe that You died for me. And here and now I trust You as my Saviour. I completely

depend upon You to take me to Heaven when I die. Amen.

If you have prayed this prayer or one similar, telling Jesus that you would trust Him for salvation, then I have some free literature I want to send that will help you as you set out to live the Christian life. All you need to do to receive your free literature is write to me:

Dr. Curtis Hutson
Sword of the Lord Foundation
P. O. Box 1099
Murfreesboro, Tennessee 37133

and say, "I have read your sermon, 'The Unpardonable Sin.' Knowing that I am a sinner and believing that Jesus Christ died for me, I here and now trust Him completely for my salvation and depend on Him to take me to Heaven when I die. Please send me the free literature that will help me as I set out to live the Christian life."

Chapter 12

False Hopes of Heaven

"Then shall the kingdom of heaven be likened unto ten virgins, which took their lamps, and went forth to meet the bridegroom. And five of them were wise, and five were foolish. They that were foolish took their lamps, and took no oil with them: But the wise took oil in their vessels with their lamps. While the bridegroom tarried, they all slumbered and slept. And at midnight there was a cry made, Behold, the bridegroom cometh; go ye out to meet him. Then all those virgins arose, and trimmed their lamps. And the foolish said unto the wise, Give us of your oil; for our lamps are gone out. But the wise answered, saying, No so; lest there be not enough for us and you: but go ye rather to them that sell, and buy for yourselves. And while they went to buy, the bridegroom came; and they that were ready went in with him to the marriage: and the door was shut. Afterward came also the other virgins, saying, Lord, Lord, open to us. But he answered and said, Verily I say unto you, I know you not."—Matt. 25:1-12.

"Many will say to me in that day, Lord, Lord, have we not prophesied in thy name? and in thy name have cast out devils? and in thy name done many wonderful works? And then will I profess unto them, I never knew you: depart from me, ye that work iniquity."—Matt. 7:22, 23.

Many who think they are going to Heaven are going to be

disappointed. All of the ten virgins went out to meet him. All thought they were ready, but only five were. Jesus said to the others, "Verily I say unto you, I know you not."

Matthew 7:22, 23 teaches that many who think they are ready for Heaven will be lost:

"Many will say to me in that day, Lord, Lord, have we not prophesied in thy name? and in thy name have cast out devils? and in thy name done many wonderful works? And then will I profess unto them, I never knew you: depart from me. . . ."

There is an old spiritual song that our black friends used to sing: "Ever'body talks about Heav'n ain't goin' there!" Those words are absolutely true. Many who think they are going to Heaven have only a false hope.

R. A. Torrey once said that a man is better off with no hope than a false hope. He went on to explain that if a man has a false hope, he will go through life thinking he is saved and never come to know Jesus Christ as Saviour, while if a man has no hope at all, he is more likely to find the true hope, the only plan of salvation, and trust Jesus Christ as Saviour.

Now what are some of these false hopes of Heaven? There is no way that I can mention them all, but I will call attention to some of the more popular ones.

One false hope of Heaven is

I. GOOD WORKS

Sometimes when I ask an individual, "If you die today, will you go to Heaven?" he responds, "I am trying." But one is not saved by trying; he is saved by trusting. There is no way we can earn Heaven. Titus 3:5 says, "Not by works of righteousness which we have done, but according to his mercy he saved us." And Ephesians 2:8, 9 plainly states, "For by grace are ye saved through faith; and that not of yourselves: it is the gift of God: Not of works, lest any man should boast."

Those referred to in Matthew 7:22, 23 thought they should be allowed into Heaven because of their works. "Lord, Lord, have we not prophesied in thy name? and in thy name have cast out devils? and in thy name done many wonderful **works**?" But Jesus said, "I never knew you: depart from me, ye that work iniquity."

If the Bible is clear on anything, it is on the matter that salvation is by grace and not by works; and it cannot be a combination of the two. Romans 11:6 says, "And if by grace, then it is no more of works: otherwise grace is no more grace. But if it be of works, then is it no more grace: otherwise work is no more work."

Grace is God's unmerited favor toward Hell-deserving sinners with no expectation of return. If it is unmerited favor, then there is nothing we can do to earn it. The fact that salvation is a gift shows that it cannot be of works. Romans 6:23 tells us that "the *gift* of God is eternal life through Jesus Christ our Lord."

Jesus said to the woman at the well, "If thou knewest the **gift** of God, and who it is that saith to thee, Give me to drink; thou wouldest have asked of him, and he would have **given** thee living water" (John 4:10). If someone gave you a new gold watch and required that you mow his lawn once a week, then the watch would not be a gift; you would have earned it by mowing the lawn. The only thing one can do with a gift is receive it.

I have often heard preachers remark at a funeral service, "Mr. __________ has gone on to his reward." But Heaven is not a reward; it is a gift. John 1:12 says, "As many as received him, to them gave he power to become the sons of God." Philip P. Bliss was right when he wrote:

Once for all, O sinner, receive it,
Once for all, O brother, believe it;
Cling to the cross, the burden will fall,
Christ hath redeemed us once for all.

Those who work for salvation render the work ineffective through a wrong motive. The Bible teaches that the only service or work acceptable is that which is motivated by love. In I Corinthians 13:3 Paul said, "Though I bestow all my goods to feed the poor, and though I give my body to be burned, and have not charity [love], it profiteth me nothing." Love is the proper motivation for service and good works. But the man who works in order to stay out of Hell is motivated by fear and thus renders the work ineffective.

Human reason tells us that we could never earn Heaven even if we had ten lifetimes in which to work. Most of us work a lifetime here and never get a home paid for; then how can we expect to pay for Heaven? If we worked ten thousand lifetimes, we couldn't earn the golden street that runs in front of one heavenly mansion! Those who are trusting their good works have a false hope of Heaven and will hear Jesus say, "I never knew you: depart from me, ye that work iniquity" (Matt. 7:23).

Is there no place for good works in the Christian life? To be sure there is. Ephesians 2:10 says, "We are his workmanship, created in Christ Jesus unto good works." Once we are saved, God expects us to serve Him, to perform good works; but we don't do it to be saved or to earn Heaven; we do it because we love Him and want to serve Him.

Someone once said:

I would not work my soul to save,
For this my Lord hath done;
But I would work like any slave,
For love of His dear Son!

O dear reader, if you are trusting good works to get you to Heaven, I urge you to abandon your unscriptural plan of salvation and trust Jesus Christ as Saviour.

Another false hope of Heaven is

II. A GOOD LIFE

When I once asked a lady if she were sure she would go to Heaven when she died, she replied, "I live a good life." When I asked a man that same question, he said, "Well, I'm not too bad." Both were trusting their good life to get them to Heaven.

Now I am all for good living. One should live as clean, moral, pure and as righteous as he possibly can; but no one goes to Heaven on his own righteousness. The Apostle Paul said concerning his own people,

"For I bear them record that they have a zeal of God, but not according to knowledge. For they being ignorant of God's righteousness, and going about to establish their own righteousness, have not submitted themselves unto the righteousness of God."—Rom. 10:2, 3.

He goes on to say in verse 4, "For Christ is the end of the law for righteousness to every one that believeth."

Jesus said, "I came not to call the righteous, but sinners to repentance" (Mark 2:17). One would be just as safe trusting his sins to get him to Heaven as he would trusting his righteousness. The Bible says in Isaiah 64:6, "But we are all as an unclean thing, and all our righteousnesses are as filthy rags." Notice the language of this text, ". . . *all* our righteousnesses are as filthy rags." God does not accept any of our righteous acts as a hope of Heaven. He didn't say our *sins* but our *righteousnesses* are as filthy rags.

Suppose a man could turn over a new leaf and never sin again, that he could live righteous until the day he dies. Then would he go to Heaven? Absolutely not! His righteous living today cannot undo his sinful past. The truth is, no one is righteous. The Bible says in Romans 3:10, "As it is written, There is none righteous, no, not one." And verse 23 says, "All have sinned, and come short of the glory of God." The only righteousness that God accepts is His own imputed righteousness. We read in Romans 10:3, "For they being ignorant of God's righteousness, and going about to establish their own righteousness, have not submitted themselves unto the righteousness of God."

When we trust Jesus Christ as Saviour, God imputes to us, that is, credits to our account, the very righteousness of God. That is what Romans 10:10 says, "For with the heart man believeth unto righteousness." The moment we trust Jesus Christ as Saviour, God accounts us righteous in His sight.

Romans 4:5 promises, "But to him that worketh not, but believeth on him that justifieth the ungodly, his faith is counted for righteousness." The Scripture says in Romans 4:3, "Abraham believed God, and it was counted unto him for righteousness."

One verse of my favorite song says,

My hope is built on nothing less
Than Jesus' blood and righteousness.

One who is trusting in his good life or his own righteousness to be saved has a false hope of Heaven. If you are trusting in your own good life to get you to Heaven, then I urge you to pray and tell the Lord that there is no way you can be righteous enough to deserve Heaven; therefore, you will trust Him completely for God's imputed righteousness.

Another false hope of Heaven is

III. ORDINANCES

Multiplied thousands are trusting baptism to get them to

Heaven. These people teach what is known as baptismal regeneration, that is, one is saved by being baptized.

We live here in Middle Tennessee where there are many Church of Christ preachers and people. These dear ones believe that one is saved by being baptized, using such verses as Acts 2:38, "Then Peter said unto them, Repent, and be baptized every one of you in the name of Jesus Christ for the remission of sins, and ye shall receive the gift of the Holy Ghost." They think the verse means be baptized in order to obtain forgiveness of sins, when it simply means to be baptized because your sins have been forgiven. It is like saying, "Take an aspirin for your headache." It doesn't mean take an aspirin in order to get a headache, but because you already have one.

One must remember that the Bible never contradicts itself, and over and over the Scriptures make it plain that one is saved by grace through faith. John 3:36 says, "He that believeth on the Son hath everlasting life." Nothing is said about baptism. John 3:18 says, "He that believeth on him is not condemned." Nothing said about baptism. Romans 10:13 says, "For whosoever shall call upon the name of the Lord shall be saved." Nothing about baptism. John 5:24 says, "Verily, verily, I say unto you, He that heareth my word, and believeth on him that sent me, hath everlasting life, and shall not come into condemnation; but is passed from death unto life." Again nothing is said about baptism.

I could fill a small book with passages which state we are saved by simply believing on the Lord Jesus Christ, that is, trusting Christ as Saviour.

A dear man asked me about Mark 16:16, "He that believeth and is baptized shall be saved; but he that believeth not shall be damned." Notice the verse carefully, "He that believeth and is baptized shall be saved"; but the rest of the verse says, "but he that believeth not shall be damned." It does not say, "He that believeth not and is baptized not shall be damned," but, "He that believeth not shall be damned."

One is damned for not believing on the Lord Jesus Christ. Believing is the determining factor, not being baptized. That is like saying, "He that getteth on the jet plane and sitteth down shall fly to Jacksonville, Florida; but he that getteth not on the plane shall not fly to Jacksonville." It is the getting on that gets you there, not the sitting down.

Now we preach that every Christian should follow the Lord in believer's baptism. But the man who is trusting his baptism is not fully trusting Jesus Christ. There is no promise in the Bible for those who partially believe on Jesus. The promise is to those who believe on Him. If a man trusts Jesus Christ 90% and his baptism 10%, then the 10% destroys the 90% because it indicates that the person is not fully trusting Jesus Christ.

The other Sunday morning while getting ready for church I turned on the television. There was a program on entitled, "The Amazing Grace Bible Class," hosted by a Church of Christ preacher. To my surprise they were singing:

My hope is built on nothing less
Than Jesus' blood and righteousness;
I dare not trust the sweetest frame,
But wholly lean on Jesus' name.

On Christ, the solid Rock, I stand;
All other ground is sinking sand.

I found myself saying, *I wish you believed what you were singing. I wish your hope were built on nothing less than Jesus' blood and righteousness. I wish you were trusting nothing else but Jesus Christ.*

The man's message contradicted the song. He taught that one was saved by being baptized. They should have sung, "My hope is built on nothing less than Jesus' blood and righteousness—and my baptism." They are not trusting Jesus only but Jesus plus their baptism. How strange that they should call the program, "The Amazing Grace Bible Class," and then teach salvation by ordinances rather than by grace through faith in the finished work of Jesus Christ!

The man who is trusting his baptism has a false hope of Heaven because he is not fully trusting Christ. Thousands of people are going to Hell depending on the baptismal waters to wash away their sins, when the Bible clearly says in Hebrews 9:22, "Without shedding of blood is no remission." How can a person sing:

What can wash away my sin?
Nothing but the blood of Jesus;

What can make me whole again?
Nothing but the blood of Jesus

and then teach that water in a baptistry washes away one's sins? Everyone who trusts Jesus Christ as Saviour should be baptized. Acts 2:41 says, "Then they that gladly received his word were baptized: and the same day there were added unto them about three thousand souls." But one is far safer not being baptized at all than he is trusting baptism to get him to Heaven. When we add anything to the substitutionary death of Jesus on the cross as a hope of our salvation, we are saying the death of Jesus Christ was not sufficient payment for our sins.

O dear friends, the blood of Jesus Christ is never inadequate. It never needs an additive.

Hallelujah, 'tis done!
I believe on the Son.
I am saved by the blood of the crucified One.

When the redeemed gather in Heaven, they won't sing, "The baptistry is worthy," but, "Thou art worthy . . . for thou wast slain, and hast redeemed us to God by thy blood out of every kindred, and tongue, and people, and nation" (Rev. 5:9).

Jesus is the Saviour, yet He never baptized anyone. "Though Jesus himself baptized not, but his disciples" (John 4:2). If baptism saved, then Jesus saved no one because He baptized no one.

Baptism is a beautiful ordinance, and every believer should obey the Lord and be baptized, but it has absolutely nothing to do with our salvation.

Another false hope of Heaven is

IV. CHURCH MEMBERSHIP

When one man was asked if he were going to Heaven when he died, he replied, "Yes, I joined the church when I was eleven years old." Many think they are going to Heaven because they belong to a church. But many church members are lost.

One of our texts says:

"Many will say to me in that day, Lord, Lord, have we not prophesied in thy name? and in thy name have cast out devils? and in thy name done many wonderful works? And then will I pro-

fess unto them, I never knew you: depart from me, ye that work iniquity."

The people in this text were evidently members of a church. They even prophesied, or preached, in Jesus' name. Some claimed that they had cast out devils in the Lord's name. These were not only church members, but they served in the church. Yet Jesus said unto them, "I never knew you: depart from me, ye that work iniquity."

Billy Sunday used to say, "Getting into a church will not make you a Christian any more than getting into a garage will make you an automobile."

Now we are for church membership. Every person who is saved should join a good, Bible-believing church where he can be taught the Word of God, grow in grace, and become a mature, effective, fruitful Christian. The order is given in Acts 2:41, "Then they that gladly received his word were baptized: and the same day there were added unto them about three thousand souls." Believe, be baptized, belong.

God is not going to ask to see the roll of every church in the world to determine who is going to Heaven. That is determined by what we do with Jesus Christ. The Bible plainly says in John 3:18, "He that believeth on him is not condemned: but he that believeth not is condemned already, because he hath not believed in the name of the only begotten Son of God." The person who has trusted Jesus Christ is not condemned; that is, he is not under sentence; he is not going to Hell. But the person who is not believing on the Son is condemned; he is under the sentence because he has not believed in the name of the only begotten Son of God.

Church membership is good, and we urge every person who has trusted Christ as Saviour to join a good, Bible-believing, soul-winning church; but it is not a prerequisite to Heaven. Faith in Christ is. Make sure that you don't equate church membership with salvation.

Some churches urge everyone to become a member whether he has trusted Christ or not, thinking that association with church people will eventually lead to salvation. But that kind of teaching and thinking is not scriptural. No one should join a church until he has first trusted Christ as Saviour. Preachers should be careful lest they lead people to believe that joining a church is the same as trusting Jesus Christ as Saviour.

When I was pastor of the largest church in the state of Georgia, we were careful to see that every individual who responded to the invitation was properly dealt with, making sure that he had trusted Christ as Saviour before accepting him as a church member.

The person who thinks he is saved because he has joined a church has a false hope of Heaven. Love the church, pray for the church, attend the church, support the church, but don't trust church membership for salvation.

Another false hope of Heaven is,

V. "I WAS RAISED IN A CHRISTIAN FAMILY"

Some think they are going to Heaven because their mother and father and kinfolks were all Christians. I have often had people say to me, "I think I'll go to Heaven; I was raised in a Christian family."

Salvation is not inherited. John 1:13 says, "Which were born, not of blood, nor of the will of the flesh, nor of the will of man, but of God." That expression, "not of blood," means that salvation does not come to one through his family. Each individual must trust Christ for himself. Every man must make his own decision. People are not saved in groups, but one at a time as they personally trust Christ.

The Bible says in John 3:16, "For God so loved the world, that he gave his only begotten Son, that whosoever believeth in him should not perish, but have everlasting life." God loved the world and gave His Son to die on the cross that all could be saved. But it is "whosoever believeth in him" who is saved.

The death of Jesus Christ on the cross was sufficient for all, but it is efficient only to those who trust Him as Saviour. We are not going to Heaven because our mother, father, brother, sister, grandmother, grandfather, wife or husband were good Christians. We are going to Heaven because we personally trusted Christ.

Another false hope of Heaven is

VI. THE SACRAMENTS

Many are trusting their confirmation to get them to Heaven.

A Catholic priest once told me that the seven sacraments were seven channels of grace and that one had to receive all seven sacraments, including the last rites, in order to be saved.

How sad that men should trust so many different things when the Bible clearly says, "Believe on the Lord Jesus Christ, and thou shalt be saved" (Acts 16:31)! How could one trust anything else when Jesus clearly said in John 14:6, "I am the way, the truth, and the life: no man cometh unto the Father, but by me"?

The same Catholic priest said no one was good enough to go to Heaven. I agreed with his statement and wanted to hear what else he had to say. He went on to explain that no one who dies is ready for Heaven. He then explained his belief about purgatory, saying that the Catholic who dies with unconfessed venial sins goes to purgatory and remains there until he is purged from all unconfessed venial sins, then he moves into Heaven. Many well-meaning Catholics pray for their departed loved ones in hopes that they will not have to stay long in purgatory. The person who is trusting his sacraments and the fires of purgatory to purge him from any unconfessed sins has a false hope of Heaven.

The Bible teaches that Christ died for all our sins—past, present and future. Isaiah 53:6 says, ". . . the Lord hath laid on him the iniquity of us all." And I Peter 2:24 says, "Who his own self bare our sins in his own body on the tree." We read in II Corinthians 5:21, "For he hath made him to be sin for us, who knew no sin; that we might be made the righteousness of God in him."

Dear friend, nothing could be clearer. All the sins we have ever committed or ever will commit were laid on Jesus two thousand years ago. And while Jesus Christ bore our sins in His own body, God punished Him in our place to pay the debt we owe, so that when we die we won't have to pay it. And those who accept Jesus and His finished work have everlasting life. On the other hand, those who will not accept Him and His finished work "shall not see life; but the wrath of God abideth on him" (John 3:36).

VII. JESUS CHRIST, THE ONLY SURE HOPE OF HEAVEN

Jesus Christ is the only sure hope of Heaven. When the Philippian jailer asked Paul and Silas, "Sirs, what must I do to be saved?" they answered, "Believe on the Lord Jesus Christ, and thou shalt be saved." "Believe" means to depend on, to rely on, to trust. We must trust Jesus Christ to take us to Heaven just like we would trust a pilot to take us across America in a jet airplane or just like we would trust the captain of a ship to take us across the ocean.

To trust Christ means the same as trusting a family doctor. When one gets sick, he puts himself in the physician's hands. He depends on the physician to perform the necessary operation to make him well. Trusting Jesus Christ means the same thing: I come to Christ admitting that I'm a sinner and admitting that I should pay for my sins. It means I believe the Bible story that Jesus loved me, and that 2,000 years ago He died for me on the cross to pay my sin debt. Then I put my case in His hands. I fully depend on Him 100% to take me to Heaven when I die. My only hope of Heaven is the fact that Jesus Christ died for me, and I am trusting Him to take me to Heaven when I die. I have no other hope. I want no other hope. I need no other hope.

Should I at the gates of Heaven appear
To answer the challenge what claim hast thou here,
What hast thou to offer? Yea, what is thy plea?
With blessed assurance my answer would be,

Of all earthly treasures nothing I've brought,
No great deeds of merit have I ever wrought;
Tho' vile and unworthy as mortal could be,
I've nothing to offer, but this is my plea,

My sins they are many, my virtues are few;
The blood of my Saviour will carry me through;
When Christ in my place died on Calvary's tree,
Hallelujah! that opened God's Heaven to me.

All that I have is Jesus,
All that I claim is Jesus,
All that I want,
All that I need,
All that I plead is Jesus.

I have been a preacher for thirty years, but I'm not trusting the fact that I'm a preacher to get me to Heaven. I have lived a pretty good life, but I'm not trusting my good life to get me to Heaven. I belong to a good, Bible-believing church; but I'm not trusting my church membership to get me to Heaven. I was baptized as an eleven-year-old boy, but I'm not trusting my baptism to get me to Heaven. I am trusting Christ alone, nothing else. If I died in the next five minutes and stood at Heaven's gate and there an angel asked, "Curtis, why should we let you into Heaven?" I would simply say, "I understand that I'm a sinner, that Jesus Christ loves sinners and died for them at Calvary. I understand from the Bible that His death fully paid what I owe as a sinner, and I am trusting Him. He is my only hope of Heaven."

In the final analysis, there are only two groups in the world: those who are trusting Christ and those who are not trusting Him. Jesus draws the line and divides the world into two groups. In John 3:36 He said, "He that believeth on the Son HATH everlasting life" —group one. "And he that believeth not the Son shall not see life; but the wrath of God abideth on him" —group two.

Those who are believing on Him, trusting Him, relying on Him, have everlasting life—not are going to have it someday, but have it this moment. "Hath" is present tense. Those who are not believing on Him constitute the other group, and the Bible says they shall not see life but the wrath of God abides on them.

DON'T DELAY; DECIDE TODAY

Dear friend, which group are you in? Are you trusting Jesus Christ? Is He your only hope of Heaven? If not, I urge you to trust Him now. If you are trusting anything other than Jesus Christ, then you are standing on sinking sand. If you are not sure you are trusting Him, then do it now. Pray this simple prayer:

> Dear Lord Jesus, I know that I'm a sinner. I do believe that You died for me. Here and now, the best I know how, I do trust You as my Saviour. I am fully depending on You to take me to Heaven when I die. Amen."

If you prayed that prayer and will write to tell me so, I have some free literature I want to send that will help you as you set out to live the Christian life. All you need do to receive your free literature is write to me at this address:

Dr. Curtis Hutson
Sword of the Lord Foundation
P. O. Box 1099
Murfreesboro, Tennessee 37133

In your letter tell me, "I have read your message, 'False Hopes of Heaven.' Knowing that I'm a sinner and believing that Jesus Christ died to pay my sin debt, I here and now fully trust Him for my salvation. I admit that He is my only hope of Heaven and depend on Him to take me to Heaven when I die. Please send the free literature that will help me as I set out to live the Christian life."

Be sure to include your name and full address.

Chapter 13

The Most Important Question Ever Asked

If I should put to those reading these lines what is the most important question facing us in the 1980's, no doubt I would get a variety of answers. Some would say the threat of nuclear war; others unemployment; others would say a balanced budget or perhaps the interest rates; some that inequities among people is the most important question. On and on we could go. All these questions are very important, and it is our prayer that they be answered correctly.

But none is the most important. The most important question facing us now was asked by Pontius Pilate two thousand years ago in Matthew 27:22, "What shall I do then with Jesus which is called Christ?" Far more depends on the right answer to that question than all other questions in the world.

Everything that is really worthwhile for time and eternity depends upon a right decision about this question. If one does the right thing "with Jesus which is called Christ," he will get everything really worth having for time as well as eternity.

On the other hand, if one makes the right decision regarding all other questions and the wrong decision regarding the question, "What shall I do then with Jesus which is called Christ?" then he will lose everything worthwhile for time as well as eternity.

Pilate asked this question nearly two thousand years ago: "What shall I do then with Jesus which is called Christ?" And because he made the wrong decision, he is lost forever, though he may have made the right decision regarding many other important questions.

Everyone who has ever lived is faced with this all-important question, "What shall I do then with Jesus which is called Christ?" Thousands upon multiplied thousands have made the right decision and are now enjoying everything worthwhile in this life and in the life to come, while others have made the wrong decision and have suffered and will suffer irretrievable loss.

I. WHAT DOES ONE GET IF HE DOES THE RIGHT THING WITH JESUS?

1. He Receives Forgiveness of All Sin

The blessed promise in Acts 10:43 is, "To him give all the prophets witness, that through his name whosoever believeth in him *shall* receive remission of sins." Everyone who believes on Jesus Christ receives remission of sins. Our "shalls" are sometimes puny and weak. We fully intend to keep our promise, but circumstances unknown to us keep us from always fulfilling our "shalls."

I may say to a friend, "I shall come to your house Saturday night," but before then I may get an emergency call that a loved one has passed away and therefore I am not able to fulfill my promise.

But when God says "shall," He knows the future. Nothing takes Him by surprise, therefore nothing will ever happen that will keep Him from fulfilling His promise.

Dear reader, you may rest assured that if you believe in the Lord Jesus Christ you "shall receive remission of sins." If the vilest sinner who ever lived believes in the Lord Jesus Christ, he receives remission of sins. He may be an outcast of society, but the promise is "*whosoever* believeth in him shall receive remission of sins."

The forgiveness of sins depends entirely upon what one does with Jesus Christ, not upon our prayers, performances, penances or promises. Whatever else you may or may not do, if you do the right thing with Jesus you get the forgiveness of *all* your sins. But if you do the wrong thing, you will not be forgiven.

I read the story of a man serving a fifteen-year sentence for manslaughter. After reading a Bible which someone had given to him, he trusted Christ as Saviour. He read the promise, "Whosoever believeth in him shall receive remission of sins." And with an excitement characteristic of little children, he walked from one side of the cell to the other.

When someone yelled, "Sit down and be still!" He cried out, "I can't keep still! My sins are forgiven!"

What a wonderful thing to know that God has forgiven me, that He no longer holds against me the sins I have committed. And this blessed forgiveness is mine when I do the right thing with Jesus!

No wonder the psalmist wrote, "Blessed is he whose transgression is forgiven" (Ps. 32:1).

But if one does the right thing with Jesus,

2. He Also Receives Peace

Isaiah 26:3 promises, "Thou wilt keep him in perfect peace, whose mind is stayed on thee: because he trusteth in thee." The words "trust" and "believe" are the same. To believe on the Lord Jesus Christ means to trust Him. Contrast this with what the Bible has to say about the wicked in Isaiah 57:20, 21, "But the wicked are like the troubled sea, when it cannot rest, whose waters cast up mire and dirt. There is no peace, saith my God, to the wicked."

Dr. R. A. Torrey stopped on the street to speak to a man about his soul.

The man said, "I don't need religion. I have everything I need without it."

Dr. Torrey replied, "There is one thing you don't have."

"What is that?" asked the man.

"Peace," said Dr. Torrey.

The startled man exclaimed, "How did you know that?"

Dr. Torrey said, "Because the Bible says 'the wicked are like the troubled sea, when it cannot rest, whose waters cast up mire and dirt. There is no peace, saith my God, to the wicked.'"

Today, when there are so many things to cause concern and worry, how wonderful to have the peace that comes by doing the right thing with Jesus.

One who does the right thing with Jesus

3. Gets Great Joy

Peter states in I Peter 1:8, "Whom having not seen, ye love; in whom, though now ye see him not, yet believing, ye rejoice with joy unspeakable and full of glory."

When I was still serving as pastor of a church, a dear lady stood one night and testified, "I have an unable-to-speak-it-out joy!" That is the kind of joy the Bible promises to those who do the right thing with Christ. It is an unspeakable joy and full of glory.

I have no doubt that some are reading these lines who are still rejecting Jesus Christ as Saviour because you think you will lose joy if you become a Christian. And maybe your fears are not unjustified, seeing that so many Christians seem to live defeated lives. But the truth is, those who trust Jesus Christ as Saviour should have greater joy than those without Christ.

Testifying of his salvation experience, a Scotsman said, "I am happier now when I am not happy than I was before when I was happy!" Christians are happier in poverty than skeptics and unbelievers are in wealth.

The story is told of an old woman dying in the poorhouse but still singing and praising the Lord. When someone asked why she was so happy since she didn't have anything seemingly to be happy about, she shouted, "Just think! I am dying in the poorhouse, but I'm going to a mansion!"

This kind of unspeakable joy is for those who, though they see not Jesus Christ, yet believe.

But the one who does the right thing with Jesus

4. Receives Eternal Life

John 3:36 promises, "He that believeth on the Son hath everlasting life." And John 5:24 states, "Verily, verily, I say unto you, He that heareth my word, and believeth on him that sent me, hath everlasting life, and shall not come into condemnation; but is passed from death unto life."

Who can fathom all the depths of the meaning that there is in these two wonderful words, "everlasting life"? The one who does the right thing with Jesus will live on forever. Though he may have made the wrong decision about every important question of the day, still if he makes the right decision about this important question, "What shall I do then with Jesus which is called Christ?" he has everlasting life.

I recall the words of a song we sang in the country church when I was a small boy:

A million years from now,
A million years from now,
We'll still be shouting victory
As to the Lord we bow.

No one will ever die,
No heart will ever sigh.
We'll just begin to live
A million years from now.

Blessed old John Newton put it this way:

When we've been there ten thousand years,
Bright shining as the sun,
We've no less days to sing God's praise
Than when we first begun.

Billy Sunday once said that if a little sparrow took one grain of sand from the earth and flew thousands of miles and deposited that grain of sand on some far-away planet, and continued making trips, until he had moved the entire earth, it would just be breakfast time in Glory.

The one who does the right thing with Jesus

5. Becomes a Child of God

John 1:12 states, "But as many as received him, to them gave he power to become the sons of God, even to them that believe on his name." The Apostle John, thinking of this, said, "Behold, what manner of love the Father hath bestowed upon us, that we should be called the sons of God" (I John 3:1). And Paul adds in Romans 8:17, "And if children, then heirs; heirs of God, and joint-heirs with Christ."

It staggers the imagination to think of being a child and heir of God and joint-heir with Jesus Christ, the infinite One, the Creator of all things, the One before whom the whole company of angels is as nothing! Do the right thing with Jesus and you become a child of God, an heir of God and a joint-heir with Jesus Christ! But do the wrong thing with Jesus and you lose forever your opportunity to become a child of God, you lose untold wealth, you lose the greatest honor ever bestowed upon an individual, and you lose the dearest Friend one could ever have!

Is it not evident, then, that the most important question facing man today and all days is, "What shall I do then with Jesus which is called Christ?"

Do the right thing with Jesus and

6. Be Justified From All Sins

What a blessed promise is Romans 5:1, "Therefore being justified by faith, we have peace with God through our Lord Jesus Christ." When one does the right thing with Jesus, God not only forgives the sin but does away with the sin so the believing sinner stands before God as if he had never committed a single sin. To be justified means just as if I had never sinned. It means God not only forgives the sin but blots it out and it no longer exists. The Bible declares God will "cast all their sins into the depths of the sea" (Micah 7:19). I heard an old preacher say, "God has cast our sins in the depths of the sea and put up a 'No Fishing' sign. Praise the Lord!"

If you do the right thing with Jesus

7. You Will Be Like Him Someday

First John 3:2 says, "Beloved, now are we the sons of God, and it doth not yet appear what we shall be: but we know that, when he shall appear, we shall be like him; for we shall see him as he is." What a glorious thought to have a glorified body like our Lord's, a body that could appear in one place at one moment, then appear somewhere else a few moments later, as He did to the Emmaus disciples; a body that could appear in a room without any windows or doors being opened, as He did for Thomas; a body that could eat broiled fish and honeycomb, as our Lord did in Luke 24:41-43!

So I put to everyone reading these lines the most important question facing man today, "What shall I do then with Jesus which is called Christ?" Will you do the right thing or the wrong thing with Him?

II. WHAT IS THE RIGHT THING TO DO WITH JESUS?

The right thing to do is found in the words of Mark 4:36,

". . . they took him even as he was in the ship." The right thing to do with Jesus is to

1. Accept Him as He Is and for What He Is

And what does He offer Himself to be? Our Sin-Bearer. The Bible says in I Peter 2:24, "Who his own self bare our sins in his own body on the tree." Every sin we have ever committed and all we will ever commit were laid on Jesus. The Bible says in Isaiah 53:6, ". . . the Lord hath laid on him the iniquity of us all." And II Corinthians 5:21 states, "For he hath made him to be sin for us, who knew no sin; that we might be made the righteousness of God in him." We must accept Him for what He offers Himself to be—our Sin-Bearer.

The greatest truth that ever coursed through my brain was this blessed truth of the substitutionary death of Jesus Christ. He became our Substitute, bearing our sins; and God punished Him in our place to pay the debt we owe so that when we die we won't have to pay it!

The Bible not only pictures Him as our Sin-Bearer but as One who paid our ransom. Mark 10:45 states, "For even the Son of man came not to be ministered unto, but to minister, and to give his life a ransom for many." His death on the cross paid what every sinner owes. Nothing could be truer than the words,

Jesus paid it all,
All to Him I owe;
Sin had left a crimson stain,
He washed it white as snow.

His cry from the cross, "It is finished," meant, among other things, that the sin debt was paid forever.

Nothing to pay! the debt is so great.
What will you do with the awful weight?
How shall the way of escape be made?
Nothing to pay—yet it must be paid!
Hear the voice of Jesus say,
"Verily thou hast nothing to pay:
All has been put to My account.
I have paid the full amount."

Nothing to pay; yes, nothing to pay!
Jesus has cleared all the debt away—
Blotted it out with His bleeding hand!

Free and forgiven, and loved, you stand.
Hear the voice of Jesus say,
"Verily thou hast nothing to pay!
Paid is the debt, and the debtor free!
Now I ask thee, lovest thou Me?"

The right thing to do with Jesus Christ is to trust Him as your Sin-Bearer and as the One who paid your sin debt. Once you trust Him, all the things promised to those who do the right thing with Jesus are yours—forgiveness of sins, peace of conscience, unspeakable joy, everlasting life, the promise that you will become a child of God, justification, and the promise that someday you will be like Him.

But after you trust Him as Saviour, there are other things you ought to do with Christ.

2. You Should Openly Confess Him Before Men

The Bible says in Matthew 10:32, 33, "Whosoever therefore shall confess me before men, him will I confess also before my Father which is in heaven. But whosoever shall deny me before men, him will I also deny before my Father which is in heaven." Romans 10:10 tells us, "For with the heart man believeth unto righteousness; and with the mouth confession is made unto salvation." Everyone who does the right thing with Jesus Christ should come out openly and publicly.

What would you think of a man who asked his new wife to ride in the back seat of the automobile as if he were ashamed of her? And what would you think of a lady who would not happily introduce her new husband? You would think there was a lack of love. Then what about the person who trusts Christ as Saviour but never tells anyone about it?

I did the right thing with Jesus when I was an eleven-year-old boy. After I had gone to bed one night, I prayed and trusted Him as my Saviour. Several months later I went forward in the church during a big August revival and made my public declaration of faith. Oh, I was a bit nervous and afraid, but I certainly wasn't ashamed. I told the people that I had trusted Jesus Christ as my Saviour.

Perhaps there are some reading these lines who have trusted Christ but have never made it public. Then attend a Bible-believing church at your first opportunity, and at the invitation, go forward and tell the preacher you have trusted Christ as Saviour.

Someone has said that too many Christians are like an Arctic river—frozen at the mouth. Dear reader, if you have trusted Christ, then tell others about it. And by all means make a public confession in a church service!

But there is something else we should do with Jesus after we trust Him as Saviour and Sin-Bearer.

3. We Should Tell Others About Him

Mark 5 records a story of Jesus' casting the demons from one who had been possessed. And the man out of whom Jesus cast the demons wanted to stay with Jesus. But Jesus said unto him, "Go home to thy friends, and tell them how great things the Lord hath done for thee, and hath had compassion on thee." We are told, "And he departed, and began to publish in Decapolis how great things Jesus had done for him: and all men did marvel."

Oh, may the dear Lord help us to publish abroad what great things the Lord has done for us. Everyone has a circle of friends he can reach for Christ. I hope that every reader will become a witness. If you don't have time to open the Bible and show someone how to be saved, at least pass out gospel tracts wherever you go.

These are the right things to do with Jesus. Who will do them now and gain all that is worth having for time and eternity?

A Choice Must Be Made

The question is, "What shall I do then with Jesus which is called Christ?" You say, "I won't decide today." Not to decide to do the right thing with Jesus is a decision to do the wrong thing. Our Lord said in Matthew 12:30, "He that is not with me is against me; and he that gathereth not with me scattereth abroad." There is no such thing as being neutral.

Jesus is standing in Pilate's hall—
Friendless, forsaken, betrayed by all:
Hearken! what meaneth the sudden call!
What will you do with Jesus?

Jesus is standing on trial still,
You can be false to Him if you will,
You can be faithful thro' good or ill:
What will you do with Jesus?

Will you evade Him as Pilate tried?
Or will you choose Him, whate'er betide?
Vainly you struggle from Him to hide:
What will you do with Jesus?

What will you do with Jesus?
Neutral you cannot be;
Someday your heart will be asking,
"What will He do with me?"

If you will do the right thing with Jesus by trusting Him as your Sin-Bearer and Saviour, then I have some free literature I want to send that will help you as you set out to live for Christ. All you need do to receive your free literature is write to me:

Dr. Curtis Hutson
Sword of the Lord Foundation
P. O. Box 1099
Murfreesboro, Tennessee 37133

In your letter say, "I have read your sermon, 'The Most Important Question Ever Asked.' I have decided today that I will do the right thing with Jesus. Knowing that I am a sinner and believing that Jesus Christ died on the cross for me, here and now I trust Him as my Saviour. I am fully depending on Him to take me to Heaven when I die. I promise to tell others about my decision. Please send me the free literature that will help me as I set out to live the Christian life."

Chapter 14

Is There Life After Death?

"If a man die, shall he live again? all the days of my appointed time will I wait, till my change come."—Job 14:14.

From the first, "Where art thou?" in Genesis 3:9 down to the last, the Bible asks and answers many great questions. Life also has its questions, but life and experience cannot answer them. For reliable answers, we must turn to the Bible.

Someone has suggested that the preacher who preaches on the great questions of the Bible and gives not his own answers but the answers of the Scriptures will discover before he is through that he has struck all the major chords of the everlasting Gospel.

One of man's greatest and most earnest questions is found in our text, "If a man die, shall he live again?" Since Job is the oldest book in the Bible, this is probably one of the oldest questions ever asked, a question that has crossed everyone's mind.

One question more than all others
From thoughtful minds implores reply.
It is breathed from star and pall,
"What fate awaits us when we die?"

SEVERAL ANSWERS TO THE QUESTION

The first answer comes from the materialist. His reply is a quick and short, "No." The materalist claims that the sum total of man is flesh, bone and blood. Ask the materialist, "Where does one go when he dies?" and he will answer, "Nowhere. Earth to earth; ashes to ashes; and dust to dust. The soul is but a function of the brain."

Napoleon once said, "Knock me on the head; where then is my soul?"

The second answer comes from the scientist. But when it comes to the question, "If a man die, shall he live again?" the scientist's lips are sealed. He has no answer. *Science* is "organized knowledge"; and *knowledge* is "of things seen." But the Bible says, "The things which are seen are temporal; but the things which are not seen are eternal" (II Cor. 4:18).

The scientist has no scientific way of proving life after death, since there is no way to test and experiment. The scientist can deal only with those things he can taste, touch, hear, see, and smell—the things having to do with the five senses. So when the scientist tells me where I came from or where I'm going, he's completely out of his field.

The third answer comes from the agnostic. That is a word invented by Thomas Huxley. It is a transliteration of the Greek word which means "unknown." The agnostic does not say for sure that there is not life after death; simply that we cannot know." He is right—if you leave out divine revelation, the Word of God.

OUR LORD'S ANSWER TO THE QUESTION

"If a man die, shall he live again?" Jesus answered that question in John 11:25, 26:

"I am the resurrection, and the life: he that believeth in me, though he were dead, yet shall he live: And whosoever liveth and believeth in me shall never die."

He answered it again when He said to His disciples in John 14:1-3:

"Let not your heart be troubled: ye believe in God, believe also in me. In my Father's house are many mansions: if it were not so, I would have told you. I go to prepare a place for you. And if I go and prepare a place for you, I will come again, and receive you unto myself; that where I am, there ye may be also."

Our Lord was about to be separated from His disciples by death, but He assured them that they would meet again. "I will. . . receive you unto myself" teaches reunion; "myself" teaches recognition in the life to come. How would the disciples know that they had been received unto the Lord unless they recognized Him?

The Hebrew writer confirmed our Lord's answer to the question, "If a man die, shall he live again?" in Hebrews 9:27: "And as it is appointed unto men once to die, but after this the judgment." Mark those words, *"after this."* There is something after death. If death were all and man ceased to exist, then what is the need for a judgment?

The book of Job confirms our Lord's answer in 19:25-27:

"For I know that my redeemer liveth, and that he shall stand at the latter day upon the earth: And though after my skin worms destroy this body, yet in my flesh shall I see God: Whom I shall see for myself, and mine eyes shall behold, and not another. . . ."

Paul confirmed Christ's answer in Philippians 1:23: "For I am in a strait betwixt two, having a desire to depart, and to be with Christ; which is far better." He did so again in II Corinthians 5:8 when he said that to be "absent from the body" is to be "present with the Lord."

No one can believe in divine revelation and not believe in life after death.

Jesus' answer confirms man's idea and instinct of immortality. The idea of immortality did not originate at the birth of Christ; it was there long before Christ came and He simply brought it to light.

In II Timothy 1:10 we read, "But is now made manifest by the appearing of our Saviour Jesus Christ, who hath abolished death, and hath brought life and immortality to light through the gospel." The great pyramids testify to the idea of immortality. Here nations buried their kings and pharaohs, and placed in the tombs the furniture and other personal items of the deceased because it was believed that the dead would live again and, therefore, would need these things in the afterlife.

Men have unearthed the skeletal remains of warriors who were buried with their spears in hand. Why were they thus buried? Because of a belief in life after death. In the afterlife these warriors, it was thought, would need their spears.

The idea of immortality is a mighty and unanswerable argument for it. Someone has said, "The intuition of immortality is written in the heart of man by a hand that writes no falsehoods."

Jesus' answer confirms man's belief in justice. There is no such thing as complete and total justice in this world. We all know of men who have committed the same crime but did not pay the same debt to society. Just this past week while my son Tony and I were driving from Atlanta back to Murfreesboro, he talked about a lady who only a few months ago had placed her infant son in an oven and left him until he died. He said, "Daddy, that woman was released and is 'Scottfree' today." Then he added, "There is just nothing right about that." I agree with him.

One politician does something for which he is turned out of office, while another does something far worse, yet still serves in public office. There must be a place somewhere, sometime when the scales of justice are perfectly balanced. Should Elijah and Jezebel in the end experience the same fate? Should Herod and John the Baptist in the end come out the same? What about Paul and Nero?

The Bible asks in Genesis 18:25, "Shall not the Judge of all the earth do right?" Of course, the answer is an absolute *yes.* Man may get by in this life; he may buy, barter and talk himself out of justice; but man's belief in justice confirms Jesus' answer that there is life after death.

Jesus' answer confirms man's thought about the incompleteness of this life and the necessity of another life, to give full expression to the talents and gifts that are in man. More than once I've heard elderly men filled with wisdom and knowledge say, "Just as you learn how to live, it's time to die." Man's intellectual possibilities are on a scale much larger than the needs of this present life.

Dr. Bob Jones, Sr., once said, "The greatest thought that ever occurred to me is that I must live somewhere forever. And if I must live somewhere forever, I'd better learn how to live."

In this life we only learn how to live, but in the life to come we will live, and live, and live.

'Tis a sweet and glorious thought that comes to me,
I'll live on, I'll live on.
Jesus saved my soul from death, and now I'm free,
I'll live on, I'll live on.

I'll live on, yes, I'll live on,
In eternity, I'll live on.

Bacon has an incomplete essay concerning fame, and at the end one reads in brackets: "[The rest was not finished.]" That comment could well be written on the death certificate and tombstone of every individual.

There is a cathedral that contains paintings of the apostles by the painter El Greco. Some are unfinished, and all one sees is the barest outline—just a hand or a foot or part of the head. In a sense, all man does in this life is leave just a sketch, an outline of what might have been done or of what he planned to do.

Jesus' answer also confirms and satisfies the affections and longings of the heart. "The heart," said Pascal, "has reasons that the mind knows nothing of."

"If a man die, shall he live again?" Only Jesus' answer can satisfy the longing heart and wipe away the tears of those who mourn over a departed loved one or friend. Jesus' answer hangs a rainbow of hope over my mother's grave. Precious memories of departed friends and loved ones are good, but the hope of meeting them again is far better. A sunset is all right; but a sunrise—that is something else!

One of the last sermons ever preached by my beloved predecessor, Dr. John R. Rice, was delivered at the Lavon Drive Baptist Church in Garland, Texas. Speaking of the afterlife, Dr. Rice said:

> I remember some things at the cemetery when Mother was buried, though I was just six. I remember that hole in the ground. No fake grass covered the clods in that country cemetery. When a little shower began, Dad knelt down by that open grave with one arm around two little boys and one arm around two little girls. I remember a kindly woman holding a black unbrella over our heads.
>
> We said goodbye to Mama. Ah, but I'll see my mother again!
>
> I went by that cemetery in Cooke County some years ago. As I stood there I said, "Mother, I'll see you again! In just a little while, I'll see you again." I know she heard, for she wasn't in that grave but watching from Heaven.
>
> Dad has gone. Dr. Bill was a good brother. We were very close. He is gone. So is my evangelist brother Joe—very dear. And Jesse and George and Ruth and Jimmy and Gertrude—all gone.

> I'll see again Dr. Bob Jones, Dr. Walter Wilson, Dr. W. B. Riley, Dr. Harry Rimmer—and how many, many others! Oh, I'll see them all again!

Yes, Jesus' answer confirms and satisfies the affections and longings of the heart.

And Jesus' answer to the question, "If a man die, shall he live again?" is absolutely true. The Bible says in Hebrews 6:18, ". . . it was impossible for God to lie"; and Titus 1:2 says, "God, that cannot lie."

There's a land that is fairer than day,
And by faith we can see it afar;
For the Father waits over the way,
To prepare us a dwellingplace there.

WHAT IS THE FUTURE LIFE LIKE?

The Bible speaks more of the fact and glory of the life to come than of the nature of it. As a matter of fact, the Bible does not reveal all there is to know about the life to come. In II Corinthians 12:2-4, the apostle said:

"I knew a man in Christ above fourteen years ago, (whether in the body, I cannot tell; or whether out of the body, I cannot tell: God knoweth;) such an one caught up to the third heaven. And I knew such a man, (whether in the body, or out of the body, I cannot tell: God knoweth;) How that he was caught up into paradise, and heard unspeakable words, which it is not lawful for a man to utter."

Paul saw things in Heaven that he could not talk about. Is it possible that our present physical bodies could not stand it if we knew all there was to know about the wonderful life to come? We would never be satisfied here again. The knowledge of the life to come would ruin us totally for this world.

But while the Bible does not tell us everything there is to know about the afterlife, it does not leave us totally in the dark. Many of the descriptions of the life to come are given in the Bible in negative terms. I mean, rather than telling us what *is* there, the Bible tells us what *is not* there.

There shall be no more curse, that is, sin.

There shall be no more death, which is the wages of sin. Sin and death are Siamese twins—they always ride together.

There shall be no more sea, the symbol of unrest.

There shall be no more pain. Never again will we hear the cries and groans of the suffering. Never again will we stand by helpless as we watch our loved ones suffer excruciating pain.

There shall be no more sorrow. The causes of all sorrow have vanished.

There shall be no more crying.

No tears in Heaven; no sorrow given;
All will be glory in that land.
There'll be no sadness; all will be gladness.
When we shall join that happy band.

There shall be no more night.

We once heard of a small boy who had been burned very badly. The pain made it so the little fellow could not sleep. As his mother sat by his bed late one night, he cried, "Mother, Mother, will morning ever come?"

Well, we have an answer for the little fellow: morning will come—the eternal morning!

Dr. George W. Truett once visited a member who was near death's door. Before he left, he shook hands and said, "You'll be better in the morning. You'll be better in the morning." The dear saint looked up and said, "Mr. Truett, I'll be *well* in the morning!" And he was! Before morning came, he had moved to the City where there is no night.

In the land of fadeless day
Lies the "city four-square,"
It shall never pass away,
And there is "no night there."

God shall "wipe away all tears";
There's no death, no pain, nor fears;
And they count not time by years,
For there is "no night there."

Heaven is a real place. In John 14:2, 3 Jesus said:

"In my Father's house are many mansions: if it were not so, I would have told you. I go to prepare a place for you. And if I go and prepare a place for you, I will come again, and receive you unto myself; that where I am, there ye may be also."

Here our Lord calls Heaven a place.

Matthew 6:19, 20 exhorts:

"Lay not up for yourselves treasures upon earth, where moth and rust doth corrupt, and where thieves break through and steal: But lay up for yourselves treasures in heaven, where neither moth nor rust doth corrupt, and where thieves do not break through nor steal."

This could only be said of a real, literal, physical place. Some think Heaven is a state of mind; but moth and rust cannot corrupt the state of mind; thieves cannot break into a state of mind. That could only be said of a real, literal, physical place.

Revelation 21:15 gives the measurements of the Holy City. If you multiplied the cubits into feet, then divided the feet into miles, you would discover that the Holy City is 1,500 miles square. This could not be said of a state of mind. It could only be said of a real, literal place.

Heaven is a place of indescribable beauty and glory. First Corinthians 2:9 describes it this way: "Eye hath not seen, nor ear heard, neither have entered into the heart of man, the things which God hath prepared for them that love him." Paul says the things that God has prepared for us have never crossed our minds.

Luke 15:10 tells us, "Likewise, I say unto you, There is joy in the presence of the angels of God over one sinner that repenteth." If there's rejoicing in Heaven over what a sinner is saved *from,* just think what he must be saved *to*!

How beautiful Heaven must be!
Sweet Home of the happy and free!
Fair haven of rest for the weary!
How beautiful Heaven must be!

When the Apostle John was describing the Holy City in Revelation 21, he could not believe what he was writing. In verse 5 he stopped as if he thought, *Surely this is too good to be true!* And the Lord said to him: "Write: for these words are true and faithful."

Heaven is a place of perfect rest. We read in Revelation 14:13, "Blessed are the dead which die in the Lord from henceforth: Yea, saith the Spirit, that they may rest from their labours; and their works do follow them."

Our black friends used to sing:

I'm gonna lay down my burdens,
Down by the riverside,
Down by the riverside,
Down by the riverside.

Heaven is a place where pressures are gone. It's the land of perfect rest.

I remember the night my mother passed away in my home. I was out making visits when one of the church members came to where I was and told me I was needed at home. When I arrived, Mother was dead. As I looked at her body lying on the bed, my first impression was, *Mother, this is the first time I've ever seen you relaxed.* There was such a look of peace on her face. I had not realized it until that moment, but my mother evidently had carried burdens every day of her life and had never totally relaxed. But she's resting now.

Heaven is a place of perfect understanding. Look at I Corinthians 13:12, "For now we see through a glass, darkly; but then face to face: now I know in part; but then shall I know even as also I am known." Often I've had friends say, "When I get to Heaven, I have a lot of questions I want to ask the Lord." I always reply, "When you get to Heaven, you'll have all the answers. You will know what the Lord knows, because the Bible says in I John 3:2, '. . . we shall be like him; for we shall see him as he is.' "

When I was a small boy in the country church, we used to sing:

Trials dark on ev'ry hand,
And we cannot understand
All the ways that God will lead us
To that blessed Promised Land;
But He'll guide us with His eye,
And we'll follow till we die;
And we'll understand it better by and by.

The songwriter had the idea, but he wasn't altogether correct. We won't understand it *better* by and by; we will *understand* it by and by. All of our unanswered questions will be answered. The bitter experiences of life, so difficult to understand and so hard to accept, will be understood. The trials that made no sense to us here will then be understood and appreciated.

We will know our friends and loved ones in Heaven. As

a preacher I have often been asked, "Will I know my mother in Heaven? Will I know my father? brothers? sisters? friends?" The answer is *yes.* ". . . then shall I know even as also I am known" (I Cor. 13:12).

On the Mount of Transfiguration, Moses and Elijah appeared with Jesus. Moses lived and died long before Elijah was born, yet on the Mount of Transfiguration, they knew each other. And Moses and Elijah were still known by their names. Jesus said, ". . . when ye shall see Abraham, and Isaac, and Jacob, and all the prophets, in the kingdom of God" (Luke 13:28). If we know Abraham, Isaac, and Jacob, we will certainly know each other.

Job said, "And though after my skin worms destroy this body, yet in my flesh shall I see God: Whom I shall see for myself, and mine eyes shall behold, and not another" (19:26, 27).

In the life to come, we will have a body. Second Corinthians 5:1 says, "For we know that if our earthly house of this tabernacle were dissolved, we have a building of God, an house not made with hands, eternal in the heavens." Our life here in the present body is like living in a tent. The tent is frail; and the older we get, the more apt the adverse winds of life to blow it over. But at death we exchange the fragile tent for a house not made with hands.

But we believe the body described in II Corinthians 5 is a temporary one which the believer occupies between death and resurrection, because, when the Lord comes, the Bible promises that even the physical body will be raised and fashioned like unto the Lord's own glorious body. The resurrection body will be the believer's permanent body in eternity. First Thessalonians 4:16, 17 says:

"For the Lord himself shall descend from heaven with a shout, with the voice of the archangel, and with the trump of God: and the dead in Christ shall rise first: Then we which are alive and remain shall be caught up together with them in the clouds, to meet the Lord in the air: and so shall we ever be with the Lord."

"If a man die, shall he live again?" Absolutely. Jesus said so, and He cannot lie.

DO THE SAVED EXPERIENCE THIS LIFE IMMEDIATELY AFTER DEATH, OR MUST THEY WAIT UNTIL THE RESURRECTION?

We have often been asked, "Do the saved go to Heaven immediately when they die?" Yes. Proof is in II Corinthians 5:8: "We are confident, I say, and willing rather to be absent from the body, and to be present with the Lord." Nothing could be plainer: wherever the Lord is, that's where the believer goes when he dies. Paul said in Philippians 1:23, "For I am in a strait betwixt two, having a desire to depart, and to be with Christ; which is far better."

To find out where the believer goes when he dies, one only has to find out where Jesus is. The Bible does not leave us in the dark. He is seated on the right hand of God. The Scripture says in Revelation 3:21, "To him that overcometh will I grant to sit with me in my throne, even as I also overcame, and am set down with my Father in his throne." Hebrews 12:2 says, "Looking unto Jesus the author and finisher of our faith; who for the joy that was set before him endured the cross, despising the shame, and is set down at the right hand of the throne of God."

When Stephen, the first martyr, was being stoned to death, he said in Acts 7:56: "Behold, I see the heavens opened, and the Son of man standing on the right hand of God."

Those who believe the Bible must believe that Jesus is in Heaven with God the Father and that, when believers die, they go immediately to be with Christ. There is no stopover, no waiting. There are only two places the Christians can ever be—in the body or with the Lord.

WHO IS GOING TO HEAVEN?

If you asked twenty people that question, it is possible you would get twenty different answers. One would say, "Those who have been baptized." Another— "Those who keep the Ten Commandments." Others— "Those who have received the seven sacraments." Still others— "Those who endure to the end." Other well-meaning and serious people would say, "Those who live good. Those who've turned over a new leaf. Those who have reformed." Some would even say, "Those who have joined the church." And on and on and on the answers go.

But what does the Bible say?

In Revelation, chapter 7, we see a heavenly scene. The Apostle John is talking:

"And one of the elders answered, saying unto me, What are these which are arrayed in white robes? and whence came they? And I said unto him, Sir, thou knowest. And he said to me, These are they which came out of great tribulation, and have washed their robes, and made them white in the blood of the Lamb."—Vss. 13,14.

Who is going to Heaven? Those who have been washed in the blood.

Have you been to Jesus for the cleansing pow'r?
Are you washed in the blood of the Lamb?
Are you fully trusting in His grace this hour?
Are you washed in the blood of the Lamb?

We realize that this terminology is not easily understood. To be washed in the blood does not mean to dip one's hand in a basin of blood. Let me see if I can explain so the smallest child can understand.

The Bible teaches that all men are sinners. Romans 3:23: "For all have sinned, and come short of the glory of God." Because we are sinners, we owe a penalty. Romans 6:23: "For the wages of sin is death." That death is more than dying with a gunshot wound or cancer. It is described as the "second death," the lake of fire in Revelation 20:14: "And death and hell were cast into the lake of fire. This is the second death."

As sinners, we owe a debt. To pay what we owe, we must die, go into Hell, and stay there forever and ever. But God loves us and wants us to be in Heaven with Him. So He sent His only begotten Son into the world. John 3:16 states, "For God so loved the world, that he gave his only begotten Son, that whosoever believeth in him should not perish, but have everlasting life."

Now here's what happened. Two thousand years ago God took every sin we have ever committed and ever will commit, and laid those sins on Jesus. First Peter 2:24 says, "Who his own self bare our sins in his own body on the tree." While Jesus bore our sins in His own body, God actually punished Him in our place to pay the debt we owe. That's exactly what the Bible means when it says, "For God so loved the world, that he gave his only begotten Son."

Romans 8:32 says, "He that spared not his own Son, but delivered him up for us all." Jesus died for the whole world. He paid the sin debt for the whole world. And the plain promise of John 3:16 is that "*whosoever* believeth in him should not perish, but have everlasting life." To believe in Christ means to depend on Him, to trust Him, to rely on Him. To believe in Christ means that He is your only hope of salvation, that you're trusting nothing else.

The songwriter explained it when he wrote:

My hope is built on nothing less
Than Jesus' blood and righteousness;
I dare not trust the sweetest frame,
But wholly lean on Jesus' name.

On Christ, the solid Rock, I stand;
All other ground is sinking sand.

One cannot trust Christ—plus his church membership. One cannot trust Christ—plus baptism, or plus his good works, or plus his promises to do better. One must trust Christ and Christ alone. There is no promise to those who partially believe on Jesus; the promise is to those who believe on Him.

To be washed in the blood means that I believe that Jesus Christ died for me, that He shed His blood as the remission for my sins; and I'm trusting Him and His shed blood as my only hope of Heaven.

Are you sure that you will go to Heaven when you die? If not, then make sure today by trusting Jesus Christ as Saviour.

DO IT NOW!

You have read the sermon entitled "Is There Life After Death?" We have shown from the Bible that there is life after death, and this life is wonderful beyond human description. We have also shown you that the only way to go to Heaven is to trust Jesus Christ as Saviour. And now we urge you to trust Him. If you will trust Him, then pray this simple prayer:

Dear Lord Jesus, I know that I'm a sinner. I do believe You died for me. And the best I know how, I do trust

You as my Saviour. I'm depending on You and nothing else for my salvation. Amen.

If you prayed that simple prayer or one similar, telling the Lord that you would trust Him as your personal Saviour, we have some free literature we want to send that will help you as you set out to live the Christian life. All you need do to receive your free literature is write to me:

Dr. Curtis Hutson
Sword of the Lord Foundation
P. O. Box 1099
Murfreesboro, Tennessee 37133

Tell me, "I have read your sermon, 'Is There Life After Death?' Knowing that I am a sinner, and believing that Jesus Christ died for me, I do trust Him as my Saviour. I'm depending on Him completely to take me to Heaven when I die.

"Please send me the free literature that will help me as I set out to live the Christian life."

Include name and full address so I can write you and send the material.

Chapter 15

How Will You Die?

"And as it is appointed unto men once to die, but after this the judgment."—Heb. 9:27.

I received a call this week from a mother, and weeping she told of her sixteen-year-old son, Ellis, who started coming on our buses to Sunday school before he was twelve. Ellis trusted Christ as Saviour, and I baptized him.

She said, "Brother Curtis, you remember Ellis. You baptized him. You remember Ellis. He must have brought at least a dozen of his friends to church, and they were saved there."

She continued, "You know, Ellis' father and I are divorced. Ellis has tried again and again to win his drunken father to Christ, but he has been unsuccessful. I had to leave him, and the younger children are with me. Ellis, who is with his father, is over sixteen now. He drove several miles this week to visit me. He said, 'Mamma, I have tried to win Daddy to Christ, but I can't. You have accepted Christ. Mamma, I want you to promise you will raise my brothers and sisters right; I want to meet them in Heaven. Mamma, I'm going to die. Daddy will never see me again, and this is the last time you will see me.'"

She wept as she said, "That sweet little thing hugged and kissed me and said, 'Good-by Mamma.' Brother Curtis, he got in the car and left. Four hours later I received a phone call that Ellis was dead."

I have thought several times this week about the untimely death of young Ellis.

I have had a couple of close calls when I actually thought I might die. I did some inventory. I asked myself a lot of questions: Am I ready to die? I know I'm saved, but am I really ready to die? Are there things I would like to correct before I die? Is there some information I should give my wife? Are there things she ought to know? Are there things my church members ought to know? Are there things I haven't yet told my children? I have never expressed my desires concerning their future. Is there some advice I need to give them? Am I really ready to die? Are there things I would like to tell my father before I die? Are there any bills I haven't paid? Am I ready to die?

I have asked myself that question over and over this week, since the lady called me about Ellis. Am I really ready to die? I'm saved. If I died I know I would go to Heaven. I have no doubt about that, but am I really *ready* to die?

That is the question I want to burn into your minds as I preach a simple sermon on, "How Will You Die?"

I call your attention to five Bible characters and how they died.

I. THE RICH MAN DIED UNPREPARED

The rich man in Luke 16 died unprepared. I am sure many thought he was well prepared. No doubt he had provided well for his family. We read in verse 19, "There was a certain rich man, which was clothed in purple and fine linen, and fared sumptuously every day." He no doubt had a good bank account. Probably he had a good insurance policy. Had anything happened to him no doubt his family would have been better off financially, as it is in the case of most of us. He had made preparations to live; **but he had not made preparations to die.**

He was like the rich farmer who had been blessed of God. His crops brought forth so plentifully that he had no place to bestow his goods. He said to himself, *Where shall I put all my goods? I know what I'll do; I'll tear down my old barns and build new ones. Then I'll say, Soul, thou hast much goods laid up in store. Take thine ease, eat, drink and be merry.* He made preparations to live; **but he made no preparation to die.**

I hear someone saying, "No one just walks out on a platform and talks about dying on Sunday morning. You Baptist preachers are always talking about dying, dying, dying." Well, you promise me you won't die, and I'll promise you I'll stop talking about dying. The Bible says, "And as it is appointed unto men once to die, but after this the judgment."

When you die, nobody is going to ask who your father was, or how much money you had in the bank, or whether you owned your own business or worked for someone else. When you die, nobody is going to ask where you went to college.

I had been speaking in Griffin, Georgia, one night and was late coming home. As I turned a sharp curve I saw lights shining. The red lights were blinking. I soon saw that a car had gone over a steep place and down an embankment. I was one of the first to get to the convertible, which was upside down and underneath were two bodies.

The question I heard asked several times was, "Are they dead or alive?" not, "What are their names?" or, "Whose fault was it?" They didn't ask, "Were they drinking?" or, "Where did they go to school?" The only thing important was: "Are they dead or alive?"

Dear friends, when you depart this world, the only thing that will matter is: Are you spiritually dead or alive? Do you know Jesus Christ as Saviour? Have you been born again?

A very wealthy man had died. After the funeral a little boy was riding in a wagon with an old man. The man was talking about how much money the deceased had. He must have been worth several hundred thousand dollars. Finally he said, "I wonder how much he left." The little fellow replied, "He left it all." When you die, you leave it all. You can't carry one dime with you.

Sam Jones was a famous Methodist evangelist who is buried in Cartersville, Georgia. One day his wife said to him, "Sam, I want you to visit the sheriff. He is very sick, and I hear that he may die. You ought to witness to him before he dies."

Sam went to see the sheriff. He said, "Sheriff, you know you are a sick man. The doctors have already told you there is a possibility you may die."

He laughed as he replied, "Sam, listen! I have faced death many times. I have been shot at, wounded and at the point of death over and over again. Sam, you need not try to frighten me with this death business! I'm not afraid to die."

Sam said, "But, Sheriff, what about the judgment?"

The sheriff shook as he said, "My God, Sam! I hadn't thought of that!"

Maybe you are brave enough to die, but what about the judgment? "It is appointed unto men once to die, but after this the judgment."

Dr. Bob Jones, Sr., told the story of a young soldier in the Civil War. This night they were sitting around the campfire; the next day they were going into an awful battle. When the young soldier appeared nervous, someone asked, "What's the matter, Bud, are you afraid to die?" The young man said, "No, I'm not afraid to die, it's what's beyond death that frightens me!"

Are you ready to die? Thank God, I can say this morning that I am. If I were to die in the next five minutes, I know beyond a shadow of doubt that I will go to Heaven.

The rich man died unprepared, "was buried; And in hell he lift up his eyes, being in torments." It says that the beggar died, "and was carried by the angels into Abraham's bosom."

There is no mention of his funeral service or of his burial. He probably didn't have one. Many beggars died in Jerusalem, and their dead bodies would be found lying on the streets the next morning. Then men would come along with something like a garbage wagon, pick up the dead body, toss it in the wagon, go down the road a little further, pick up another dead body, throw it on the wagon, then go dump them all on the garbage heap.

The beggar died. They dragged his body off the street, threw it in the cart and wheeled it away. He had no funeral, no flowers, no singing—nothing. But he was carried by angels to Abraham's bosom. He died prepared, while the rich man died unprepared. The beggar didn't go to Heaven because he was poor, and the rich man didn't go to Hell because he was rich. The rich man went to Hell because he rejected Jesus, and the poor beggar went to Heaven because he accepted Christ and was born again.

Don't die unprepared. Trust Jesus Christ as your personal Saviour.

II. ANANIAS DIED UNCLEAN

Another Bible character died unclean. His name was Ananias. We have the story in Acts 5. I have no reason to believe that Ananias was not a Christian. Ananias and Sapphira, his wife, sold their possession. Ananias brought part of the money and laid it at the apostles' feet, saying, "We sold our property for so much and here is all the money we got for it." He lied, because he and his wife had agreed to keep back part of the price. I think the hypocrite was saved, but he was professing something that he didn't really do. He was professing full dedication, full surrender—"I have sold my property and here is all the money I got."

It is one thing to profess to have some kind of experience and be Spirit-filled; it is another thing to be Spirit-filled and have the fruit of the Spirit. It is one thing to sing, "I surrender all," but another thing to be surrendered.

If you were to die this morning, would you die unclean? Would you die as a hypocrite, professing to be a good Christian, when you know you are not? Is there envy, strife, bitterness and hatred in your heart? Is your heart cold and hard? Is there any known, tolerated, unconfessed sin in your life? If you died today, would you die an unclean Christian? Confess your sins and allow God to forgive and cleanse you as He promised to do in I John 1:9: "If we confess our sins, he is faithful and just to forgive us our sins, and to cleanse us from all unrighteousness."

III. JUDAS DIED UNFAITHFUL

I don't think Judas lost his salvation, for he was never saved. In John 6:70 Jesus said, "Have not I chosen you twelve, and one of you is a devil?" Verse 71 says, "He spake of Judas Iscariot the son of Simon: for he it was that should betray him, being one of the twelve." He served when it was easy to serve. When Jesus first made His appearance, I get the idea He was popular.

When I read of the life of Jesus, I see the crowds flocking to hear Him, and I see Him trying to get away from the crowds. He rushes away; and by the time He crosses the sea, the crowd is on the other side. Thousands gather about Jesus. He has become so popular that people say, "Let's make Him King!" He has just fed the 5,000, plus women and children. They want a king who can feed them.

Judas says, "I want to get on the bandwagon! This is the crowd

I would like to follow, the crowd that is after Jesus!" It was popular then to follow Him, so Judas joins in. "As a matter of fact, I'd like to be the treasurer," he says, so he is made treasurer.

One day Jesus announced, "He that eateth my flesh, and drinketh my blood, dwelleth in me, and I in him. . . . This is that bread which came down from heaven. . .he that eateth of this bread shall live for ever" (John 6:56-58). This statement offended some, and they began to walk away. The crowd became small. Jesus looked at the disciples and asked, "Will ye also go away?" Peter answered, "Lord, to whom shall we go? thou hast the words of eternal life" (vss. 67, 68). Jesus told them, "The foxes have holes, and the birds of the air have nests; but the Son of man hath not where to lay his head" (Matt. 8:20).

It got tough to stay with the crowd that followed Jesus. The Devil put it in their hearts to get rid of Him, and they went after Him. Judas said, "I used to follow Him, but the crowd is not as big as it was. The glamour is gone. There is no cheering, nobody clamoring to make Jesus King now. Rather, they want to crucify Him. I think I had better get out while the getting is good!"

So Judas sold Jesus for thirty pieces of silver, the price of a dog. He made what he could and got out. Later he went out and hanged himself. After some time, his body fell and his bowels gushed out. He died unfaithful.

I would rather die this morning than to know I would live another six months and die unfaithful.

In 1962 I read carefully and prayerfully the 13-point covenant that Christmas Evans made with God. Somehow I felt I should write my own. I don't remember everything I wrote down and sealed in an envelope. But I remember one thing: *Lord, let my days be no longer than my usefulness to Thee.*

I meant it then, and I mean it now. I would rather be nailed up in a coffin alive and buried, than to know I would live another day and influence somebody in the wrong direction. God grant that I shall not die unfaithful, as Judas did.

IV. STEPHEN DIED UNAFRAID

What a deacon was Stephen! A deacon out spreading the Gospel, not gossip. Stephen, out on the street corner preaching, telling people how Jesus died on a cross, how He was buried and how

He arose again the third day. The crowd stopped their ears and became angry. They ran toward Stephen and gnashed on him with their teeth. They actually bit him, gnashed on him with their teeth like dogs; but Stephen kept on preaching. They stoned him until he died, but Stephen died unafraid.

If somebody were to walk into your church this morning and say, "Everybody who intends to stay on the Lord's side, stand up. We are going to take you out and put you before a firing squad," how many of you would stand? Would you go all the way? If communism takes over and the communists say, "We are going to pull down all the fundamental churches, leaving only a few showcase churches," how would you react? If you were told, "You cannot tell folks how to get saved. And we will tell you what to preach," would you be back next Sunday morning?

Dr. Bob Jones, Sr., said, *The test of a man's character is what it takes to stop him.* Would you stop?

One night a man coming home from a masquerade party in a Devil's costume ran into the church, scaring them to death. People began running for the doors. He announced, "I'm the Devil. I came to get you!" This one lady a little overweight, got wedged in the nearest door. As the Devil ran toward her, she said, "Wait a minute! Before you get me, let me say something. I have been coming out here every Sunday morning and night for years. I have been singing in this church and shouting with the rest of them. But I want you to know I have been on your side all the time!"

How many would be like her? Would you say, "I sat over there and smiled when Dr. Hutson preached about separation and clean living. I said, 'Amen,' but in my heart I didn't agree with him. I've been on your side all the time"?

Stephen died unafraid. Give us men who can face the mouth of lions and sing "Amazing Grace." Give us some Polycarps who can face a martyr's death and declare boldly, "Eighty and seven years have I served Him, and He has never one time failed me. I'll not deny Him now." Give us some young men like Timothy who was in charge of the Word of God; and when they came to get the Word, he hid it and said, "You will not have it." They replied, "If we can't get the Word of God from you, we will fix you so you can never read it." So they took red hot irons and burned out his eyesockets, then hung him upside down. His new wife came, put her head near the ground and near his face and begged him to tell them where the Word of God was; but when he wouldn't, they killed him. Give us some Christians who, if need be, are placed on the rack; and when they come to take them off the rack, they can say, "The presence of God is so real on the rack, leave us here."

God help us to die unafraid. "The Lord is my light and my salvation; whom shall I fear? the Lord is the strength of my life; of whom shall I be afraid?" (Ps. 27:1).

How will you die? Unprepared? Unclean? Unfaithful? Unafraid?

V. PAUL DIED UNASHAMED

Paul stood for Christ when it wasn't popular. The Christians lived in the catacombs in Paul's day. They were the offscouring of the earth. They were considered nothing. Paul took his stand with that crowd. He died unashamed.

He was in a damp and dark prison. I imagine it was rat-infested and water was dripping down on him. Paul said:

> *"Of the Jews five times received I forty stripes save one. Thrice was I beaten with rods, once I was stoned, thrice I suffered shipwreck, a night and a day I have been in the deep; In journeyings often, in perils of waters, in perils of robbers, in perils of mine own countrymen. . . In weariness and painfulness, in watching often, in hunger and thirst, in fastings often, in cold and nakedness. Beside those things that are without, that which cometh upon me daily, the care of all the churches."*—II Cor. 11:24-28.

Do you think Paul thought, *Oh, I have gone through Hell. I think I'll write Timothy a closing note before they come to take me out and cut off my head?*

Did Paul tell him, "Timothy, I have gone through Hell. It's not worth it. I have scars from the crown of my head to the sole of my feet. I had to write the letter to the Galatians in large letters because I could hardly see! Some of the letters were not even written by me, but were dictated to secretaries who penned them down. I have about lost my eyesight. My back hurts. Now in a few minutes my head will be cut off. I hear them sharpening the swords. Timothy, give it up. Quit preaching now and get out of the ministry. You are coming to no good end" —is that what he wrote?

No! When he heard them sharpening the swords he said:

"Endure hardness, as a good soldier of Jesus Christ. . . Fight the good fight of faith. . . Preach the word; be instant in season, out of season; reprove, rebuke, exhort with all longsuffering and doctrine. For the time will come when they will not endure sound doctrine; but after their own lusts shall they heap to themselves teachers, having itching ears. . . I have fought a good fight, I have finished my course, I have kept the faith: Henceforth there is laid up for me a crown of righteousness, which the Lord, the righteous judge, shall give me at that day: and not to me only, but unto all them also that love his appearing. . . the time of my departure is at hand."

And the enemy took him out and cut off his head. But he died unashamed!

There are several things of which a Christian should not be ashamed. He should not be ashamed of the clear, simple Gospel of Christ. Paul said in Romans 1:16, "For I am not ashamed of the gospel of Christ: for it is the power of God unto salvation to every one that believeth; to the Jew first, and also to the Greek." He should not be ashamed to suffer.

The Bible reminds us in I Peter 4:16, "Yet if any man suffer as a Christian, let him not be ashamed; but let him glorify God on this behalf." No believer can be everything he ought to be without experiencing some suffering. The Bible says in II Timothy 3:12, "Yea, and all that will live godly in Christ Jesus shall suffer persecution." Christian persecution is not trouble in general. Everybody has that. Vance Havner says, "Christian persecution is trouble you get into that you would not have gotten into if you had not been a Christian." No Christian should be ashamed to suffer for Christ.

We should not be ashamed of the second coming. We believe in the visible, physical, literal return of Jesus Christ and in the imminent coming of Christ for His own, the pretribulation rapture of the church. The Bible says in I John 2:28, "And now, little children, abide in him; that, when he shall appear, we may have confidence, and not be ashamed before him at his coming."

We are not ashamed of the Bible, God's Holy Word. We stand without apology for the verbal inspiration of the Scriptures. We not only believe the truths contained in the Bible, but we believe the words that convey those truths are God's words. Jesus said in Mark 8:38, "Whosoever therefore shall be ashamed of me and of my words in this adulterous and sinful generation; of him also shall the Son of man be ashamed, when he cometh in the glory of his Father with the holy angels."

When I was a small boy in a country church, we used to sing an old song which went something like this:

I'm not ashamed to own that
Jesus came and died on Calvary;
That by His blessed, free atonement
He prepared a place for me;
And fixed it so that I with Him
Might forevermore be free.
Oh, praise the Lord, I'm not ashamed.

I'm not ashamed to speak for Jesus!
I'm not ashamed to praise His name!
I'm not ashamed to own His blessing!
Oh, praise the Lord, I'm not ashamed!

DON'T DIE UNPREPARED

Dear friend, how will you die? Be sure you don't die unprepared. And the only way to be prepared to meet Jesus in death is to trust Him completely for salvation. If you have never trusted Him, then trust Him today.

If you will trust Him and write to tell me so, I have some free literature I want to send that will help you as you set out to live the Christian life. All you need do to receive your free literature is write to:

Dr. Curtis Hutson
Sword of the Lord Foundation
P. O. Box 1099
Murfreesboro, Tennessee 37133

In your letter say, "I have read your sermon, 'How Will You Die?' I am not sure that I am prepared for death. I do want to go to Heaven when I die. Knowing that I am a sinner and believing that Jesus Christ died on the cross for my sins, I here and now trust Him as my Saviour. From this moment on I am totally depending on Him for my salvation and to take me to Heaven when I die. Please send me the free literature that will help me as I set out to live the Christian life.

"I will not die unprepared. I have trusted Jesus Christ as my Saviour."

Be sure to include your name and address.

Chapter 16

The Perfect Fool

I call your attention to the Gospel of Luke, chapter 12, the familiar parable of the rich fool.

"And one of the company said unto him, Master, speak to my brother, that he divide the inheritance with me. And he said unto him, Man, who made me a judge or a divider over you? And he said unto them, Take heed, and beware of covetousness: for a man's life consisteth not in the abundance of the things which he possesseth. And he spake a parable unto them, saying, The ground of a certain rich man brought forth plentifully: And he thought within himself, saying, What shall I do, because I have no room where to bestow my fruits? And he said, This will I do: I will pull down my barns, and build greater; and there will I bestow all my fruits and my goods. And I will say to my soul, Soul, thou hast much goods laid up for many years; take thine ease, eat, drink, and be merry. But God said unto him, Thou fool, this night thy soul shall be required of thee: then whose shall those things be, which thou hast provided? So is he that layeth up treasure for himself, and is not rich toward God. And he said unto his disciples, Therefore, I say unto you, Take no thought for your life, what ye shall eat; neither for the body, what ye shall put on. The life is more than meat, and the body is more than raiment. Consider the ravens: for they neither sow nor reap; which neither have storehouse nor

barn; and God feedeth them: how much more are ye better than the fowls? And which of you with taking thought can add to his stature one cubit? If ye then be not able to do that thing which is least, why take ye thought for the rest? Consider the lilies how they grow: they toil not, they spin not; and yet I say unto you, that Solomon in all his glory was not arrayed like one of these. If then God so clothe the grass, which is to day in the field, and to morrow is cast into the oven; how much more will he clothe ye, O ye of little faith? And seek not ye what ye shall eat, or what ye shall drink, neither be ye of doubtful mind. For all these things do the nations of the world seek after: and your Father knoweth that ye have need of these things. But rather seek ye the kingdom of God; and all these things shall be added unto you. Fear not, little flock; for it is your Father's good pleasure to give you the kingdom. Sell that ye have, and give alms; provide yourselves bags which wax not old, a treasure in the heavens that faileth not, where no thief approacheth, neither moth corrupteth. For where your treasure is, there will your heart be also."—Vss. 13-34.

Notice the words in verse 20:

"But God said unto him, Thou fool, this night thy soul shall be required of thee: then whose shall those things be, which thou hast provided?"

Jesus said, "Whosoever shall say to his brother, Raca, shall be in danger of the council: but whosoever shall say, Thou fool, shall be in danger of hell fire" (Matt. 5:22). We should not lightly and foolishly call someone a fool. But I have every right to say that the man in this parable was a fool, because God called him a fool. God knew well what the man had done, what the man had thought; and He said, "Thou fool. . . ."

Several times in the Bible men are called "fools" or "foolish." In Luke 24:25 Jesus said, "*O fools*, and slow of heart to believe all that the prophets have spoken."

The Lord says a man is a fool who is slow of heart to believe that all the Bible is the Word of God. We wonder what He would think of a person who flatly denied it.

In Matthew 25 Jesus said of the ten virgins, "Five of them were wise, and five were *foolish*." He said, "They that were *foolish* took their lamps, and took no oil with them."

Psalm 14:1 says, "The *fool* hath said in his heart, There is no God." The man who denies the existence of God is a fool, the Bible says.

It is not a light thing to be called a fool by Almighty God. But here in this text God said, "Thou fool. . . ."

There are at least six reasons why God considered this man a fool.

I. HE WAS CONCERNED ONLY WITH THINGS

The word "things" is mentioned many times in the Bible. Matthew 6:33 says, "But seek ye first the kingdom of God, and his righteousness; and all these *things* shall be added unto you." In this verse Jesus was speaking of clothing and food and the necessities of life. We are not to worry about *things.*

Someone has said the Apostle Paul had *things* right in his life. In Philippians 3:7 he said, "But what *things* were gain to me, those I counted loss for Christ. Yea doubtless, and I count all *things* but loss for the excellency of the knowledge of Christ Jesus my Lord: for whom I have suffered the loss of all *things*, and do count them but dung, that I may win Christ." Then in verse 13: "Brethren, I count not myself to have apprehended: but this one thing I do, forgetting those *things* which are behind, and reaching forth unto those *things* which are before, I press toward the mark for the prize of the high calling of God in Christ Jesus."

I have lived long enough and been blessed enough of God to know by experience as well as by Scripture that you can get too occupied with *things*—material things. We can get too concerned about clothing, about houses, about automobiles, about salary, about security, about bank accounts, about money—things. . . things . . . *things.* The first reason this man was a fool was that he was concerned only with *things.*

There are two reasons why we should not be overly concerned with things.

1. The Tyranny of Things

One can get to the place where he no longer possesses things, but things possess him. We can become like one of the wealthiest men in the world who collects money like a stamp-collector collects stamps. His money possesses him. He even has a pay telephone in his house so if friends use the phone, he won't have to pay for the calls! He has enough money to live thousands of lifetimes; but he no longer possesses his money; his money possesses him.

There is danger in this. You can reach the place where you have so much property and *things* that all you think about is your possessions— "my *things.*" *I've got so much land this way, and so much land that way, and so many miles of land that way, and so much land that way.*

George Truett tells of visiting a wealthy man in Texas. As they stood on the porch, the man pointed north and said, "Dr. Truett, I own so many miles of land in that direction." Then pointing south he said, "I own so many miles of land in that direction." Then pointing east and west he said, "I own so many miles of land in that direction and that direction."

Dr. Truett then pointed to Heaven and asked, "And how much do you own in that direction?"

The tyranny of *things. Things* can enslave you. I know men who seemingly have everything there is to own, yet they are still miserable. When in the evening news they read that the price of gold has fallen, they can't sleep at night. They can't enjoy breakfast for reading the stock report. All their investments are in this world.

Some of the most miserable people are millionaires who are constantly worried about money. They have it made today, but what happens if the dollar is devalued? What happens if the price of silver and the price of stocks go down? They fear there will be another Great Depression and they will be left with nothing.

When visiting with businessmen, I have asked, "Do you own this business?" and had them reply, "Oh, no. This business owns me," meaning they were slaves to the business, that they could no longer do what they wanted to do; the business now dictated their lives. That's the tyranny of *things.*

2. The Temporality of Things

Things are temporal; they are going to pass away. Second Corinthians 4:18 says, "While we look not at the things which are seen, but at the things which are not seen: for the things which are seen are temporal; but the things which are not seen are eternal."

The automobile is temporal—it will pass away. The house is temporal—it will pass away. Property is temporal—it will pass away. How well we know it! It passes away a lot faster than we suspected it would. Somebody said, "Money talks." One fellow said, "Yeah. Mine says, 'Goodby.'"

I am not against having things, but I am against things having me. There's a big danger, and it is not usually faced by the fellow born with a lot, but by the one who had nothing most of his life. He scrapes and works and toils and puts forth effort and accumulates a little something. And if he's not careful, *things* will possess him.

But they are temporal; they pass away. Says II Peter 3:10,11: "The earth also and the works that are therein shall be burned up. Seeing then that all these *things* shall be dissolved, what manner of persons ought ye to be in all holy conversation and godliness."

I am thinking of a Christian friend who recently passed away. He trusted Christ as Saviour, and I have had good fellowship with him. When I heard of his death, my first thought was: *Well, they both retired a few years ago. They surely had a good income and were just getting to where they could really travel and "enjoy life." But now their things are worth nothing.*

Someone has said, "When you die, the only thing you will have is a six-foot hole in the ground." Then after pondering a minute he added, "As a matter of fact, you won't have the hole in the ground; it will have you." How true. Job said, "Naked came I out of my mother's womb, and naked shall I return thither: the Lord gave, and the Lord hath taken away; blessed be the name of the Lord" (1:21).

Your billion dollars won't amount to one dime after you are dead. Things are temporal; things pass away.

II. HE CONSIDERED HIS EARTHLY GOODS HIS OWN

Notice how he talks:

"And he thought within himself, saying, What shall I do, because I have no room where to bestow my fruits? And he said, This will I do: I will pull down my barns, and build greater; and there will

I bestow all my fruits and my goods. And I will say to my soul. . . ."

"My. . .my. . .my. . .my. . . ." He considered as his own the things God had entrusted to him.

You are not a good Christian if you consider things your own. You say, "You're judging." No, I'm just trying to help you. I'm not saying that you are not going to Heaven, but that you are not a *good* Christian until you get to the place where you surrender claim to everything you have and recognize everything you own as belonging to the Lord. We are stewards in charge of somebody else's possessions.

We shouldn't look at our giving as, "How much shall I give to God?" but, "How much of God's money shall I keep for myself?" You will give more when you look at it as not belonging to you but to God, and you are simply His steward in charge of His possessions.

Someone has said, "Not the tenth, but the whole dollar belongs to God; not only the dollar, but the billfold the dollar is in; not only the billfold, but the pants the billfold is in; and not only the pants, but the man in the pants." The Bible says, ". . .ye are not your own? For ye are bought with a price" (I Cor. 6:19,20).

Christian, everything you have belongs to the Lord—lock, stock and barrel. This man was a fool when he considered his earthly goods his own. He didn't see his rightful place as a steward.

III. HE THOUGHT THINGS WOULD SATISFY HIS SOUL

Verse 19 says, "And I will say to *my soul, Soul,* thou hast much goods laid up for many years; take thine ease, eat, drink, and be merry." *"Soul. . .* take thine ease. . . ." He thought things would satisfy his soul.

Have you lived long enough to find that not true? I used to think that if I ever made $100.00 a week, that would be wonderful, fantastic! (That was when I was making $70.00 every two weeks, and my wife was making $80.00 plus every two weeks, giving me an inferiority complex.)

Then one day when I began earning $100.00 a week, I wasn't satisfied! Then I thought if I could earn $150.00 a week, I would be satisfied. Don't look at me like that! You are not satisfied either! Some of you who make $300.00 or $400.00 or even $500.00 a week are still not satisfied. You want a raise every six months. Not only that—you want more time off! And more benefits! The more we get, the more we want, because *things* never satisfy. Ecclesiastes 6:7 says, "All the labour of man is for his mouth, and yet the appetite is not filled."

When I first got my Buick—a gift from the church—I thought, *I am somebody! This thing has leather seats, air-conditioning, power windows, power steering, power brakes, two-tone paint, stereo radio, spoke wheels, and everything!*

It's not too hot in Georgia in January, but I rode around all day with the windows rolled up and the air-conditioning wide open! I had to listen to that FM stereo radio with two speakers in the front and two in the back. I would lie down across the seats and smell the leather! I thought, *This is something! This is fantastic!*

But now I don't ride around with the air-conditioning on in January. I don't drive around just to listen to the radio. I don't ride up and down the highways smelling the leather. I've gotten used to it.

Things don't satisfy. As long as we are in this world, we will never be satisfied. David said in Psalm 17:15, "I shall be satisfied, when I awake, with thy likeness." No child of God will ever be completely satisfied until he is changed in a moment, in the twinkling of an eye, and made like our Lord.

I used to go to a certain place to buy my suits. I thought then that if I could ever own a suit that cost $100.00 instead of $29.95, I would be satisfied. But I wasn't.

I am trying to show that this man thought *things* would satisfy. "If I just had more corn, if I just had another barn, if I only had a bigger crop, if I had more goods. . . . Soul, you could be easy with that." But when he got his bigger crops, his bigger barns, and more goods, *things* didn't satisfy his soul.

The songwriter said:

The world will try to satisfy that longing in your soul.
You may search the wide world o'er, but you'll be just as before!
You'll never find true satisfaction until you've found the Lord,
For only Jesus can satisfy your soul.

If you could have the fame and fortune, all the wealth you could obtain.
Yet, you have not Christ within, your living here would be in vain.

There'll come a time when death shall call you, riches cannot help you then,
So come to Jesus, for only He can satisfy your soul.

Only Jesus can satisfy your soul,
And only He can change your heart and make you whole;
He'll give you peace you never knew, sweet love and joy and Heaven, too,
For only Jesus can satisfy your soul!

You may make a million; you may own a house on the lake and a house in the mountains; you may have a yacht—no matter what you have, *things* never satisfy. We are not built like that. The old pilgrims used to say, "Man's heart is three-cornered, and a round world can never fill a three-cornered heart."

IV. HE PLANNED FOR TIME, NOT FOR ETERNITY

He said, "Soul, thou hast much goods laid up for many years; take thine ease, eat, drink, and be merry." He had goods for *many years.* He planned for time—years. "It's enough to do me five years, ten years, twenty years. Man, I'll have a good time!"

That old adage, "Eat, drink, and be merry, for tomorrow we die," is one of the Devil's lies. You can't be merry by eating and drinking; and tomorrow you don't die. You live forever and ever. There was a time when you did not exist, but there will never come a time when you will cease to be. You are going to live somewhere forever.

Dr. Bob Jones, Sr., once said, "The greatest thought that ever occurred to me is that I must live somewhere forever."

This man planned for time, not for eternity. "All I need now is a little more money over here, bigger barn there, a better crop here, a few more servants; and I will have it made!" But he died! "This night thy soul shall be required of thee: then whose shall those things be which thou hast provided?"

Riding on a train, Dr. B. H. Carroll started a conversation with a young man.

"Young man, what's your name?"

The fellow told him.

"Where are you going?"

"I'm going to such-and-such a town."

"After that, what are you going to do?"

"I'm going to school over there."

"After that, what are you going to do?"

"I'm going four years there and get my education."

"After that, what?"

"Well, after that, I'm going to get my diploma."

"After that, what?"

"After that, I suppose I'll start my own business."

"After that, what?"

"I'm going to work at my business and try to make a success."

"After that, what?"

"After I've made a success in business, I plan to build a chain of stores."

"After that, what?"

"I'm going to make a lot of money."

"After that, what?"

"I'm going to put money in the bank and prepare for old age."

"After that, what?"

"Well, I guess by then I'll be old."

"After that, what?"

"I'm going to retire."

"After that, what?"

"I'm just going to take it easy and live off the money I've made and enjoy life."

"After that, what?"

"Uh. . . after that, I guess I'll die."

Dr. Carroll said, "After that, what?"

The fellow said, "I don't know. I never thought about it."

He had only planned for *time.* He knew the answer to every question about time. He had made *all* his plans for *time,* but there his plans stopped. He made no plans for eternity.

What about you? When you die, after that, what? Where? Have you made plans for that?

A little girl overheard her uncle say about her father, "Bob has his business insured. He's made preparations; but I wonder about Bob's soul. I wonder if he has trusted Christ as his Saviour."

The little girl went back home, and that night at supper she said, "Daddy, Uncle Joe said today that you had your property and your business insured; but, Daddy, do you have your soul insured?"

He looked at her and said, "No, honey, I don't."

He had made plans for *time* but not for eternity.

Isn't it strange? We are only going to be here about seventy years, yet we make most of our plans for time rather than eternity.

Suppose a man had two stores—a small store with only a few dollars invested, and a large store with millions and millions invested. If he gave all his time and attention to the little store, would you think him a fool? Of course. Then isn't a man a fool who does all his planning and preparation for this life of only a few years when he is going to live in the other world forever? After a man has been in Hell for thousands of years, he will still look back and say, *How foolish I was to give so much time, effort, planning, energy and money for the few short years I lived on earth!*

This man, this fool, planned for time, not for eternity.

V. HE THOUGHT HIS SOUL WAS HIS OWN

Did you ever hear anybody say, "I'm the pilot of my own ship"? Have you seen the bumper sticker that reads, "God is my Co-Pilot"? That sounds good, but you better look at it again. The problem is, God is Co-Pilot to too many people when He should be Pilot. A co-pilot is somebody you call on in case of emergency, when the pilot has had a heart attack or something else has happened to him while in the air. Jesus should be our Pilot. He should run our lives. We should not call on Him only in case of emergency. He is not just a stand-by, not simply a spare tire. He is everything!

The man in this parable thought his soul was his own: "I will say to *my* soul, Soul, thou hast much goods laid up for many years." Your soul is not your own. You belong to God by right of creation, but that doesn't mean you are His or that you are going to Heaven. Once you trust Him, He owns you by right of redemption and regeneration. It is not your soul.

We read in I Corinthians 6:19 and 20: "What? know ye not that your body is the temple of the Holy Ghost which is in you, which ye have of God, and ye are not your own? For ye are bought with a price. . . ." The Bible says we are "bought with a price," indicating the purchase was expensive. If we are bought, we know there was a price involved; but when we say concerning a certain item, "He paid a price for that!" we mean it was expensive.

The Bible says in I Peter 1:18, "Ye were not redeemed [bought] with corruptible things, as silver and gold. . . But with the precious [valuable] blood of Christ." Jesus Christ has the absolute right of ownership over every individual in the world. We owe our very existence to Him.

VI. HE THOUGHT HE HAD PLENTY OF TIME

He said, "Soul, thou hast much goods laid up for *many* years. . . ." Little did he know that the flowers which would be put on his grave were already in the florist shop. Little did he know that his would be the next funeral conducted in that city, that he would never see another sunrise.

Young people sometimes say, "Religion is for old people who are ready to die. I have plenty of time. I want to live it up." The man in our text thought he had "many years," but he died that very night.

I preached on soul winning here, and a man whom I had led to Christ got so burdened about his brother that he called him long distance to try to win him to Christ. When he couldn't he drove to Florida to try to lead him to Christ. But his brother laughed and said, "I'm only in my twenties, man. Don't worry about me. I have plenty of time!"

The man came back to Atlanta, Georgia, and told me the sad story. The next week they found his brother who had "plenty of time" in a desolate area in Florida shot six times with a thirty-eight revolver by a hitchhiker he had picked up.

His body was flown back to Atlanta, and I conducted his funeral. All I could think of was what the man had said: "I'm young. I've got plenty of time. I'm only in my twenties," yet a week later I was preaching his funeral.

You don't have plenty of time. That's the most idiotic, foolish thing one can say. The wise man is the one who, when he sees a thing ought to be done, says, "I'll do it now." The fool is a man who, when he sees a thing ought to be done, says, "Yes, I know it ought to be done, but I'll do it tomorrow."

There is no surer way of success in this life—let alone the life to come—than this: When you see a thing ought to be done, do it immediately.

The clock of life is wound but once,
And no man has the power

To tell just when the clock will stop—
At late or early hour.

To lose one's wealth is sad indeed;
To lose one's health is more;
But to lose one's soul is such a loss
That no man can restore.

You don't have plenty of time. Do it now. . .NOW. If there's the least inkling in your heart, if the Holy Spirit indicates any desire at all in your heart to be saved, don't wait a moment about it; do it now.

On the end of Billy Sunday's tabernacles was printed in large letters: GET RIGHT WITH GOD; DO IT NOW!

This rich farmer thought he had plenty of time. You don't have plenty of time. The gasoline is in the ambulance at Turner's Funeral Home now that will take somebody to the graveyard this week, one who does not suspect it is he. The embalming fluid is there now that will be pumped into somebody's dead body next week, but that person has no idea that it is he.

How foolish to gamble with eternity, to say, "I have plenty of time," then die without an opportunity to call upon Christ! Some will lift up their eyes in Hell in the next few minutes and say, "O God, I was going to get right! I didn't know this accident was going to happen!" "I didn't know there was going to be this tornado come through and kill thirty-five people!" "I didn't know I was going to be shot by a hitchhiker!"

If we could uncap Hell and have the inhabitants march across this platform, we would find that not one planned to go to Hell. Everybody in Hell planned to get saved, but "a little later." The road to By-and-By leads to the house of Never. "Not this morning; I have plenty of time." "I want to wait." "I'm sitting too far back in the house." "It's too far down the aisle." "It's a big church, and I'll wait and get saved in a little church"—just anything to keep from doing it now. "You can't live it," the Devil says. "Don't be a hypocrite." "When I think I can be perfect, I'll get saved." "The church is full of hypocrites." Yes, and Hell is full of people who said they didn't want to be hypocrites.

Now is the time. Second Corinthians 6:2 warns, "Behold, now is the accepted time; behold, now is the day of salvation." Again we are urged in Hebrews 3:7,8, "To day if ye will hear his voice, harden not your hearts."

Did you ever think how fast "now" is? "Now" is over before you get it said. If I said, "Do it now," you're already late. If you did it any time after I said "now," you were late. "Now" is as soon as you say it.

That's how quickly Jesus wants you to get saved—NOW. Salvation is instantaneous. You don't say, "I am *being* saved." You either say, "I am saved," or, "I'm not saved." You'll never hear anybody say, "I'm in the process of being saved." It happens too fast. You are either saved or lost. You have either trusted Him or you have not. You are not in the process.

Have you trusted Jesus Christ as your personal Saviour? Are you fully depending on Him to take you to Heaven? If not, do it now. Now is the only time you have. We have no promise of tomorrow.

TRUST CHRIST TODAY

You have read the sermon, "The Perfect Fool," which was preached at the Forrest Hills Baptist Church when I was pastor. More than eighty precious people trusted Christ as their Saviour the Sunday this sermon was preached.

Now I urge you, dear reader, to trust Christ as your personal Saviour. Don't be like the rich fool in this parable who thought he had many years, and don't give all your time and attention to the present rather than the eternal. Being saved is a very simple matter. Jesus said, "For God so loved the world, that he gave his only begotten Son, that whosoever believeth in him should not perish, but have everlasting life" (John 3:16).

Two thousand years ago God allowed His Son Jesus Christ to go to the cross and die for our sins. The Bible teaches that Jesus bore our sins in His own body; and while He was bearing our sins, God punished Him in our place. That's what John 3:16 means when it says, "For God so loved the world, that he *gave* his only begotten Son." God gave Jesus in our place, as our Substitute, to pay our sin debt; and the clear promise of Scripture is that "whosoever believeth in him should not perish, but have everlasting life."

The whole problem seems to be with the word "believe." To

believe on Christ simply means to trust Him, to depend on Him, to rely on Him. It means that we put our full confidence in Him and trust Him only for our salvation and depend on Him only to take us to Heaven when we die.

Do you know that you are a sinner? Do you really believe that Jesus Christ died on the cross for you? If so, will you trust Him now? If you will trust Him, I have some free literature I want to send that will help you as you set out to live the Christian life. All you need do to receive your free literature is to write me a letter:

Dr. Curtis Hutson
Sword of the Lord Foundation
P. O. Box 1099
Murfreesboro, Tennessee 37133

And say, "I have read your sermon, 'The Perfect Fool.' Knowing that I am a sinner and that Jesus Christ died for me, I do here and now trust Him completely as my Saviour and am totally depending on Him to take me to Heaven when I die. Please send me the free literature that will help me as I set out to live the Christian life." Then include your name and full address.

Chapter 17

"There They Crucified Him"

"And there followed him a great company of people, and of women, which also bewailed and lamented him. But Jesus turning unto them said, Daughters of Jerusalem, weep not for me, but weep for yourselves, and for your children. For, behold, the days are coming, in the which they shall say, Blessed are the barren, and the wombs that never bare, and the paps which never gave suck. Then shall they begin to say to the mountains, Fall on us; and to the hills, Cover us. For if they do these things in a green tree, what shall be done in the dry? And there were also two other, malefactors, led with him to be put to death. And when they were come to the place, which is called Calvary, there they crucified him, and the malefactors, one on the right hand, and the other on the left. Then said Jesus, Father, forgive them; for they know not what they do. And they parted his raiment, and cast lots. And the people stood beholding. And the rulers also with them derided him, saying, He saved others; let him save himself, if he be Christ, the chosen of God. And the soldiers also mocked him, coming to him, and offering him vinegar, And saying, If thou be the king of the Jews, save thyself. And a superscription also was written over him in letters of Greek, and Latin, and Hebrew, THIS IS THE KING OF THE JEWS."—Luke 23:27-38.

I call your attention to verse 33: "And when they were come

to the place, which is called Calvary, there they crucified him, and the malefactors, one on the right hand, and the other on the left." I choose for a text and the subject of my message four words found here: *"There they crucified him."*

I have four divisions in the sermon, and each division will comprise one word found in the text. The first division—*"there"*; the second division—*"they"*; the third division—*"crucified"*; the fourth division—*"him." "There they crucified him."* "There" —the place; "they" —the people; "crucified" —the purpose; "him" —the Person.

It will be easy to remember; and I hope you will remember it a long, long time.

I. "THERE"—THE PLACE

Somebody said, "Little is much when God is in it." The more I read the Bible, the more I am convinced of that fact as it pertains to certain verses found in the Bible. That is particularly true of this verse, ". . . there they crucified him." "There." Where? Within the vicinity of the city of Jerusalem.

Someone said the *holiest* Person who ever lived died the most *unholy* death ever experienced in the most *holy* place on earth. The name of the place where He was crucified is *Calvary*, according to this text. The parallel reading in Matthew says the name of the place is called in the Hebrew *Golgotha.* Calvary is a Greek word for the Hebrew *Golgotha,* and they both mean the same, "the place of the skull." ". . . there they crucified him." There—"the place of the skull."

"The skull" speaks to me of several things.

First, it speaks to me of sin. Had there been no sin, there would be no skull. Death is a result of sin. Romans 5:12 says, "Wherefore, as by one man sin entered into the world, and death by sin; and so death passed upon all men, for that all have sinned." When I see the skull I think about sin. The skull is a result of sin.

I have said again and again that Jesus Christ was our Sinbearer, that in His own body He bore our sins on the cross (I Pet. 2:24)—not part of our sins, not some of our sins, not most of our sins, but blessed be God, *all* our sins. He bore them in His own body on the tree. And the Bible says in Isaiah 53:6: "The Lord hath laid on him the iniquity [or the sins] of us all." There Jesus Christ, in a sense, became the greatest of all sinners, though He

Himself never committed one single sin in all His life. He was the greatest sinner in the sense that on the cross He was bearing all the sins of all the world, and every sin ever committed by any person who has ever lived or ever will live was being borne by Jesus on the cross when He died there two thousand years ago. Had He not borne the sins of all the world, then the possibility of salvation for all the world would never be.

The death of Jesus on the cross is sufficient for all, but it is efficient only to those who believe.

I do not believe in a limited atonement. I believe that Jesus Christ died for the whole world, because that is exactly what the Bible says: "He is the propitiation for our sins: and not for our's only, but also for the sins of the whole world" (I John 2:2). John 3:16: "God so loved the world, that he gave his only begotten Son."

The skull speaks of sin, and Jesus Christ settled the sin question at Calvary. He bore our sins, and His death was the *full* payment that God had demanded for our sins.

"There they crucified him." Calvary, *Golgotha,* "the place of the skull."

Second, it not only speaks to me of sin, but of death. Death is the penalty of sin. Had there been no sin, there would be no death. Sin is the sting of death. One thing that makes death miserable is that death itself is a penalty for sin, and there is a sting in death. "There"—the place of death; the Just dying for the unjust that He might bring us to God (I Pet. 3:18). He who knew no sin bore all the sin of all the world, suffered the death that every sinner deserves to die, satisfied the just demands of a holy God and made salvation possible to whosoever will. He cried out from the cross, "It is finished." Everything necessary for the salvation of the world has been completed and nothing else has to be done. It is now accomplished. Nothing can be added to; nothing can be taken from it. "It is finished!" Glory to God! That is one of the greatest sentences in all the Word of God.

Third, "there," the place of the skull, speaks to me of emptiness. Here is a skull. The brain once there is gone. It is an empty thing. What could I say of Jesus Christ emptying Himself, making Himself of no reputation? According to Philippians, chapter 2, He literally emptied Himself and came to earth, God in human flesh. Not wanting to give away His divinity, He concealed His deity and appeared to men as a Man. "There," the skull speaks of emptiness.

Fourth, "there," the place of a skull, speaks of the end of human wisdom. The brain that once functioned is now dust. It is a strange thing; but you will never make an unsaved world understand how men can live through One who died, how we can be justified by One who was made a curse, how we can be cleared from all guilt by One who became guilty in our place. Talk about the death of Jesus Christ on the cross in the sinner's place for the purpose of our justification to an unsaved world, and they wag their heads and call it foolishness.

A preacher brought a wonderful sermon on the substitutionary death of Jesus. Afterwards a man came to him and said, "I want you to know that the idea of Jesus Christ dying on a cross and paying some debt that I owe as a sinner is all foolishness to me."

The preacher said, "Well, Sir, I guess you know that you agree perfectly with the Apostle Paul."

"No," he said, "I didn't know it."

The preacher turned to I Corinthians 1:18 and read, "For the preaching of the cross is to them that perish foolishness; but unto us which are saved it is the power of God."

The word "there" deserves an entire sermon; but to have time for the other three words, we must leave it and go on.

II. "THEY"—THE PEOPLE

"There they crucified him." Who? You say, "The Jews did it." This charge has been laid to the Jews for years. They have been referred to as the Christ-crucifiers, as the God-murderers, and because of this they have been persecuted as the ones who crucified our Saviour.

To be sure, the Jews must take their part of the blame for His death. It was the Jews who laid hold upon Him in the Garden of Gethsemane. Jesus Christ stood before Annas and Caiaphas, their high priests. He was tried by the Sanhedrin. His own people, the Jews, called Him a blasphemer worthy of death. It was the Jews who cried out, "Crucify him, crucify him." It was the Jews who took counsel against Him to put Him to death. So the Jews must share their part in the responsibility for the death of

Jesus Christ on the cross. "There they crucified him." Who? The Jews.

However, it was the Romans, not the Jews, who actually killed Him. So the Romans must take their part of the blame for the crucifixion of Jesus. The Jews didn't have the power to put anyone to death. The Jews were under Roman rule and could only try a man and declare him worthy of death; but the final decision was with the power of Rome. The power of capital punishment was not committed to the Jews but only to the hands of the Romans. When Jesus came before the Sanhedrin, they found Him worthy of death; but they had to go to Pilate, the Roman governor, in order to get the death penalty. Pilate said to Jesus in John 19:10, "I have power to crucify thee, and have power to release thee," or, "to let thee go." Pilate wasn't just bluffing; nor was he simply trying to frighten Jesus when he said, "I have power to crucify thee," or "I have power to release thee." He did have that power. As the Roman governor, that authority was in his hands. He could say, "Crucify him," and the soldiers would obey; or, he could say, "Let Him go," and the soldiers would release Him. So the authority to put Jesus to death was in the hands of the Roman governor.

Pilate turned Him over to the Roman soldiers. Who scourged Jesus? The Romans. Who spit in Jesus' face until the spittle ran down His beard? The Romans. Who put the purple robe on His back? The Romans. Who placed the reed in the hand of Jesus? The Romans. Who bowed and mocked Jesus Christ and said, "Hail, king of the Jews!"? The Romans. Who laid the two-hundred-pound cross upon the back of Jesus and compelled Him to carry it a bloody mile? The Romans. Who laid Jesus down upon that cross and drove the nails through His hands and feet? It was the Romans. Who divided His clothing among them? The Romans. Who sat at the foot of the cross and gambled for His cloak that was woven without seam? The Romans. Who put the inscription over the cross, "Jesus of Nazareth the King of the Jews"? It was the Romans.

Why do I say it was the Romans? Because the Jews went to the Romans and begged them to change the inscription. "Write not, The King of the Jews; but that he said, I am King of the Jews." The Jews did not want to recognize Jesus Christ as their king, so requested the Roman government to change the inscription.

Pilate answered, "What I have written I have written."

Who sealed the tomb in which Jesus was laid? The Romans. Who stood guard around that tomb daring the world to molest it? It was the Romans. So the Jews are not alone in their blame, guilt and crucifixion of Jesus. The Romans, the Gentiles, are also responsible. But I believe if the Romans had not given authority for Jesus Christ to be crucified, the Jews would have taken Him into their own hands and crucified Him, just like they later killed Stephen.

On the other hand, I believe if the Jews had not tried Jesus because of His claim to the Messiahship, the Romans would have taken Jesus Christ and crucified Him without the Jews, as they later did James and Paul. Both Jews and Gentiles are guilty of His crucifixion. "There *they* crucified him."

The Jews—yes. The Romans—yes. And you and I. In the final analysis, it was your sin, my sin, that nailed Jesus Christ to the cross. We are as much responsible for the death of Jesus as the Jews who cried, "Crucify him, crucify him!" As much responsible for the death of Jesus as the Romans who drove the nails through His hands and feet. That was our hammer that drove the nails because our sins nailed Christ to the cross.

A man once dreamed that he was witnessing the scourging of Jesus. In his dream he screamed, "Stop it! Stop it! Stop it!" When the Roman soldier with the scourge in his hand looked around, the man saw his own face!

If you close your eyes and visualize the Roman soldier scourging Jesus Christ until His inner organs lie at His feet in a pool of blood, and if your imagination is as vivid as mine, you can see yourself with a scourge in your own hand laying the stripes on the back of the Son of God.

"There they crucified him." Who? You and me.

'Twas I that shed the sacred blood;
I nailed Him to the tree;
I crucified the Christ of God;
I joined the mockery.

Of all that shouting multitude,
I feel that I am one;
And in that din of voices rude,
I recognize my own.

Around the cross, the throng I see,
Mocking the Sufferer's groan;
Yet still my voice, it seems to be,
If I had mocked alone.

We were there! "There they crucified him." We did it! Our sin did it! Those still without the Saviour are in the throng.

III. "CRUCIFIED"–THE PURPOSE

"There they crucified him." "Crucified." He died the most ignominious, shameful, horrible death the world has ever known! Crucifixion involved the extreme limit of suffering. The victim was scourged.

If I had the voice of angels, the vocabulary of scholars and the ability to speak like an orator, I could have you standing and weeping; I could have you prostrate on the floor if I could paint for you the awful picture of the crucifixion of Christ.

The Romans soldiers were not careful where they laid that scourge with a cat-o'-nine tails. I will be conservative and say there were only five lashes in that scourge. At the end of each lash was a sharp fishhook-like object made of metal or stone or bone. When they hit the victim across his naked back with it, it would sink into his flesh; and when they retrieved it, it plowed furrows in his back. The victim was struck at least 39 times, which meant 195 plowed furrows in his back—as if one had taken a sharp knife and lashed him 195 times. "There they crucified him."

The Roman soldiers were not careful where they laid the scourge. The early historian Josephus says that often a man's eyes and teeth were knocked out from the scourging as the lash wrapped around his head at times. He says that often the victim would stand in a pool of blood with his inner organs lying at his feet; not many people lived through the scourging.

"Crucified." Get hold of that word! If He must die, why die like this? Why not simply die with a heart attack or of old age? Crucifixion involved the extreme limit of suffering.

After the scourging, the victim was nailed to a piece of rough wood–first through his hands, then through his feet. The cross victim did not die suddenly, because no vital organ was injured. He would stay there for hours, hanging between Heaven and earth as if rejected by both.

God said, "I don't want Him," and turned His back. The world said, "We don't want Him," and turned its back. Jesus died alone, without one friend! He was forsaken that the believer may never be forsaken.

The cross victim endured the most excruciating agony because of his position. One medical doctor said such victims died of suffocation. He then proved his point by saying that the victim would pull with hands and push with his feet in order to get his breath. As the weight of his body pulled him down, his breath was cut off until he nearly suffocated; then he would push back up again in order to breathe.

Usually the victim hung on that cross for six hours, pushing up and down, up and down, with his raw back grating against the rugged wood. The sufferings of Jesus on the cross depict the sufferings of Hell.

The Roman soldiers, in order to speed up death, would often break their victim's legs. Once the legs were broken, the cross victim could no longer push up to get his breath and thus died of suffocation. Any medical doctor knows you don't speed a man's death by breaking his legs; you simply inflict more pain. But if he died from suffocation because he could not push up and get his breath, then breaking his legs would speed his death.

Now, when they came to Jesus Christ, He was already dead, so they didn't break His bones. Jesus didn't die from suffocation but gave "his life a ransom for many." Excruciating pain!

Six long hours our Lord hung on that cross! "There they crucified him."

If the Son of God had to die, why such a death? For one reason—to fulfill Bible prophecy. The Old Testament had pictured the crucifixion in detail. Psalm 22 is called the Crucifixion Psalm. It begins with, "My God, my God, why hast thou forsaken me?"—one of the very expressions of Jesus as He hung on the cross, actually the fourth cross utterance. The Psalm tells how His bones were out of joint and not a bone of His body was broken. Psalm 22 is a graphic description of the crucifixion of our Lord.

Crucifixion as a mode of execution was not practiced by the Jews, only by the Romans. Yet we have a graphic description of the crucifixion even before Rome. I would have to believe the Bible is the Word of God if I didn't have anything except Psalm 22. So would any other honest person!

If He must die, why such a death? Because of prophecy—yes. But He didn't die on the cross just because of prophecy. He must die that way. There is no other way for us to go to Heaven. The Bible says, "Cursed is every one that continueth not in all things which are written in the book of the law to do them" (Gal. 3:10). There is a curse pronounced upon the lawbreaker, and the curse is death. Everyone has broken the law. The Bible says, "All have sinned, and come short of the glory of God" (Rom. 3:23). Everyone is cursed.

Jesus was the only Person to never break the law. He kept it perfectly. And Jesus, though not under the curse, died on the cross for us. The death of the cross victim was so horrible that one nailed to the cross was always accounted guilty. Christ on the cross was accounted guilty in our place. The guilt was so real that God punished Him as if He were the sinner.

Galatians 3:13 tells us that He "hath redeemed us from the curse of the law, being made a curse for us: for it is written, Cursed is every one that hangeth on a tree." The death of Jesus on the cross has redeemed us from the curse, which is death, the second death, the lake of fire, Hell. The Lord's death on the cross means that no one has to go to Hell. If one trusts Christ as Saviour, he is redeemed from the curse of the law.

IV. "HIM"—THE PERSON

"There they crucified him." Who? First Corinthians 2:8 says, "They. . . crucified the Lord of glory." He was a Man among men, God incarnate. Jesus Christ was as much Man as any man in this room. He knows the pain you bear, the tests you endure.

Hebrews 4:15 gives us this comfort: "For we have not an high priest which cannot be touched with the feeling of our infirmities; but was in all points tempted like as we are, yet without sin." One version says, "apart from the sin nature." Jesus Christ did not have the sin nature, but He had all the temptations we have. He was a Man. There is a Man in Glory. He knew fatigue as a Man. The Bible says, "Jesus therefore, being wearied with his journey, sat thus on the well" (John 4:6). When He lay down in the ship and went to sleep, He was a Man. He knew hunger as a Man. The Bible says, "When he had fasted forty days and forty nights, he was afterward an hungred" (Matt. 4:2). He was a Man. If He had not been a Man, there would be no salvation. As God in Heaven, He could love us, but He couldn't die for us. But as a Man, He could die for us and redeem us from the curse of the law.

In a parade held in honor of a great man who had gone on, his fellow-townsmen marched through the city carrying a banner which read, "He was one of us."

We could start such a march in honor of Jesus and wave the banner, "He was one of us." Because He was "touched with the feeling of our infirmities," He was one of us. He knows what we go through. You say, "Nobody understands what I go through. I can't explain it to my mother. Nobody understands." Wait a minute. Somebody understands. He was a Man among men. "There they crucified him."

But He was also a Man above men. We often hear it said, "Jesus was a good man." So was Confucius. So was Mohammed. So are a lot of other men. Jesus had some good philosophies; a lot of other men had good philosophies. But Jesus is a Man above men. "God so loved the world, that he gave his only begotten Son. . . ." Another version reads, ". . . he gave his only-begotten [unique] Son." Unparalleled! Confucius doesn't come near the hem of Jesus' garment. Mohammed doesn't come within ten billion miles of this Man above men.

That is why they said, "Never man spake like this man" (John 7:46). He spoke with authority. He was a Man above men because He was more than man; He was God.

And this bunch of pussy-footing, Caspar Milquetoast, potato-string backboned, rose-water squirting, take-it-easy, start-nowhere-end-up-same-place modernistic preachers who deny the deity of Jesus Christ ought to get out of the ministry! Or should I say, take their flag down—they are already out of the ministry!

Jesus was God in the flesh, born of a virgin.

A lawyer walked into a pastor's office, sat down and said, "Now, Pastor, when I heard you preach, I thought you sounded like one of those old-fashioned preachers who believe in the virgin birth."

"I am, Sir," the pastor replied.

He said, "Oh, you don't believe that!"

Then the pastor said, "Yes, I believe that a virgin conceived and bore a Son; and that Son was Jesus Christ the Son of God."

"But just suppose, Pastor, a young woman about six months with child came walking into your office and said, 'Well, I'm expecting a baby; and this is my boyfriend. He hasn't touched me. I conceived miraculously by the Holy Spirit.' Would you believe that girl?"

He thought surely the pastor would say no, but instead, he replied, "If it had been told by the prophets seven hundred years before she conceived; and if, when she conceived, the boyfriend had a visit from an angel who said, 'Fear not to take unto thee Mary thy wife: for that which is conceived in her is of the Holy Ghost'; if, when that baby was born, Wise Men traveled from afar and brought gifts to worship; if a star guided them to where the baby lay; if hundreds of years before he was born the Bible named the place of his birth; and if before he was born it was told in detail with a thousand prophecies minutely fulfilled how he would die on the cross, be buried in a borrowed tomb, be raised from the dead; and if, when he was raised from the dead, many of the saints came out of their graves and went into the Holy City with him; and if when he went back to Heaven, an angel stood by and said, 'This same Jesus, which is taken up from you into heaven, shall so come in like manner as ye have seen him go'; and if, when he left, he said, 'I will come again'—I would believe it!"

So would I. So would every other reasonable person with any Bible knowledge. The parallel breaks down before it gets out of the lawyer's mouth.

Jesus is the unique Son of God. He was a Man among men, but He was a Man above men. He was God in human flesh. I want to throw my hat over a windmill and shout, "Hallelujah!"

He was not only a Man above men and a Man among men, but He was a Man for men. When Jesus died on the cross, He was dying for us, a Man for men.

In the final analysis, there are only two proposed schemes or plans of salvation. One is that man saves himself. The other revealed plan is that God saves a man by the substitutionary death of Jesus. The first proposed scheme teaches that man saves himself by doing something or promising to do something. Some say one is saved by keeping the Ten Commandments. Others say one is saved by receiving the seven sacraments. Still others insist that one is saved by being baptized. Another group argues, "If you endure to the end and don't slip up anywhere down the road, you will be saved." Anyone who teaches these things teaches that man saves himself.

There are only two proposed ways of salvation. Either a man saves himself or God saves him. And I say the latter is true—God saves a man. For if man could save himself, God would have never allowed His Son to go through what I have partially described in this message. Man cannot save himself. Only God can save him.

"There they crucified him." Who? The Lord of Glory. A Man among men, a Man above men, a Man for men.

Dear friend, He died for you. He suffered your Hell and paid your sin debt in full. Hebrews 2:9 says, "He tasted death for every man." No one need miss Heaven. Jesus has done everything necessary for our salvation.

Isn't that the most wonderful story you have ever heard? Doesn't it make you want to go to the housetop and yell, "There they crucified him!"

What have you done about it? Yonder sits a couple who did something about it last night. There sits another one with his son this morning. But you haven't done anything about it. You know He died for you. You know I'm telling you the truth. And you go on rejecting Jesus Christ. You say, "I'm young, and I want to have a good time. After I get old and can't enjoy life, then I'll get saved." No! Now is the time to do something about it.

An old Englishman died alone in the night. The next morning they found him with his right hand clenched tightly, and in it was a silver cross. I don't know what the Englishman was thinking when he died. No one will ever know, this side of eternity, but maybe he was thinking of that old hymn:

Nothing in my hand I bring,
Simply to Thy cross I cling.

"There they crucified him."

DECIDE TODAY!

Dear reader, you have read my sermon, "There They Crucified Him." I recall very vividly the morning I delivered this message.

I had such great liberty and sensed in a very powerful way the presence of Christ. Over one hundred trusted Jesus Christ as Saviour in the services that day, and I am trusting that many who have read this message will claim that same Saviour.

All you need do to be sure of everlasting life is to admit that you are a sinner, believe that Jesus Christ did die on the cross for you, and trust Him completely for salvation. Won't you please trust Him now?

If you will, then pray this simple prayer:

> Dear Lord Jesus, I know I'm a sinner. I do believe You died for me, that Your death on the cross paid my sin debt. Here and now I do trust You as my Saviour. From this moment on, I am depending on You to take me to Heaven when I die. Help me to live for You and to be a good Christian. Amen.

If you prayed that simple prayer and will write to tell me so, I have some free literature I want to send that will help as you set out to live the Christian life. All you need do to receive your free literature is to write to me at this address:

Dr. Curtis Hutson
Sword of the Lord Foundation
P. O. Box 1099
Murfreesboro, Tennessee 37133

Say, "I have read your sermon, 'There They Crucified Him.' I know that I'm a sinner and do believe that Jesus Christ died for me on the cross. I believe His death was full payment for my sins, and I am trusting Him completely for my salvation. I promise to go to church at my earliest convenience and tell the preacher that I have trusted Christ after reading your sermon. Please send me the free literature that will help me as I set out to live the Christian life."

Be sure to include your name and full address.

Chapter 18

Five Fearful Facts

1. **Not Everyone Is Going to Be Saved**
2. **More People Will Be Lost Than Will Be Saved**
3. **Many Expecting to Be Saved Will Be Lost**
4. **No One Will Be Saved After Death**
5. **This Could Be Your Last Opportunity to Be Saved**

The Great Authority, the Lord Jesus Himself, is speaking:

"Enter ye in at the strait gate: for wide is the gate, and broad is the way, that leadeth to destruction, and many there be which go in thereat: Because strait is the gate, and narrow is the way, which leadeth unto life, and few there be that find it. Beware of false prophets, which come to you in sheep's clothing, but inwardly they are ravening wolves. Ye shall know them by their fruits. Do men gather grapes of thorns, or figs of thistles? Even so every good tree bringeth forth good fruit; but a corrupt tree bringeth forth evil fruit. A good tree cannot bring forth evil fruit, neither can a corrupt tree bring forth good fruit. Every tree that bringeth not forth good fruit is hewn down, and cast into the fire. Wherefore by their fruits ye shall know them. Not every one that saith unto me, Lord, Lord, shall enter into the kingdom of heaven; but he that doeth the will of my Father which is in heaven. Many will say to me in that day, Lord, Lord, have we not prophesied in thy name? and in thy name have cast out devils? and in thy name done many

wonderful works? And then will I profess unto them, I never knew you: depart from me, ye that work iniquity."—Matt. 7:13-23.

I speak this morning on "Five Fearful Facts." The five facts are found in this passage I read.

The Bible is filled with some wonderful, wonderful verses.

"The Lord is my shepherd; I shall not want" (Ps. 23:1). What a tremendous statement! Then the psalmist enumerates the things we shall not want, if the Lord is our Shepherd.

"Let not your heart be troubled: ye believe in God, believe also in me. In my Father's house are many mansions: if it were not so, I would have told you. I go to prepare a place for you" (John 14:1,2). What a tremendous promise!

A verse I have claimed so many times is Romans 8:28: "And we know that all things work together for good to them that love God, to them who are the called according to his purpose." Nothing ever happens to the surrendered believer that is not working together for his good.

I was thinking the other day of these three facts concerning myself as a Christian. The Bible says that:

1. All things are mine;
2. All things work together for me;
3. I can do all things.

A fellow couldn't want much more than these promises from the Word of God, could he!

While there are many wonderful and comforting passages in the Bible, there are also some very solemn truths, some fearful facts.

The first fearful fact is:

I. NOT EVERYONE IS GOING TO BE SAVED

Though very basic and very simple, yet the note ought to be sounded again and again: not everyone is going to be saved. I am going to narrow that down. Every one in this congregation is not going to be saved. I would like to hope that you will be. I would like to think that every person who has ever heard me preach will go to Heaven. But the Bible indicates that many whom I have spoken to and tried to win to Christ will stand at the white throne judgment to be judged, then to be cast into the lake of fire.

I will be there, too, not to be judged, but to witness their judgment, and, in a sense, to condemn them; because Jesus said of one generation that another generation would rise up against them in judgment "and condemn it: because they repented at the preaching of Jonas; and, behold, a greater than Jonas is here" (Matt. 12:41). This has to be at the white throne judgment because that is the only judgment for unbelievers.

So the Bible clearly implies that some of us who have preached the Gospel will stand face to face with those to whom we have preached and will condemn them in the day of judgment and testify: "Yes, that man heard me preach the Gospel. I witnessed to him. I told him how to be saved. We prayed together. I urged him to trust Christ, but he rejected the Saviour. Yes, he stood that morning, trembling, with hands white as he gripped the pew and said, 'Not now, Preacher.' "

I am thinking of a man to whom I witnessed one Saturday night. Eleven o'clock came and passed. . . midnight. . . one o'clock—I was still pleading with him to trust Christ as Saviour.

Early Sunday morning I was in my office in the church when the phone rang. The voice on the other end said, "Would you preach So-and-So's funeral?"

I sort of laughed as I asked, "Is this some kind of a joke?"

"No. Last night he committed suicide."

I said, "He couldn't have! He was with me until one o'clock this morning!"

"But after he left you, he took his own life. Now, would you preach the funeral?"

I don't know whether that man trusted Christ—I hope he did. But if he did not, he will stand at the white throne judgment; and I will stand there and have to say, "I pleaded with that man three hours the night he died, begging him to trust Christ as Saviour; and he would not."

The sad and fearful fact is that not everyone is going to be saved.

I know the universalists teach that everyone is going to be saved, that because God is so loving and so good, He will not permit anyone to go to Hell forever and ever and ever.

I answer: The only way we know what God will do is either by judging what He has done in the past or having God Himself tell us what He will do. We cannot reach our conclusions by human reasoning. We find the facts only in the Bible. The source of error is ignorance of the Word of God. Jesus said, "Ye do err, not knowing the scriptures, nor the power of God" (Matt. 22:29). You must push out of your mind human reasoning and take what God says.

In the past God has done things people did not think He would do.

Let me take you back before the creation of the world. In our imagination, let us stand before man or the worlds were ever created. Angels were already created because Job 38:7 says "all the sons of God shouted for joy" as God framed the worlds and hung them on nothing.

Suppose we are standing by and there are some angels gathered around talking one with the other. One says, "You know, I heard that God Almighty is going to create a world." Another says, "Yes, I heard that, too, from a very reliable source." They continue conversing. Another angel speaks, "After God creates this world, I hear He is going to create a man—a mortal, intelligent being, not one like us. He is to be made a creature of choice, one with a will to choose, to do what he wills."

Says another angel, "Do you suppose when God creates this beautiful world and puts man in it, He will ever allow any suffering or sorrow?"

I know what the other angel will answer: "No. God will never allow any suffering or sorrow in a world He will create. His world will be only beautiful and perfect."

"Do you suppose God will ever allow death, pain and disease?"

"Oh, no—not in the world He creates!"

But we live now six thousand years this side of man's creation, and we know the sad story. God has allowed trouble and sorrow, sickness and disease. So the angels would have been wrong in their reasoning.

We stand now on this side of creation where men die looking forward to the end and culmination of all things. We know we are not going to be here forever; death will come to one and all. So we reason: *When a man dies, will God allow him to go into Hell and stay there forever and ever and ever? Could a loving God allow this to happen?*

I answer: The only way to know is to judge by what He has done in the past or have Him tell us in His Word.

In the past, in the Old Testament, God caused the earth to open and allowed men to fall into Hell through a crevice in the earth. In the past, God did allow men to suffer. And this Book makes one thing clear: men who die without Jesus Christ go to Hell and stay there forever and ever and ever and ever.

The Bible says, "The rich man. . .died, and was buried; And in hell he lift up his eyes" (Luke 16:22). You say that is a parable, an illustration. Then, if it is, Hell has to be worse than the illustration, because no illustration fully illustrates what it is trying to illustrate.

I could stand here all day long and illustrate how an apple tastes. I could describe the taste: "It is like biting a juicy pear." But no matter how I try to describe the taste, when you bite the apple for yourself, you would say that any description of mine comes short of what I am endeavoring to illustrate.

So giving you the benefit of the doubt, we will say that the story of the rich man and Lazarus is a parable or an illustration. Then you will have to admit that Hell is something worse than that described in Luke 16:19 and following.

Not only that, but Jesus said, "If thine eye offend thee, pluck it out: it is better for thee to enter into the kingdom of God with one eye, than having two eyes to be cast into hell fire: Where their worm dieth not, and the fire is not quenched" (Mark 9:47,48). Jesus said Hell is so bad that if your foot offend, it is better to lay your foot on a chopping block, take an ax and chop it off just like you would chop a limb in two, than have two feet and go into Hell fire.

Now, I am not suggesting that inflicting self-punishment or pain will bring salvation. Salvation comes by grace through faith. The only way to Heaven is by trusting Jesus Christ as your Saviour. Jesus said, "I am the way, the truth, and the life: no man cometh unto the Father, but by me" (John 14:6).

A fellow said to me, "Preacher, you say that God is going to punish the wicked forever and ever and ever and ever; and after billions of years they are still being punished. Could anyone possibly live long enough to commit enough crimes and be bad enough to have to be punished for a year, two years, three years [and he kept going]. . . a thousand years, ten thousand years? In his seventy or eighty years, can a man merit enough punishment to last indefinitely?"

I answered him by saying that the time taken to commit the crime does not determine how long the punishment will last. A man can commit a crime in fifteen seconds that will get him life in prison.

I read in the newspaper that a man in Texas was sentenced to nine life sentences when he was found guilty of the torture and murder of nine children. It didn't take him long to commit those horrible crimes, but look how long he will be behind bars! The length of time has nothing to do with it.

Another fellow said, "Dr. Hutson, could any of your children do anything so bad that would cause you to put them in fire and burn them forever and ever and ever?"

I answered, "No, they could not."

"Well, are you telling me, Sir, that you are a more loving father than God who is the Father of us all? Are you telling me that you wouldn't punish your children forever and ever for some wrong they committed, but that God would—that He would put one of His children in Hell to burn forever and ever and ever and ever?"

"I am not saying that. The truth is, God will not punish even one of His children in Hell for a moment! As a matter of fact, they won't even have the smell of smoke on them, because God's children are going to Heaven to be with Him forever and ever and ever and ever."

"Well, we are all God's children," he argued.

I said, "Why?"

"Because God created us all."

Then I thought of what Billy Sunday said and answered him: "He created the donkey, too. Is he your brother?"

We are not God's children by creation; we are God's children by regeneration, as a result of faith in the finished work of Jesus.

II. MORE PEOPLE WILL BE LOST THAN WILL BE SAVED

Think about that for a minute. With all our efforts to evangelize the world, with all the great soul-winning churches, with all the evangelists, with all the radio broadcasts, with all the missionaries and with all the other efforts, still more people are going to be lost than are going to be saved.

In the first two verses I read, Jesus said,

"Enter ye in at the strait gate: for wide is the gate, and broad is the way, that leadeth to destruction, and many there be which go in thereat: Because strait is the gate, and narrow is the way, which leadeth unto life, and few there be that find it."

The way to life, Jesus said, is a strait and narrow way and few will find it; but the way to Hell and destruction is a broad way, and many will go that way.

I have heard sermons on this Scripture; and, in my own opinion, men have made the wrong inference from this expression, "strait is the gate, and narrow is the way." They have made it say that if you want to go to Heaven, it is a little bitty narrow gate and a very, very strait way, like walking a tightrope. And you will be saved if you can squeeze through that little narrow gate and can walk that tightrope and not fall off, not even wobble one bit. The moment you step out of the way, that is the end. You go to Hell.

When I was young, these verses made me think that when I trusted Jesus Christ as Saviour, I had to be absolutely perfect; and if I ever did make one mistake, I would be lost. But that is a contradiction of salvation by grace through faith. When Jesus said, "Strait is the gate and narrow is the way, which leadeth unto life, and few there be that find it," He was saying there is only one way to be saved. It is narrow, not broad. When the Bible says, "Believe on the Lord Jesus Christ, and thou shalt be saved," it is giving the one and only narrow way—faith in Jesus Christ and what He did on the cross. The broad way says faith in Jesus—plus baptism, plus keeping the Ten Commandments, plus enduring to the end, plus doing this, plus doing that—adding everything.

I am narrow-minded when it comes to salvation. You say, "But I am broad-minded." Yes, some folks are so broad-minded that they are flat-headed. It is a strait and narrow way. Jesus died on the cross and paid our sin debt; you trust Him to go to Heaven. No room there for man's ideas about religion. No room there for man's ideas and opinions about how to go to Heaven. That is narrow!

The broad way will be filled with men. When we think of the broad way, we think about drunkards, harlots, whoremongers and everyone of that sort. When we think of the broad way, we think about people who teach baptismal regeneration, those who teach that Jesus Christ is not the Son of God but a good man who set an example and if we follow His example, we will go to Heaven.

The drunks, the bums, the derelicts, the harlots, the adulterers are not on any road; they are outside. To me, the ways represent the true way of salvation and the false ideas about salvation. Those who do not adopt any form of religion are not in any way, but are only drifters, lost and without Christ. Those on the broad way are religionists trying to get to Heaven through their own ideas, their own ways to be saved.

More people are going to be lost than are going to be saved. There will be more religious people in Hell than people who are not religious.

The third fearful fact is:

III. MANY EXPECTING TO BE SAVED WILL BE LOST

Jesus said, "Many will say to me in that day, Lord, Lord, have we not prophesied in thy name? and in thy name have cast out devils? and in thy name done many wonderful works?"

Here is a crowd ready to go in but unsaved. I can almost hear them now: "Where's my mansion, Lord? I know it has to be downtown somewhere, on one of those big, wide, golden boulevards on a corner lot. Lord, Lord, we have prophesied in Your name. Boy, You ought to have heard us! We let 'em have it! We preached in Your name! We cast out devils in Your name! We did many mighty, wonderful works! We performed miracles! We did it all!"

Do you mean people can do all that and still be lost? Yes. Many people expecting to be saved will be lost. What a sad day when Jesus says to those people, "I never knew you: depart from me, ye that work iniquity."

The fourth fearful fact is:

IV. NO ONE WILL BE SAVED AFTER DEATH

When you die without Christ, there will be no chance of salvation then. Jesus will pronounce, "I never knew you: depart from me."

"Well, give us another opportunity. If we had it to do over again, we would be saved!"

I am amazed at the ignorance of professedly intelligent people. Some talk about reincarnation, which means we live on the earth not once, but many times. They can't give one reason why they believe in it, they just believe in it because it sounds good to them.

Well, tell us about it. How will we be? They tell how we will have a rebirth of the soul in another body, how we will reappear after death in another and different form, etc., but give not one single proof, not one intelligent reason for their belief; they just want to believe this false doctrine.

Now, I am talking about intelligent people who have been to college and have so many degrees behind their names that they look like thermometers—these talk about getting a chance to come back and try it over again.

One fellow said, "We are going to have a chance to come back and do it all over."

Another fellow said, "Have I been here before?" (He wasn't being funny; he really wanted to know.)

The first fellow answered, "Yes, you have been here before."

"Then what was I?"

He told him, and the man believed him!

If I could, I wouldn't want to come back. I'm afraid I would make a bigger mess the second time around. I know my weaknesses too well to want to come back.

But if we could come back a thousand times, at the close of each lifetime we would be a failure because of our old sinful, depraved nature.

God sent His Son to live a perfect, sinless life and to take our sins in His own body and die on the cross because He knew we could not live a perfect life.

None will be saved after death. Death is the end. When you die, your destiny is sealed.

The fifth fearful fact is:

V. THIS COULD BE YOUR LAST OPPORTUNITY TO BE SAVED

What do I mean by that? Two things: First, you may die before you have another opportunity to trust Christ as Saviour.

I led a man to Christ in this church whom we visited one night in the Doraville area. We made one call after the other. A girl had come to Sunday school on the bus. I visited the family. We prayed together, and all the family wept and received Christ. They are here this morning. When I preached on soul winning, this fellow got burdened about his younger brother. He called him, then drove all the way to Florida to witness to him. He gave him the plan of salvation and begged his brother to receive Christ as Saviour. But he said, "I'm just twenty years old. Man, I have plenty of time to think of religion!"

The man, a member of our church, came back to Atlanta. The next week came a call from Florida saying his brother had been found dead in a field beside a road in an isolated area. A hitchhiker had unloaded a gun into his side.

His body was brought to Atlanta, and I preached the funeral of the one who a little over a week before had said, "I'm just twenty years old! I've got plenty of time."

Why was that fellow shot to death by a hitchhiker? Why wasn't it some other fellow? Do you think God was trying to say, "You don't have as much time as you think"?

I am just saying we never know how much time we have left.

The son of a preacher friend was out a few weekends ago swimming. He was a good swimmer. The son left saying, "I'll be back at such and such a time." He didn't come back—he drowned, this college-age kid.

Who knows! This could be your last opportunity to be saved.

Second, Jesus could come back. Any Bible student knows that Jesus could come for His own at any minute. Nothing else has to happen. The rapture could take place as quick as a wink. And those who have heard the Gospel and had an opportunity to be saved, yet rejected Christ, will not have another opportunity after the rapture of the church. The Bible says:

"For the mystery of iniquity doth already work: only he who now letteth will let, until he be taken out of the way. And then shall that Wicked be revealed, whom the Lord shall consume with the spirit of his mouth, and shall destroy with the brightness of his coming: Even him, whose coming is after the working of Satan with

all power and signs and lying wonders, And with all deceivableness of unrighteousness in them that perish; because they received not the love of the truth, that they might be saved. And for this cause God shall send them strong delusion, that they should believe a lie: That they all might be damned who believed not the truth, but had pleasure in unrighteousness."—II Thess. 2:7-12.

Those who have said, "I won't be saved; I don't want Jesus; I don't want to accept Christ"—after the rapture of the church, God will send them strong delusion; and they can't be saved if they want to.

What can I say to get you to come and trust Christ? I wish I knew. You say, "You are trying to frighten us into being saved." If I could frighten you into being saved, I would scare the daylights out of you! You say, "You are not supposed to get saved by fear." The Bible says, "Noah...moved with fear, prepared an ark to the saving of his house" (Heb. 11:7). If I can lead you to trust Christ as your Saviour by showing you the importance of doing it now, then I want to do it.

Trust Him Now

Dear friend, you have just read my sermon, "Five Fearful Facts." I urge you to trust Christ as your personal Saviour now. It is a fearful but scriptural fact that those who do not trust Christ as Saviour before death will spend an endless eternity in the lake of fire.

It is possible that this could be your last opportunity, so please do not delay. Death could overtake you, or Jesus could come before you have another opportunity to trust Christ.

I have explained to you that the only way to reach Heaven is by simple trust in Jesus' death on the cross as full payment for your sins. Will you this moment trust Jesus Christ as your Saviour? If you will, then pray this simple prayer:

> Dear Lord Jesus, I know that I'm a sinner and do believe that You died for me. The best I know how I trust You as my Saviour. From this moment on, I am depending on You to take me to Heaven when I die. Now help me live for You and be a good Christian.

If you prayed this prayer and will write to tell me so, I have some free literature I will send that will help you as you set out to live the Christian life. All you need do to receive your free literature is to mail a letter to me,

Dr. Curtis Hutson
Sword of the Lord Foundation
P. O. Box 1099
Murfreesboro, Tennessee 37133

In it say, "I have read your sermon, 'Five Fearful Facts.' I know that I am a sinner and do believe that Jesus Christ died for me. Here and now I trust Him as my Saviour. I am fully depending on Him to take me to Heaven when I die.

"Please send me the free literature that will help me as I set out to live the Christian life."

Then sign it and give your full address.

Chapter 19

Touching ALL the Bases

(Preached on special "Baseball Day '84" at the Shiloh Hills Baptist Church, Kennesaw, Georgia, April 8, 1984. There were many Little League Baseball players and coaches in the congregation, including members of the World Champion Little League Team from Marietta, Georgia, and their coach.)

I am happy to be here on this special "Baseball Day '84." I'm an athlete myself. I had athlete's feet one time! I love sports and all kinds of athletic competition. If two doodle bugs were crawling down the street, I would stop and cheer for one of them. I am almost as bad as the fellow who watched so many football games on television that his wife said, "Honey, you love football better than you do me." Without taking his eyes away from the TV screen, he said, "That may be so, but I like you better than I do basketball."

It is a special joy to have several players from the 1983 World Champion Little League Baseball Team in the service today, along with their coach.

I bring you a message this morning using some baseball terminology on the subject, "Touching All the Bases." In order for the player to be safe at home, all bases must be touched.

I think it is scriptural to speak on this subject. Paul frequently used the sports of his day to illustrate the truth he was teaching. In writing to the Corinthians, he said, "Every man that striveth for the mastery is temperate in all things. Now they do it to obtain a corruptible crown; but we an incorruptible" (I Cor. 9:25).

In I Timothy 4:8 he said to Timothy, "Bodily exercise profiteth little: but godliness is profitable unto all things." The writer to the Hebrews makes us think of one of our great baseball stadiums when he says, "Wherefore seeing we also are compassed about with so great a cloud of witnesses, let us lay aside every weight, and the sin which doth so easily beset us, and let us run with patience the race that is set before us" (12:1).

In the light of these Scriptures, I believe we have the sanction of the Bible for using an athletic event to illustrate and interpret the truth we are endeavoring to teach. Not only is it scriptural to use baseball terminology to illustrate the truth; but when you talk about baseball, nearly everyone knows what you are talking about and you don't have to explain.

However, I did hear of a young lady who went to a baseball game with a young man and arrived late. They had already played three innings. She said to the young man, "I wonder what the score is?"

He looked at the scoreboard and said, "Nothing to nothing."

She exclaimed, "That's fine. We haven't missed anything yet!"

But most people do understand baseball games. I am going to do my best this morning to make everyone in this auditorium understand exactly what they must do to be safe at Home, to be sure that they will go to Heaven.

As far back as I can remember, we went to church. Some of my earliest memories are of attending an old country church in this greater metropolitan Atlanta area. I can still hear the preacher as if it were yesterday. I heard what he said, but I didn't understand what he meant. He said such things as: "Jesus died for you that you may go to Heaven." As a boy, the age of some of you here this morning, I wondered how in the world a Man dying on a cross could get me to Heaven! I thought I could get to Heaven better with an airplane or rocket of some kind.

Then I heard him say, "Ye must be born again!" He said, "Except a man be born again, he cannot see the kingdom of God." I got the idea from his sermon that if I were not born again, I would not make Heaven; but I had no idea what being born again meant, since he didn't explain it to me. Through the years I have learned that my experience was not unique. Many go to church Sunday after Sunday, week after week, month after month; they hear expressions and sermons but never really understand exactly what is being said.

Everyone who is not yet a Christian has some reason or excuse as to why he is not. The excuse most often given is, "I read the Bible, but it doesn't make sense. I go to church and listen, but I don't understand it." The Bible says in I Corinthians 2:14, "But the natural man receiveth not the things of the Spirit of God: for they are foolishness unto him: neither can he know them, because they are spiritually discerned." The Bible is one Book that you can't understand as you should until you know the Author of the Book. But after you know Christ as personal Saviour, the Bible takes on new meaning, a new light.

While it is difficult for the unsaved to understand the Bible, they can understand enough to be saved.

And I want to share with you this morning very simply what you must understand in order to get to Heaven. You may not do anything about it, but at least you will know what you have to do in order to make Heaven your Home.

Acts, chapter 8, records the story of the conversion of the Ethiopian eunuch. He had been to church and was on his way home. He was riding in a chariot with his Bible lying on his lap, open to Isaiah 53, and was reading, "He was wounded for our transgressions, he was bruised for our iniquities: the chastisement of our peace was upon him; and with his stripes we are healed. All we like sheep have gone astray; we have turned every one to his own way; and the Lord hath laid on him the iniquity of us all" (vss. 5,6). But he didn't understand what it said.

An evangelist named Philip, obeying the instructions given by God, joined himself to the chariot; and as the two rode along together, the evangelist asked, "Understandest thou what thou readest?" And the man replied, "How can I, except some man should guide me?" Then he asked the evangelist, "Of whom speaketh the prophet this? of himself, or of some other man?" And the Bible says that Philip "began at the same scripture, and preached unto him Jesus."

Now they had not been riding very long before the eunuch saw a body of water and said, "See, here is water; what doth hinder me to be baptized?" And Philip answered, "If thou believest with all thine heart, thou mayest." Immediately the eunuch said, "I believe that Jesus Christ is the Son of God." And according to Acts 8:38, they commanded the chariot to stand still; and both Philip and the eunuch went down into the water, and Philip baptized the eunuch. And verse 39 ends by saying, "And he went on his way rejoicing."

There are three things you must understand to be saved.

When a baseball player hits the ball out of the park for a home run, he must be sure to touch every single base in order to be safe when he arrives at home. If he fails to touch first base and the opposing team appeals, he is called out by the umpire. He may have knocked the ball far enough for a home run; but if he fails to touch any base, he can be called out.

Keep those three bases in mind because they represent three things I want to share with you regarding this all-important matter of salvation.

I. FIRST BASE

Base number one is: you must realize that you are a sinner. That is what the eunuch is reading in Isaiah 53:6, "All we like sheep have gone astray; we have turned every one to his own way; and the Lord [that is Jehovah in Heaven, the Father] hath laid on him [Jesus] the iniquity of us all."

The most difficult thing I have to do as an evangelist is make people see that they need to be saved, especially when I address young people such as this group, because, for the most part, here are young people who are moral, clean, pure, obedient, honest and trustworthy, and with great character. But the Bible says, "All we like sheep have gone astray." That means, though I am a preacher and have been preaching since I was twenty years old, I am not perfect. It means, though the pastor of this church is a very nice gentleman, he is not perfect.

Now it does not say how far astray we have gone, but it does say, "All we like sheep have gone astray," and that is what this man is reading in the Bible. Some may have gone astray to drunkenness, some to dope addiction, some to disobedience to parents; some may even have gone astray to immorality, but everybody has gone astray.

The Bible says in Romans 3:23, "All have sinned, and come short of the glory of God." To "come short" means "to miss the mark." Suppose I hang a target on the wall and give everyone in this building a dart. I say, "Do your best to hit the bull's eye. Give it everything you've got!" And each one throws a dart at the target. One misses the bull's eye by a quarter of an inch, another by a sixteenth of an inch, another by a foot, another the entire target, and still another, the entire wall! After a thousand darts were thrown, there would be darts all over the wall, in the target, and on the floor, but not one single dart in the bull's eye.

Looking at the congregation I would say, "There is no difference." And you would say, "Wait a moment! What do you mean, no difference? There is one boy who missed it by only a sixteenth of an inch and another who missed it by twelve feet!" I would say, "No difference because ALL came short of the bull's eye!"

Ladies and gentlemen, boys and girls, when God Almighty looks down on the human race, He doesn't say, "There's a good man and there's a bad man and that man is awful!" God looks down and, according to Romans 3:22, says, "There is no difference." Then He explains, "For all have sinned, and come short of the glory of God."

To go to Heaven, one must be absolutely perfect. But the Bible says nobody is perfect—all have come short!

When I went to high school, one had to have a grade average of 70 to pass. If one averaged anything less than 70, he had to repeat the grade. A boy who averaged 65 was in the same predicament as one who averaged 35, though there was a 30-point difference. Both had failed to pass.

A lot of things I have never done. I have never murdered anybody. I have never robbed a bank. But I am in the same predicament as the man who has murdered 35 people and robbed every bank in town. Why? Because all have come short of the glory of God. None of us are perfect. We all need to be saved.

The Bible reminds us in James 2:10, "For whosoever shall keep the whole law, and yet offend in one point, he is guilty of all." It is plain that if we offend in one point, we are guilty of breaking the whole law. And who hasn't offended at least in one point?

I want to tell you honestly and plainly that first base is simply this: *you must admit that you are a sinner.* Jesus did not come to save righteous people. He "came not to call the righteous, but sinners to repentance" (Luke 5:32). Nobody is saved except sinners. Salvation is for sinners. If I went to Heaven, took a paint brush and wrote across the gate, FOR SINNERS ONLY, God would come out, smile and say, "That is absolutely right! I came not to call the righteous, but sinners to repentance. They that are whole need not a physician."

Millions of people disqualify themselves for Heaven and will be called out because they don't touch first base. They won't admit they are sinners. They say, "I'm not bad. I try to live good. I go to church and read my Bible. I pay my bills." But that is not the issue. You only qualify for your sonship when you recognize your sinnership.

In Shoreham, England, several years ago, a savings and loan association celebrated their 40th anniversary. Some of the directors decided it would be a good thing to give away some great prizes and have a beauty contest. So they did. Someone came up with the idea: "Since it is our 40th anniversary, let's give the prizes only to a lady who is over 40 years old!" But they ran into a problem. The ladies beautiful enough to win the contest wouldn't admit they were 40 years old!

Now you may leave here shaking your head when I tell you this, but God has a wonderful Heaven He wants to give away! But He will not give it to anybody who will not admit he is a sinner.

Not every person has committed the same sins, but every person has sinned. And you don't have to commit every sin in the catalog to be lost. You must touch first base. You must admit that you are a sinner.

II. SECOND BASE

Then you must touch second base. You not only must understand that you are a sinner, but you must understand that Jesus died for sinners. We call that "a sacrifice." A sacrifice in baseball is when you advance because somebody else is out. The greatest sacrifice ever made was not in a World Series game but the sacrifice Jesus made at Calvary two thousand years ago! We call it the substitutionary death of Jesus.

Now you may not believe this, but here is what happened two thousand years ago. God took every sin you ever have committed and every sin you ever will commit and laid those sins on Jesus

Christ, just like I lay this Bible on my hand. That is exactly what the Bible says, and that is what the eunuch was reading in Isaiah 53:6, "And the Lord hath [past tense] laid on him the iniquity of us all."

We get excited when our favorite player hits a home run. But, brother, God Almighty hit a home run for everybody! Nobody need die on base. Everybody can come Home because He knocked the ball slap over the fence two thousand years ago! Every sin you have ever committed—I am talking about the little sins and the big sins—ALL OF THEM!

If I said, "Everybody who wishes to go to Heaven come down the aisle, get on your knees and confess your sins," all of you would be in a bad predicament, because there is no one in this building who can remember all the sins he has ever committed. Little things you have forgotten about, big things that still nag you—you worry about these. But a lot of little things are just as bad in God's sight as the big things. He doesn't classify sins as small, medium and large. All your sins, large and small, were laid on Christ.

Every time I was disobedient to my parents, God laid that on Jesus. Every lie I have ever told since I was a baby, God laid that on Jesus.

My sin—oh, the bliss of this glorious tho't—
My sin—not in part, but the whole—
Is nailed to the cross and I bear it no more,
Praise the Lord, praise the Lord, O my soul!

I am talking about the sins that Hitler committed! I am talking about the sins Mussolini committed. I am talking about the sins the mass murderer committed. I am talking about the sins of the rapist. The Bible says in I John 2:2, "And he is the propitiation for our sins: and not for our's only, but also for the sins of the whole world." Now you may never do anything about it, but you will not change this fact—your sins, every one of them, were laid on Jesus Christ two thousand years ago.

The Bible says in I Peter 2:24, "Who his own self bare our sins in his own body on the tree." Second Corinthians 5:21 states, "For he hath made him to be sin for us, who knew no sin." That is exactly what the Bible says. And while Jesus Christ bore all our sins in His own body—watch it, like I hold this Bible in my hand—

God actually punished Him in our place to pay the debt we owe. And while He was suspended between Heaven and earth on that cross, as if rejected by both, He uttered seven things. Three utterances came before the darkness; three utterances came after the darkness, and one utterance came during the darkness. The sixth utterance was, "It is finished!" When He said, "It is finished," you can believe the ball went over the fence, up in about the 18th row of the grandstand! Hallelujah! I mean it went totally out of the park and is lost forever! When God said, "It is finished," you mark it down, IT WAS FINISHED!

You may reject it, but you cannot do away with the fact that two thousand years ago Jesus Christ died on the cross in your place, suffered your Hell, paid your debt; and if anybody gets Home, he goes Home on His sacrifice! Nobody makes it any other way.

Now listen! I try to live good, but I had as soon trust my sins to get me to Heaven as to trust my righteousness. Isaiah 64:6 says, "All our righteousnesses are as filthy rags."

So you have to touch first base: you have to admit that you are a sinner. And you have to touch second base: you have to believe that Jesus Christ made the sacrifice, that His death on the cross paid what you owe as a sinner. You must believe that. There is no other way to be saved, no other way to get Home safe.

III. THIRD BASE

Then you have to touch third base. It is one thing to know that I am a sinner; it is another thing to know that Jesus Christ died for me on the cross. But I am not going to Heaven just because I recognize I'm a sinner and believe He died for me. This eunuch saw water and said, "Here is water; what doth hinder me to be baptized?" And Philip gave this simple answer: "If thou BELIEVEST with all thine heart, thou mayest."

He said, "I believe that Jesus Christ is the Son of God." They stopped the chariot, went down into the water; Philip baptized him, and the eunuch went on his way rejoicing!

Third base is *trusting Jesus Christ as Saviour*. Third base is *depending on Jesus Christ for salvation*. That is what Philip said to the eunuch: "If thou BELIEVEST. . . ."

Nearly everybody I meet says, "I have always believed in

Christ!" I have never in my life met an atheist. There may be some but I have never met one. I have met some skeptics who were not sure. I have met some agnostics who were ignorant about it. But I have never met a man who said, "I don't believe there is a God."

To believe in your mind that there is a God is not what it means to believe on the Lord Jesus Christ. Don't miss that. To believe in your mind that Jesus Christ died on the cross is not what the Bible means when Philip said to the eunuch, "If thou believest with all thine heart. . . ." The Bible word "believe" means to trust, to depend on, to rely on.

I can believe an airplane will fly and never make a trip. I can believe that when I dismiss you in a few minutes, the buses are going to take you to the Atlanta Stadium to watch the Atlanta Braves play. I can believe that and never make the trip. I can believe the bus drivers are trustworthy, that if I get on the bus, they will deliver me safely to the Stadium. I can believe that and never go to the Stadium. I must not only believe the bus is going to the Stadium, but I must get on the bus and trust my life to a bus driver and say, "Old Boy, wherever you go, I'm going! If you go the Stadium, I'm going to the Stadium. If you go to Florida, I'm going to Florida. I'm on the bus, and you are the driver."

To trust Jesus Christ as your Saviour means to say, "I know I'm a sinner. I have touched first base. I believe He made the supreme sacrifice; He died for me. I have touched second base. I am nearly Home; I am nearly Home! I not only know I'm a sinner and believe He died for me, but I am headed for third. I will trust Him as my Saviour. If I die today, I will die depending on Him to get me to Heaven."

I'm a Baptist. I'm Baptist born and Baptist bred; and when I die, I'll be Baptist dead. I'm a Baptist. But if I go to Heaven in the next thirty minutes and they say, "Why should we let you in?" I will not say, "Because I'm a Baptist." I have better sense than that. If I go to Heaven in the next thirty minutes, and they say, "Why should we let you in?" I will not say, "Because I lived good." I know better than that. I have come short. I missed the bull's eye, too. If I go to Heaven in the next thirty minutes, and they say, "Why should we let you in?" I will say, "Because I touched all the bases. I know I'm a sinner. I believe Jesus Christ made the supreme sacrifice. And I am trusting Him as my Saviour, and I am safe at Home!"

When you admit you are a sinner, believe Jesus Christ died for you and trust Him and Him alone and nothing else to get you to Heaven, you will be safe at Home!

That is what the Bible means when it says, "Believe on the Lord Jesus Christ, and thou shalt be SAVED!" Why not say "safe"? I like that baseball term, "SAFE!" Not out, SAFE! Why? Because I believed on the Lord Jesus Christ, and I'm SAFE.

IV. THE UMPIRE'S DECISION IS FINAL

When the player crosses home plate and the umpire says, "Safe," who is going to argue with that?

You will remember this play. I got so mad when I saw it I could hardly stand it! I was watching an Atlanta Braves' game. I don't remember who the left fielder was, but the guy hit a ball; and the left fielder caught the ball on the run inside the foul line, at least ten or fifteen yards inside the foul line. I was so excited! I was screaming and hollering! I was having a fit! He caught it, and he kept running. He crossed the foul line, ran into a fence, and dropped the ball! And the dumb umpire flagged the hitter to keep running. I said, "That umpire is crazy! He is nuts! Anybody with one eye saw he caught the ball fifteen or twenty yards inside the foul line. That guy was out the minute he caught it! I know baseball!" I argued and fussed, and I wasn't the only one. Sports writers across the country said the ball shouldn't have been in play when the left fielder hit the fence. For several days I read articles in papers all across America.

One day I read an article in which the umpire pulled the rule book on them. He quoted from the rule book, "If a man catches the ball and collides with an object and drops the ball, the ball is still in play." It didn't say how long he had to hold it. He could have held it until he grew whiskers and then ran into the fence and dropped it and it would still have been in play, according to the rule book. Well, when he pulled the rule book on me, I shut up. The rule book had the final say.

I'm going to tell you something. When the Umpire pulls the Rule Book on you, your religion won't mean much then. What you thought and argued and screamed about and fussed about all your life won't mean beans then; because the great Umpire is going to have the final say. And the Rule Book says, "He that believeth on the Son hath everlasting life."

You may say, "But I lived good! I gave a tithe! I went to church!"

It doesn't say, "He that lives good is saved." It says, "He that believeth on the Son hath everlasting life." If you didn't trust Christ as Saviour, you will be out!

"But I hit the ball out of the park!"

"You are out!"

"Why?"

"You didn't touch all the bases."

On the other hand, if the umpire says, "Safe," you are safe! They can run around like a bunch of bumblebees, pick up dirt and throw it, spit on the ground, jump around and do flips; but the umpire just walks around with his hands folded, "SAFE!" And you go by what he says, no matter what happens.

You must touch all the bases: "I understand I'm a sinner. I believe Jesus Christ made the supreme sacrifice. I am trusting Him as my Saviour, and I will make it Home safe." That settles it. But you have to make dead sure you touch all three bases: Admit that you are a sinner; believe that Jesus died for you; trust Him and nothing else to get you to Heaven. And according to the Rule Book and the great Umpire, you will be SAFE.

Trust Jesus Christ Today

After preaching the sermon, "Touching All the Bases," several people came to trust Jesus Christ as Saviour, including many Little League ballplayers and coaches. And now we urge those reading these lines to make that same decision.

If you will admit that you are a sinner, believe that Jesus Christ died on the cross for you and trust Him completely for salvation, then pray this simple prayer:

> Dear Lord Jesus, I know that I'm a sinner and do believe that You died for me. Here and now I fully trust You as my Saviour and depend on You to take me to Heaven when I die. Please help me to live for You and to be a good Christian. Amen.

If you prayed that simple prayer and will write and tell us so, we have some free literature we want to send that will help you as you set out to live the Christian life. All you need do to receive your free literature is write to me:

Dr. Curtis Hutson
Sword of the Lord Foundation
P. O. Box 1099
Murfreesboro, Tennessee 37133

In your letter say, "I have read the sermon, 'Touching All the Bases.' I understand that I'm a sinner and do believe that Jesus Christ died on the cross for me. Here and now I trust Him completely for my salvation and depend on Him to take me to Heaven when I die. Please send me the free literature that will help me as I set out to live the Christian life."

Be sure to include your name and full address.

Chapter 20

The Blood of Jesus Christ

"*But if we walk in the light, as he is in the light, we have fellowship one with another, and the blood of Jesus Christ his Son cleanseth us from all sin.*"—I John 1:7.

The basic message of the Bible is in that expression, "The blood of Jesus Christ his Son cleanseth us from all sin." Everyone who has ever taught or studied, knows that the basic fundamental of teaching is repetition, whether you are teaching in kindergarten, grade school, high school, university or in a postgraduate school. The world knows this. That is why you hear cigarette and other ads repeated over and over again.

One preacher asked another, "How do you make a point stick when you are preaching a sermon?"

He replied, "First, I tell them what I am going to tell them. Second, I tell them. Then I tell them what I done told them!"

He knew the importance of repetition.

I read somewhere that you have to see something seventeen times before it registers.

Remember the schoolteacher who made you write over and over again, "I will not talk in class. I will not talk in class"? I had such a teacher who made me write that five hundred times! Why? Because she knew that the basic fundamental law of teaching is repetition, and if I wrote it enough, sooner or later I would remember it. Repetition is the secret of learning.

A great teacher generations ago was asked by one of his scholars, "How many times do you repeat a lesson? Four times?"

The teacher replied, "Forty times, four hundred times, four thousand times, if necessary. Repeat the lesson over and over until the pupils you are teaching get what you are trying to say."

The greatest Teacher the world has ever known is the Holy Spirit.

In I John 2:27 we read: "But the anointing which ye received of him abideth in you, and ye need not that any man teach you: but as the same anointing teacheth you of all things, and is truth, and is no lie, and even as it hath taught you, ye shall abide in him."

Again, Jesus said in John 14:16,26, "And I will pray the Father, and he shall give you another Comforter, that he may abide with you for ever. . . But the Comforter, which is the Holy Ghost, whom the Father will send in my name, he shall teach you all things, and bring all things to your remembrance, whatsoever I have said unto you."

The Holy Spirit, being the greatest Teacher of all, knows that the fundamental law of teaching is repetition. So with illustration after illustration, type after type, declaration after declaration, throughout the Bible the Holy Spirit teaches this truth, "The blood of Jesus Christ his Son cleanseth us from all sin."

I. THE PROCLAMATION OF THE BLOOD

Throughout the Bible the message of the blood is proclaimed over and over again.

The Old Testament is divided into three parts: the Law, the Prophets and the Psalms. This division is accepted both by Jews and Gentiles, and it is also a division that is accepted by our Lord Jesus Christ. In Luke 24:44 Jesus said, "All things must be fulfilled, which were written in the law of Moses, and in the prophets, and in the psalms, concerning me."

The heart of the Law, in my opinion, is the book of Leviticus. The heart of Leviticus is the description of the feast. The heart of the feast is the day of atonement, described in chapters 16 and 17. And in the heart of the description of the day of atonement is this verse, "The life of the flesh is in the blood: and I have given it to you upon the altar to make an atonement for your souls: for it is the blood that maketh an atonement for the soul" (17:11).

What is the Holy Spirit saying in the heart of the Law? "The blood of Jesus Christ his Son cleanseth us from all sin."

The second division of the Old Testament is the Prophets. I believe the heart of the Prophets is the book of Isaiah. In searching for the heart of the book of Isaiah we inevitably come to chapter 53. Martin Luther said concerning Isaiah 53: "It is so precious that it ought to be written on parchment of gold and lettered with diamonds."

In the twelve verses in this chapter there are twelve mentions of the substitutionary death of Jesus. I would say the heart of Isaiah 53 is verse 6: "All we like sheep have gone astray; we have turned every one to his own way; and the Lord hath laid on him the iniquity of us all."

What is He saying in the heart of the Prophets? "The blood of Jesus Christ his Son cleanseth us from all sin."

The Psalms is the third division of the Old Testament. Surely I am correct in saying that Psalms 22, 23, 24 is the heart of the Psalms. Psalm 22 is the cross chapter—we have the Suffering Saviour. Psalm 23 is the crook chapter—we have Jesus, the Good Shepherd, in the present life. Psalm 24 is the crown chapter—we have Jesus reigning as King of kings and Lord of lords.

In Psalm 22 we find in prophecy the description of the sufferings of Christ on the cross. And verse 1, "My God, my God, why hast thou forsaken me?" was fulfilled when Jesus hung on the cross two thousand years ago and cried out, "My God, my God, why hast thou forsaken me?" (Matt. 27:46).

Here we have by implication, "The blood of Jesus Christ his Son cleanseth us from all sin."

Like the Old Testament, the New Testament has three main divisions: the Gospels, the Epistles and the book of Revelation.

What would you say is the heart of the Gospels? Most people would no doubt say the book of John. John was written that "ye might believe that Jesus is the Christ, the Son of God; and that believing ye might have life through his name" (20:31).

If John is the heart of the Gospels, which chapter do you think is the heart of the Gospel of John? I would say John, chapter 3.

And if you asked, "What is the heart of John, chapter 3?" I must say it is verse 16, "For God so loved the world, that he gave his only begotten Son, that whosoever believeth in him should not perish, but have everlasting life."

What is the Holy Spirit saying in the heart of the Gospels? The same thing He said in the heart of the Law, the same thing He said in the heart of the Prophets, the same thing He said in the heart of the Psalms: "The blood of Jesus Christ his Son cleanseth us from all sin."

The second division in the New Testament is the Epistles. Now it may be difficult to say this or that book is the heart of the Epistles, but after studying the Bible, it is the opinion of this preacher of the Gospel that the book of Romans is the heart of the Epistles. And I would have to say the heart of Romans would be chapter 5, which deals with justification by faith. And to me the heart of Romans, chapter 5, is verses 8 and 9: "But God commendeth his love toward us, in that, while we were yet sinners, Christ died for us. Much more then, being now justified by his blood, we shall be saved from wrath through him."

What is the Holy Spirit saying in the heart of the Epistles? The same thing He said in the Law, in the Prophets, and in the Psalms, and in the Gospels: "The blood of Jesus Christ his Son cleanseth us from all sin."

The last division in the New Testament is the book of Revelation. To me the heart of the book of Revelation is chapter 1. And chapter 1, verse 5, says, "Unto him that loved us, and washed us from our sins in his own blood."

What is the Holy Spirit saying in the book of Revelation? The same thing He said in the Law, in the Prophets, in the Psalms, in the Gospels and in the Epistles: "The blood of Jesus Christ his Son cleanseth us from all sin."

Now do you wonder why Satan has made an attack upon the blood of Christ? Do you wonder why Satan has gotten some denominations to take out of their hymnals all songs dealing with the blood of Jesus? Do you wonder why some preachers never preach on the blood of Jesus Christ?

The Holy Spirit puts the emphasis on the blood, the blood, the blood, the blood—"The blood of Jesus Christ his Son cleanseth us from all sin."

The best way Satan can attack me is to get me off on a tangent.

If he can get me away from preaching "the blood of Jesus Christ his Son cleanseth us from all sin," he has succeeded. He may get me off on some pet doctrine to the exclusion of preaching the cross. And when I cease to preach "the blood of Jesus Christ his Son cleanseth us from all sin," Satan has won a victory.

I honestly believe God Almighty cannot bless the preacher, or church, or Sunday school teacher, or soul winner, or missionary, or evangelist who goes away from preaching the blood of our Lord Jesus Christ. This is a must in gospel preaching.

Throughout the Bible the blood of Jesus runs like a scarlet thread from Genesis to Revelation.

II. THE PROMISE OF THE BLOOD

The promise of the blood goes back as far as Genesis 3:15 where immediately after man sinned, God Almighty promised a Redeemer. You say, "How did He do that?" He said to Satan, "The seed of the woman shall bruise thy head, and thou shalt bruise his heel."

When He spoke of the Seed of the woman, He prophesied the virgin birth of our Lord Jesus Christ. You see, God knew the importance of Jesus' being the virgin-born, spotless, sinless Son of God. God knew that Jesus had to be the virgin-born Son of God, and He promised that kind of Redeemer.

Every time you see in the Bible a little lamb slain and his blood spilt, God is saying, "I am going to send a Redeemer." Every time you see little doves killed and their blood spilt, God is saying, "I am going to send a Redeemer." When in the book of Genesis God slew an innocent animal and the skins provided clothing for Adam and Eve, God was saying, "I am going to send a Sacrifice to die for you. His blood is going to be shed, and in the shedding of blood, there will be a covering for your sin."

If I had time I could preach for months on the types, illustrations and examples throughout the Bible where God was promising that Jesus Christ would come and die for our sins.

III. THE PROVISION OF THE BLOOD

Not only did God promise the blood, He also provided the blood. One day when John was baptizing, Jesus came on the scene, and

John said, "Behold the Lamb of God, which taketh away the sin of the world" (John 1:29).

Wait a minute! "Lamb of God"—what does that mean? That here is God's sacrificial Lamb. Back in Exodus, chapter 12, the Israelites had to provide their own little lamb that was to be without spot and blemish. That lamb had to be killed and its blood applied to the doorposts. God said, "When I see the blood, I will pass over you."

Here in John 1, John said, "Wait! This is God's Lamb. You don't have to search to find a little lamb that doesn't have a spot or blemish. God has already searched and found the Lamb. Here He is. He qualifies. He is without spot, without blemish. He never sinned. There are no flaws in His character. He is the sinless Lamb of God." God Almighty sacrificed His own Son in our place at Calvary two thousand years ago.

You say, "The Jews killed Him." Somebody else says it was the Roman soldiers. No. It was God who sacrificed Jesus. Isaiah 53:10 tells us, "It pleased the Lord to bruise him," to "make his soul an offering for sin." John 3:16, "God so loved the world, that *he* gave his only begotten Son." Romans 8:32, "*He* that spared not his own Son, but [freely] delivered him up [to the death] for us all . . . ." God promised the blood, but, praise His name, He also provided the blood!

When God turned His back on His own Son and Jesus cried out, "My God, my God, why hast thou forsaken me?" God provided the blood. In providing the blood, He provided a Substitute. We should have been there, but He took our place. He who knew no sin was made sin for us.

Not only did He provide a Substitute, but He provided satisfaction. God's justice had to be satisfied. God Almighty cannot sacrifice His justice on the altar of His love. He is Love, but He is also just.

If a judge passed sentence on a guilty individual, we could not say the judge didn't love that individual. We could only say he was just. The judge must be just. And the greatest Judge of all—God—must be just.

But suppose a judge said, "You are guilty of murder and now you are sentenced to die in the electric chair," then if that same judge should lay aside his robe and say, "Now, you may go free;

I will die in the electric chair in your place," then the judge would be just, but he would also demonstrate his great love.

Not only did God say to man, "When you sin, you will die, for the wages of sin is death," He also said, "I love you so much that I am going to come into the world in the form of My Son and die for you." That is love, friends—real love!

He provided a Substitute, He provided satisfaction for His own justice, then He provided a Saviour. The angel said, "Unto you is born this day in the city of David a Saviour." I like that expression, "Unto you—[y-o-u]—is born. . . ." When I read that I feel I am somebody! God took me into account, and He knows my name. When I read, "Unto you. . .," I know He is talking directly to me.

I am almost like the elephant and rooster who crossed the bridge together. When they got across to the other side, the little rooster looked up at the elephant and said, "Big boy, did you feel that thing shake when we crossed it?"

When I read that verse, "Unto *you* is born. . .," I feel like looking in the Devil's face and saying, "Did you feel that bridge shake when Jesus and I went across it?" He loves *me*. He gave Himself for *me*! God promised the blood, and God provided the blood.

IV. THE POWER OF THE BLOOD

Many songs have been written trying to depict the power of the blood.

Would you be free from the burden of sin?
There's pow'r in the blood, pow'r in the blood;
Would you o'er evil a victory win?
There's wonderful pow'r in the blood.

Say! Be free from your burden of sin? Yes. Get the victory over evil? Yes. How? Through the blood. Oh, the power of the blood of Christ!

There is the power of forgiveness in the blood, according to Ephesians 1:7: "In whom we have redemption through his blood, [even] the forgiveness of sins." For years I didn't believe this. Why? Because my actions proved I didn't believe it. I thought the power of forgiveness was in my ability to feel sorry for my sin, or in my ability to agonize, when the power of forgiveness is in the blood. "In whom we have redemption through his blood, the forgiveness of sins."

All you have to do is say, "Dear Lord Jesus, I have sinned, but Your blood was shed for me at Calvary, and the Bible says if we confess our sins, You are faithful and just to forgive us. I am confessing mine, and I know it is forgiven and cleansed because You said so. If the Devil reminds me of it, I am going to quote to him I John 1:8,9. And if he reminds me again, I am going to quote those two verses until he flees."

Many Christians won't forgive themselves after they have sinned. But the power of forgiveness is not in the way you feel but in the blood.

Not only is there power of forgiveness in the blood, but there is power of cleansing. God not only forgives sin, He also cleanses it. He fixes us so we are like we were before we ever sinned. Those verses in I John 1:8,9 read: "If we say that we have no sin, we deceive ourselves, and the truth is not in us. If we confess our sins, he is faithful and just to forgive us our sins, and to cleanse us from all unrighteousness." "Cleanse" means a continual cleansing.

A fellow who thought that one could fall from grace tried to illustrate the point to another who believed in eternal security. Standing by the riverbank he took out of the mud a rock which was muddy and dirty. He put the rock into the stream and washed it clean, then he showed it to his friend who believed in eternal security and said, "You see that? The rock is clean." Then putting the rock back into the mud he said, "That is my salvation. I can be cleansed one minute and the next minute be back just like I was."

His friend who believed in eternal security took the rock out of the mud, washed it in the stream and said, "See that rock?" Then throwing it out in the middle of the stream, he said, "That is my salvation. It will never get dirty again. The water continually keeps it clean."

There is power in the blood for continual cleansing.

There is power in the blood for reconciliation. How is man reconciled to God? Second Corinthians 5:19 says that "God was in Christ, reconciling the world unto himself." Man, not God, needs reconciliation. To reconcile means to bring back together two who have been at outs. Colossians 1:20 says, "And, having made peace through the blood of his cross, by him to reconcile all things unto himself."

How are we reconciled? Through the blood. Our sin separates us from God, but Ephesians 2:13 tells us, "Ye who sometimes were far off are made nigh by the blood of Christ." According to Strong's Concordance, the Greek word for "nigh" is *eggus*, meaning "to squeeze." You who were sometimes afar off have been squeezed up close by the blood. It is almost enough to make one shout!

Listen! You who were afar off have been made nigh by the blood. Reconciliation. How? Jesus shed His blood for my sins. He knows my sins are gone, and He receives me back on the basis of the shed blood of Jesus Christ.

Not only is there power for forgiveness, power for cleansing, and power to reconcile, but the blood also has power to redeem us.

He bought us! That means one day we belonged to somebody else, then Jesus came along and paid the price to purchase us. First Peter 1:18,19 says:

"Forasmuch as ye know that ye were not redeemed with corruptible things, as silver and gold, from your vain conversation received by tradition from your fathers; But with the precious blood of Christ, as of a lamb without blemish and without spot."

The word "precious" means "valuable." Say, we were bought at infinite price! We were bought with the precious blood, the valuable blood of our Lord Jesus Christ. He bought you, He owns you, He paid for you. He didn't make the down payment like some religions teach—that "Jesus died for you to get you started on your way to Heaven, but you have to keep up the installments by keeping the Ten Commandments, going to church, receiving sacraments," etc. Oh, He didn't just pay the down payment—He paid it in full.

When in John 19:30 He cried out on the cross, "It is finished," He meant, "It is finished." "Finished" means "the end of it." When salvation's plan was finished, nothing else had to be done.

You may never come to Jesus Christ. You may never be saved. But—you could be. You need nothing but the blood. And it has already been shed for you. He has already paid what you owe. There is nothing else to do. All you need do is come to Jesus Christ and say, "I believe You died for me. I believe You paid what I owe. And the best I know how I will receive You, trust You." Then you will be saved.

Dr. A. J. Gordon told a touching story while pastoring in Boston. He had studied one Saturday until his eyes were tired from reading. He closed his Bible to take a walk and refresh himself for further study later.

As he walked in the street, he saw a child coming from the field with a cage in his hand. In the cage were some field birds.

Dr. Gordon stopped him and asked, "Son, what do you have there?"

"Oh, just some birds."

"Where did you get them?"

"I trapped them."

"What are you going to do with them?"

"Play with them."

Dr. Gordon then asked, "What are you going to do with them after you are through playing with them?"

"Feed them to my cat."

Dr. Gordon looked at the cage and the little wild birds. They were not making a sound as they huddled on the bottom of the cage. The great preacher said he could almost see their little hearts vibrating with fear.

Dr. Gordon couldn't stand the thought of those little field birds being fed to a cat, so he said, "Son, would you sell me those birds?"

"Mister, you don't want these birds, just field birds. You can go trap some yourself."

"No," said he, "I want those birds that are in that cage, and I am willing to pay for them." Taking some money from his pocket he said, "How much do you want for those birds?"

"Mister, they are only wild birds. They are not canaries. They can't sing."

Said Dr. Gordon, "Whether they can sing or not, I want those birds. How much do you want for them?"

Finally the little boy said, "Well, if you insist, I'll sell them to you for two dollars, and give you the cage."

Dr. Gordon gave the boy two dollars and took the birds and the cage.

The little boy walked away but looked back to see what the "crazy" man wanted with the birds. Dr. Gordon was holding the cage, just looking at the frightened birds. They were looking up at Dr. Gordon as if they knew they were going to their death.

The preacher walked a few blocks, then turned into an alley. Looking to see that nobody was watching, he then opened the door of the cage and said, "Fly out, little birds! Fly out!"

But they were so afraid they wouldn't fly. Dr. Gordon tapped the bottom of the cage and repeated, "Fly out, little birds, you are free!"

One by one each little bird got up, shook itself, went to the opening of the cage and flew away. Dr. Gordon said that as they flew out of the cage it seemed as if one by one they chirped, "Redeemed! Redeemed! Redeemed!"

When I read that story, I pictured myself in a cage. Thousands of years ago Satan trapped us. Jesus saw our hopeless condition and one day said to God the Father about Satan, "What is he going to do with those birds?"

God replied, "He's going to play with them."

"And after he is through playing with them—what is he going to do with them?"

God answered, "He's going to torment them eternally in Hell."

Jesus said, "Would You sell them to Me?"

"Are You sure You want those birds? If You buy those birds, they will nail You to the cross. If You buy those birds, they will plait a crown of thorns and push it down on Your brow. If You buy those birds, some of them won't live for You. If You buy those birds, they will beat You with a lash, spit in Your face and pluck Your beard out. Are You sure You want those birds?"

Jesus said, "Yes, Father, I know I want them. I will lay down My life—I will die for them."

And two thousand years ago when Jesus on the cross cried, "My God, my God, why hast thou forsaken me?" He was opening the door of the cage.

I didn't know it until I was eleven years old. At eleven I was still afraid and shaking and my heart trembled. I didn't know the door had been opened. But Jesus took His nail-pierced hand, tapped the bottom of the cage and said, "Go on, little bird. You are free."

I couldn't believe it. You mean, "I just trust the Lord Jesus and rely on Him, and lean on Him and I am free?"

"Yes. Go on, little bird. You are free."

He is saying to someone today, "The cage is open. You are free." But the little birds won't fly out. Would you try it? I know it is unbelievable. I hardly believe it myself. It is unbelievable to think that all I had to do was trust Him. But as unbelievable as it is, it is true. The door is open. Fly out, little bird. You are redeemed!

Will You Trust Christ Right Now?

You have just read the sermon, "The Blood of Jesus Christ." Dear friend, when Jesus died on the cross, He was dying in your place to pay what you owe. We see in Hebrews 2:9 that He tasted death for every man. If you will trust Christ today as your Saviour, and write to tell me so, I have some free literature that I want to send you to help in your Christian life. All you need do is mail a letter to me:

Dr. Curtis Hutson
Sword of the Lord Foundation
Box 1099
Murfreesboro, Tennessee 37133

In your letter say, "I do believe that Jesus Christ died for me. I believe He became my Substitute on the cross. I believe He fully paid my sin debt, and today, the best I know how, I do trust Him as my Saviour. I have prayed and told Jesus that I trust Him. Please send me the free Christian literature that will help me as I set out to live the Christian life."

Then be sure to include your name and full address.

Chapter 21

Two Blind Men Healed

"And when Jesus departed thence, two blind men followed him, crying, and saying, Thou son of David, have mercy on us. And when he was come into the house, the blind men came to him: and Jesus saith unto them, Believe ye that I am able to do this? They said unto him, Yea, Lord. Then touched he their eyes, saying, According to your faith be it unto you. And their eyes were opened; and Jesus straitly charged them, saying, See that no man know it."—Matt. 9:27-30.

There were many blind people in the Eastern countries. I have read that at one time, for every one hundred persons, at least twenty were blind, ten had sight in only one eye and twenty others had some eye affliction.

The fact that He healed so many blind people is an indication that many were blind in Jesus' day. There was blind Bartimaeus; there was the healing of the blind man in John, chapter 9, and others.

I am impressed in the Bible how Jesus was attracted to the needy. It seems the more needy the individual, the more He was attracted.

For instance, in John, chapter 5, at the Pool of Bethesda, He was seemingly attracted to the man with the greatest need. The one He healed had been stricken with an infirmity for thirty-eight years.

Where human sorrow was most conspicuous, divine power was most compassionate. Mercy met misery on its own ground. What an encouragement for the sinner! Romans 5:20 says, "But where sin abounded, grace did much more abound."

In the story I have read, Jesus healed two blind men. Blindness is a picture of the unsaved man. All men without Christ are blind. They have intellectual light but not spiritual light. Everyone comes to Jesus under a cloak of darkness.

In that wonderful song, "Amazing Grace," John Newton described his own salvation experience by saying, "I once was blind, but now I see." Second Corinthians 4:3,4, tells us, "But if our gospel be hid, it is hid to them that are lost: In whom the god of this world hath blinded the minds of them which believe not."

In this story of two blind men seeking Christ, I want us to consider several things:

I. THE SEEKING BLIND MEN

The Bible says, "And when Jesus departed thence, two blind men followed him, crying, and saying, Thou son of David, have mercy on us." Notice first, **they were earnest.** The word which describes their appeal is: *crying.* "Two blind men followed him, *crying. . . .*" This implies that the men were earnest, energetic, pathetic, imploring, pleading and beseeching. How eager they were! Far too many unsaved people are indifferent to their need.

I have had the happy opportunity of leading thousands to Christ. I remember witnessing to a man once, and when I explained that Jesus Christ had died to pay his sin debt, he shrugged his shoulders and said, "What do I care? I don't want anybody to do anything for me. I'll take care of myself!" I could not believe what my ears were hearing. The man seemed so indifferent. Indifference is the dry rot of the church, but in many cases, indifference is the damnation of the sinner.

There was no indifference on the part of these two seekers. They were earnest.

Notice secondly, **they were persistent.** Verse 27 says, "Two blind men followed him." Think of that a moment. Two blind men followed Him. The Bible continues in verse 28, "And when he was come into the house, the blind men came to him. . . ." Remember, they were blind.

It is not easy for two blind men to follow anyone. It must have been difficult for them to follow Jesus. I am sure they had to ask others which way He went. And sometimes He would almost get away from them. It must have been frustrating—two blind men following Jesus. But they were persistent. They would not give up! Being blind—I am sure they kept their ears open for every sound so as not to lose Him. Oh, how I wish that unsaved men were as persistent in finding Jesus!

Not only were they earnest and persistent, but thirdly, **they had a definite object in prayer.** They knew what they wanted—their sight. There was no beating around the bush with these men. Too many blind souls do not know what they want. They seem to beat the Devil around the bush.

When I first started leading souls to Christ, I thought it was better for the person to pray his own prayer rather than me lead him. But after several experiences, I found it is wiser to lead the unsaved man in prayer. When he is left on his own, he will pray for everything except the main thing. He may pray, "Lord, make me a better father. Lord, I thank You for this preacher. Lord, make me a better husband. Lord, help me to live a better life." And he may never get around to saying, "Dear Lord, I am a sinner. I do believe that You died for me, so here and now I do trust You as my Saviour."

These blind men had a definite object in their prayer. They knew what they wanted. When the unsaved man comes to Christ for salvation, his prayer need not be long, but it should be to the point.

Then in the fourth place, **they confessed their own unworthiness.** They cried, "Thou son of David, have mercy on us." They were not asking for justice. If the sinner received justice, he would be in Hell. There was no talking about merit with these two blind men.

When we come to Christ for salvation, we must approach Him as condemned criminals. Nobody ever receives his sonship until he recognizes his sinnership. Jesus Christ came to save sinners, and if we expect to go to Heaven, we must realize that we are sinners and trust Christ as personal Saviour.

And now that we have seen the seeking blind men, notice:

II. THE SAVIOUR'S QUESTION TO THEM

"Believe ye that I am able to do this?" His question concerned their faith. He did not ask what kind of characters they had been, nor if they would do right after they had received their sight. He was not so much concerned with their reputation or their resolution. His question was: "Believe ye that I am able to do this?"

No one is ever saved because he promises to do better. He is saved because Jesus Christ died for him, and he trusts Jesus Christ as Saviour. "For by grace are ye saved through faith; and that not of yourselves: it is the gift of God: Not of works, lest any man should boast" (Eph. 2:8,9). Faith has a receptive power. Faith is not the Saviour. It is an attitude of the soul through which Jesus saves.

As a young boy, I lived with my family in a little two-room house. Near the back porch was a well where we drew water for drinking and bathing. Many hot afternoons I have gone to that well to draw water to quench my thirst. That bucket and rope could not quench my thirst. On the other hand, I could let that bucket down into the well and draw it up and the fresh water quenched my thirst.

Faith is the bucket. Faith never quenched the thirst of a poor sinner, but faith could reach out and take hold of a Saviour who gives living water, springing up into everlasting life so that we would never thirst again.

Often people have said to me, "I don't think I have enough faith to be saved." Dear friend, the Bible never says how much faith you must have. It simply says, "Believe on the Lord Jesus Christ, and thou shalt be saved. . . ."

You can take a little faith and get a mighty big Saviour. It is not the degree of faith, but the object of faith that makes faith important. Take whatever faith you have, put it in Christ, and you will have everlasting life.

Notice, too, that the question concerned their faith in Jesus. The question was not, "Believe ye that ye are able to save yourselves?" Or, "Believe ye that ye are able to live up to a certain set of rules which will produce your salvation?" The question was not, "Believe ye that ordinances and sacraments are able to save you?" The question was: "Believe ye that *I am* able to do this?"

A dear lady was dying. Not having peace in her heart about

salvation, she sent for the priest, who prayed and read the Scriptures. Still she was not satisfied. After trying several things, he suggested that she receive communion, and so brought in the bread and wine. After she had received communion, the priest asked, "Did it help you?" Weeping, the lady cried, "I don't need it. I need Him!"

The Bible never says, "Believe and be saved." It is always very careful to tell us in whom we must believe.

For instance, John 3:16 says, "That whosoever believeth *in him* should not perish, but have everlasting life." Then verse 36, "He that believeth on *the Son* hath everlasting life." The person who is trusting in Jesus Christ for salvation has everlasting life. But the one who is trusting anything other than Jesus Christ, no matter how good the thing may be, the Bible says that one "shall not see life; but the wrath of God abideth on him."

Now notice: the question concerned faith for a specific thing. The question was not, "Do you believe that I am able to raise the dead?" Or, "Do you believe that I am able to unstop deaf ears?" The question was not, "Do you believe I healed the woman with the issue of blood?" The question was: "Do you believe that I am able to do *this*?"

I visited a man in the hospital, and before leaving the room I asked, "Have you ever trusted Christ as your Saviour?"

"Oh, yes," he replied. "I certainly have." I knew the man's background and knew that he did not attend church regularly, so I wondered if he had really trusted Christ as Saviour.

I continued: "Would you mind telling me about it?"

He said, "Well, when they took me down for the operation the other day, I told Jesus before I left the room that if I came out of the operating room, He would have to do it and I told Him I was trusting Him to bring me through safely."

I said, "That is wonderful. Is there another time when you have trusted Christ?"

"Why, yes. A number of times."

"Could you tell me about another experience?"

"During the Depression," he said, "when people were out of work and jobs were hard to find, I went several weeks without a job. My family was hungry. We had nothing to eat. And one day when

I left the house, I prayed as I walked along the street, 'Lord, I'm not going back home today until You give me a job.' I meant that. And before the day was over I had a good job."

"That's wonderful. You have trusted Christ for your health, and it was given back to you. You have also trusted Christ for a job, and you got it. But now let me ask you this: Has there ever been a time when you prayed, 'Dear Lord Jesus, I am a sinner. And I owe a sin debt, but I believe You died on the cross to pay my sin debt. And I will trust You as my Saviour. And if I die, I will trust You to get me to Heaven'?" I waited for his response.

There was silence for a moment, before he said, "No. I've never trusted Him for that."

"Well, just like He gave you a job when you trusted Him, and just like He gave you health when you trusted Him, He will give you everlasting life if you will trust Him for that. Now would you pray with me and trust Him for salvation?"

He agreed. And with his hand in mine, he repeated a simple sinner's prayer telling Christ He would trust Him as His Saviour. The man was saved, and I took the Bible and led him to the assurance of salvation.

If any person will come to Christ and say, "I know You can save me: therefore, I trust in You completely," that person will not be turned away.

Charles Spurgeon told the story of a dog in his garden. "I threw a stick at the dog to run him away," said Spurgeon, "but the dog picked up the stick in his mouth and brought it to me, wagging his tail. Immediately," said Spurgeon, "he and I were friends. Because he trusted me, he conquered me."

Now one other thing about the Saviour's question. It was a reasonable question. I say it was reasonable because they had followed Him into the house. If they did not believe, then why did they pray, and why did they follow Him into the house?

Many of you have come here this morning without the Saviour. In a few moments I am going to ask you to trust Jesus Christ. And my question is reasonable. The fact that you came to church this morning indicates that you are interested. It shows that you have some concern. It is reasonable that I should ask you to trust Christ.

Now notice:

III. THE ANSWER THEY GAVE

"Jesus saith unto them, Believe ye that I am able to do this?" There was no hesitation in their answer—"Yea, Lord."

Everything depends upon the right answer to the question, "Do you believe that Jesus Christ is able to save you?"

Can you say, "Yes, Lord"?

There was no making of excuses. There was no putting it off. The answer was, "Yea, Lord."

Suppose someone offered you a million dollars. Would you say, "Well, I believe it's real money. And I know I need a million dollars, but I want to put it off awhile. I need to think about it"? Certainly not. You would accept it immediately. And if there were any reason you should not have the million dollars, you would be careful not to let others know about it.

Suppose a man is on death row awaiting execution, and one day someone walks in with a pardon and says, "I've got good news. In my hand I hold a pardon from the governor."

What would you think if the prisoner said, "Well, I know I need a pardon. And if I don't get a pardon, I'll be executed in a few days. To be honest, I would like to have a pardon, but I don't want to rush into it. Let me think about it awhile"? You would think the man crazy, and he would be. If a man were offered a pardon, he would jump at it.

When Jesus Christ offers to save all who will trust Him, I wonder that they do not jump at it. But in many cases rather than jumping at it, people began making excuses as to why they should not have a pardon and be justified and given everlasting life. The answer of the blind men was immediate.

Now finally notice:

IV. THE LORD'S RESPONSE TO THEIR ANSWER

"Then touched he their eyes, saying, According to your faith be it unto you. And their eyes were opened" (vss. 29,30). The Lord's response was immediate.

The moment a man trusts Jesus Christ, he has everlasting life. The believer is not put in a position to have everlasting life eventually, provided he meets other conditions. Everlasting life is a present possession. John 3:36: "He that believeth on the Son *hath* everlasting life. . . ." Salvation is instantaneous and complete.

The moment the blind men believed, they were healed. It makes no difference how deep you have gone into sin, nor how hard your case may seem to be—if you will trust Jesus Christ for salvation, you will have everlasting life the moment you believe.

'Twas grace that taught my heart to fear,
And grace my fears relieved;
How precious did that grace appear
The hour I first believed!

Trust Christ Now

You have read the sermon, "Two Blind Men Healed." They believed that Christ was able to meet their specific need, so they trusted Him and received their sight immediately.

If you have never trusted Jesus Christ as your personal Saviour, have never trusted Him for salvation and everlasting life, won't you believe that He is able now to meet your need? And, like the blind men, won't you say, "Yea, Lord, I believe"?

If you will trust Jesus Christ as your Saviour, pray this simple prayer: "Dear Lord Jesus, I know that I am a sinner. I need forgiveness and everlasting life. I do believe that You died for my sins. And the best I know how I do trust You as my Saviour. Now help me to live for You and to be a good Christian."

If you have prayed the above prayer, and you will trust Christ as Saviour, I have some free literature that I want to send you which will help you in your Christian life. Just write me:

Dr. Curtis Hutson
Sword of the Lord Foundation
P. O. Box 1099
Murfreesboro, Tennessee 37133

In your letter say, "I have read your sermon, 'Two Blind Men Healed.' I know that I am a sinner. I do believe that Jesus Christ died to pay my sin debt, and I am trusting Him as my personal Saviour.

"Please send me the free literature that will help me to live the Christian life."

Be sure to include your name and address.

Chapter 22

"By Grace Alone, Through Faith Alone"

"*For by grace are ye saved through faith; and that not of yourselves: it is the gift of God: Not of works, lest any man should boast.*"—Eph. 2:8,9.

"By grace alone, through faith alone," was the Reformers' motto in Zurich. That chorus, written by Bill Harvey, is printed inside the front cover of *Soul-Stirring Songs & Hymns*, published by the Sword of the Lord Publishers. "By grace alone, through faith alone" is also the Bible teaching regarding salvation. The Scripture says, "For by grace are ye saved through faith."

I. BY GRACE ALONE

The Bible teaches that men are saved by grace. Grace is the unmerited favor of God.

If you could gather in one great assembly a representative of every religion in the world and spend thousands of hours discussing the question, "What must I do to be saved?" in the final analysis, you would have only two doctrines regarding salvation: One, God saves man; two, man saves himself.

Those who teach the second doctrine say that man saves himself because of what he is, or because of what he does, or because of what he knows, or because of what he feels.

Man is not saved because of what he is. People have said to me, "I have been a Christian ever since I was born." But no one is a Christian until he is *born again*. It is impossible to inherit salvation. John 1:12,13 states, "But as many as received him, to them gave he power to become the sons of God, even to them that believe on his name: Which were born, not of blood. . . ."

"Not of blood" means that salvation doesn't come through the bloodline. One is not a Christian because his parents are or because his grandparents were. Men are born sinners. "The wicked are estranged from the womb: they go astray as soon as they be born, speaking lies" (Ps. 58:3). "Behold, I was shapen in iniquity; and in sin did my mother conceive me" (Ps. 51:5). Men are sinners by birth as well as by choice, having inherited their sin nature from their parents and they from their parents—all the way back to the first man, Adam. So the Bible declares in Romans 5:12, "Wherefore, as by one man sin entered into the world, and death by sin; and so death passed upon all men, for that all have sinned."

Not only does every man have a sin nature, but every man has committed sins. First John 1:10 says, "If we say that we have not sinned, we make him a liar." And Romans 3:23 states, "For all have sinned, and come short of the glory of God." If salvation were by character, then all would be lost because there are no perfect people.

Somewhere I read,

> There is so much good in the worst of us, and so much bad in the best of us, that it hardly behooves any of us to condemn the rest of us.

But according to John 3:18 we are already condemned: "He that believeth not is condemned already, because he hath not believed in the name of the only begotten Son of God."

Man is not saved because of what he is. Isaiah 64:6 states, "But we are all as an unclean thing, and all our righteousnesses are as filthy rags." Note carefully the teaching here: our righteousnesses are as filthy rags. Not our worst but our best is like dirty rags in the sight of God. God is so much holier than man that our best is like dirty rags in His sight. To hold our righteousness up before God would be like holding the brightest light known to man before the sun. With the brightness of the sun as a background, our brightest light would appear dark.

The only way a person can ever be righteous before God is to have the imputed righteousness of God Himself, which, according to Romans 3:22, is "by faith of Jesus Christ unto all and upon all them that believe."

Man is not saved because of what he does. That is, there is no salvation by works. Titus 3:5 says, "Not by works of righteousness which we have done, but according to his mercy he saved us." And our text says, "For by grace are ye saved through faith; and that not of yourselves: it is the gift of God: Not of works, lest any man should boast."

Some argue that the book of James teaches salvation by works, quoting James 2:24, "Ye see then how that by works a man is justified, and not by faith only." A good rule of thumb to follow in Bible interpretation is never use an obscure passage to contradict a number of clear ones.

For instance, Ephesians 2:8,9; Romans 5:1; Titus 3:5, and many other passages plainly teach that man is not saved by works.

When the Bible says in James 2:24 that man is justified by works, you must consider the context. Verse 18 of the same chapter states, "Yea, a man may say, Thou hast faith, and I have works: shew me thy faith without thy works, and I will shew thee my faith by my works."

Notice carefully the teaching here. James said, "*Shew me* thy faith without thy works, and I will *shew thee* my faith by my works." The believer can only demonstrate his faith to others by his works. Since faith is invisible, you cannot know whether I am trusting Christ as Saviour unless I show you by my works. So when the Bible speaks of being justified by works, it has reference to being justified before men, not before God. We are justified before God by faith, but we are justified before men by works.

Romans 5:1 says, "Therefore being justified by faith, we have peace with God through our Lord Jesus Christ." This is not a contradiction of James 2:24. Romans 5:1 speaks of being justified before God. James 2:24 speaks of being justified before men. Let me give an example.

When I was a small boy, there was a country store just down the street from the school I attended. It was operated by an elderly lady who lived alone. One night she was murdered and the store robbed. The evidence seemed to point to a certain individual in the community. He was arrested and after a long trial was acquitted by the jury. He never served time. He was justified in the sight of the law, but nearly everyone in our neighborhood thought the man was guilty.

I remember hearing men say to my father, "I don't know how he got out of it. Everybody knows he killed that woman." And to this day that man is not justified before the men in that community. Because of his behavior, some still think he is guilty of murder.

If a man worked for salvation, the motive behind the work would render it ineffective. First Corinthians 13 teaches that any service not motivated by love for Christ will not be rewarded at the judgment seat. If man worked to be saved, the motive would not be love but fear lest he should go to Hell.

Jesus said in Matthew 7:22,23,

"Many will say to me in that day, Lord, Lord, have we not prophesied in thy name? and in thy name have cast out devils? and in thy name done many wonderful works? And then will I profess unto them, I never knew you: depart from me, ye that work iniquity."

Here are men in judgment whose only claim for Heaven is their wonderful works. And Jesus says to them, "I never knew you: depart from me."

Works sometimes take the form of sacraments such as baptism or communion. It is sad that many are trusting the fact that they have been baptized to get them to Heaven. Baptism is not a saviour. I'm a Baptist. I believe in baptism; and when I was pastor, I baptized more converts than any pastor in the state of Georgia—baptizing converts every week for more than fourteen years. But baptism is not an instrument of salvation. What man needs is not form but faith. The person who is trusting his baptism is not fully trusting Jesus Christ, and there is absolutely no promise in the Bible to those who partially believe on the Lord Jesus Christ. One must believe completely, wholeheartedly, and without reservation. His only hope of Heaven must be Jesus. If it is Jesus—plus anything, then the plus becomes more important than Jesus in that one dies and goes to Hell for not having the plus, whatever it is.

Some think they are saved because they have received communion, but receiving Christ is not receiving communion; it is trusting Him as Saviour.

So the Bible plainly teaches in John 1:12, "But as many as received him, to them gave he power to become the sons of God, even to them that believe on his name." Receiving is believing.

Sometimes works take the form of reformation. Well-meaning evangelists and pastors have made men believe that if they quit their sinning they will be saved. Now I am for living right, I am for reforming, but I am not for reformation as an instrument of salvation.

Old Sam Jones, the Methodist evangelist, used to preach on "Quit your meanness." But a man is not saved by quitting his meanness. He is saved by trusting Jesus Christ as Saviour.

A saloonkeeper in Detroit heard Billy Sunday's sermon on booze, walked the aisle and said, "If I'm as mean as he says I am, then I am going to quit the business." But that did not make a Christian out of him.

A man said to Dr. Bob Jones, Sr., "Bob, just as soon as I get on my feet, I'm going to become a Christian." Dr. Bob wisely replied, "A man is not saved by getting on his feet; he is saved by getting on his face."

Remember this: you don't get better to get saved; you get saved to get better. You can't get better until you do get saved.

Nothing either great or small,
Nothing, sinner, no;
Jesus did it, did it all,
Long, long ago.

'Til to Jesus' cross you cling
By a simple faith;
Doing is a deadly thing,
Doing ends in death.

Cast your deadly doing down,
Down at Jesus' feet;
Trust in Him, in Him alone,
Stand glorious and complete.

Man is not saved by what he knows. Salvation does not come wrapped in a diploma. I am for education. One should get all the education possible in line with his calling. But I would as soon trust my sins to get me to Heaven as to trust my education. Christianity is not culture. The Bible does not say, "He that knoweth hath everlasting life" but ". . . he that believeth." The promise in John 3:36 is, "He that believeth on the Son hath everlasting life." You go to Heaven heart first, not head first.

Man is not saved because of what he feels. Faith must never be confused with feelings. Many a man has died and gone to Hell waiting on a feeling. I have had hundreds say to me, "Not yet; I don't have the right feeling." One does not have to have any feeling to accept an invitation. And the sweet invitation in the Bible is, "Come unto me, all ye that labour and are heavy laden, and I will give you rest" (Matt. 11:28). He didn't say, "Come if you have a certain feeling"; only, "Come." Feelings are not the basis of what we believe; they are the result of it.

Elmer Johnson received a telegram: "Mother passed away. Funeral Wednesday. Signed, Bill." Very upset, Elmer rushed to his mother's home; but to his surprise she greeted him at the door. He couldn't understand. His brother Bill was still at home with his mother, and Elmer thought the telegram was from him. Later he learned that the note was from a friend named Bill.

Now Elmer Johnson's feeling did not change the fact. When he first read the note, he thought his own mother had died. But his feelings had nothing to do with the fact. The fact was, she was still alive.

That is why I say feelings are not the basis of what we believe; they are the result of it. I feel good, but I don't know I'm saved because I feel good; I know it because the Bible says so, and I feel good because I know I am saved.

As I mentioned earlier, in the final analysis there are only two doctrines regarding salvation: either God saves man, or man saves himself. But we have seen that man does not save himself because of what he is, because of what he does, because of what he knows, or because of what he feels. If man doesn't save himself, then God saves him.

The Bible plainly teaches that only God can save a man, and that man's only part in salvation is described in the Bible word "believe." Salvation is not by a mixture of grace and works. It is either by grace or by works. Romans 11:6 says, "And if by grace, then is it no more of works: otherwise grace is no more grace. But if it be of works, then is it no more grace: otherwise work is no more work."

Salvation is either a gift or it is earned, and Romans 6:23 makes it plain that it is a gift: ". . . but the gift of God is eternal life through Jesus Christ our Lord." So does John 3:16: "For God so loved the world, that he gave his only begotten Son." Jesus said to the woman at the well in John 4:10, "If thou knewest the gift of God, and who it is that saith to thee, Give me to drink; thou wouldest have asked of him, and he would have given thee living water."

II. BY FAITH ALONE

"For by grace are ye saved through faith; and that not of yourselves: it is the gift of God: Not of works, lest any man should boast."—Eph. 2:8,9.

Notice the teaching here: by grace through faith. God has already done His part when He allowed Jesus Christ to die on the cross in our place to pay our sin debt. Titus 2:11 states, "For the grace of God that bringeth salvation hath appeared to all men." The grace of God brought salvation, but Jesus Christ must be received by faith.

Our Lord divides the world into two groups—believers and unbelievers. In John 3:36 He said, "He that believeth on the Son hath everlasting life: and he that believeth not the Son shall not see life; but the wrath of God abideth on him." So each of us is a believer or an unbeliever in God's Son. The believer has everlasting life—that is the promise of God. The unbeliever "shall not see life; but the wrath of God abideth on him"—that is the warning of God.

In John 3:18 Jesus said, "He that believeth on him is not condemned: but he that believeth not is condemned already, because he hath not believed in the name of the only begotten Son of God." The believer is not condemned, is not under sentence. The sentence has been lifted. The unbeliever is condemned already. He is not going to be condemned at some future judgment because he could not live up to certain standards or because of certain sins in his life; he is condemned already because "he hath not believed in the name of the only begotten Son of God."

Verse after verse after verse says that man is saved by believing, by faith alone. John 3:16, "For God so loved the world, that he gave his only begotten Son, that whosoever believeth in him should not perish, but have everlasting life." John 3:14,15, "And as Moses lifted up the serpent in the wilderness, even so must the Son of man be lifted up: That whosoever believeth in him should not perish, but have eternal life." And Mark 16:16 warns, "He that believeth not shall be damned." In the words of Galatians 3:26, "For ye are all the children of God by faith in Christ Jesus."

The problem is with the word "believe." The Bible word means more than giving mental assent to a fact. "Believe" means to trust, to depend on, to rely on. The person who is depending on Jesus Christ, Him alone and nothing else, has everlasting life, according to the plain promise in the Bible. And he that does not believe, does not depend, does not rely on Christ "shall not see life; but the wrath of God abideth on him."

The person who preaches like this is sometimes accused of teaching "easy believism." Easy believism is not a Bible expression but an invention by men. The truth is, it is not easy to get one to believe on Christ. It is difficult for a man to fully trust Jesus Christ and nothing else for salvation. It was not easy for me to put the matter of my salvation into His hands and rely totally on Him for a home in Heaven. If you think it is easy, try getting a Catholic to stop trusting his church and the sacraments for salvation. If you think it is easy to get a man to believe on Christ, try to get a Church of Christ man to stop trusting his baptism and trust only in Jesus. If you think it is easy, try to get the man who is working for salvation to stop trusting his works and rely totally on Jesus Christ. Easy believism? There is no such thing.

Salvation is by grace alone, through faith alone.

But what about repentance? Repentance is not a separate act from believing. It is included in the Bible word "believe." When Nicodemus asked in John 3:4, "How can a man be born when he is old? can he enter the second time into his mother's womb, and be born?" Jesus told him plainly how to be born again. In verses 14 and 15 He said, "As Moses lifted up the serpent in the wilderness, even so must the Son of man be lifted up: That whosoever believeth in him should not perish, but have eternal life." And He continued in verse 16, "For God so loved the world, that he gave his only begotten Son, that whosoever believeth in him should not perish, but have everlasting life." In verse 18 He said, "He that believeth on him is not condemned." In verse 36 He said, "He that believeth on the Son hath everlasting life."

Since Jesus did not use the words "repent" or "repentance" in His conversation with Nicodemus, we must conclude one of three things: repentance is not necessary to salvation or Jesus didn't really give the clear plan of salvation to Nicodemus or repentance is necessary to salvation and is included in the word "believe" which Jesus did use. I conclude that repentance is necessary to salvation, but it is included in the word "believe," found 99 times in the Gospel of John.

The problem with repentance is that some people teach it as reformation. But repentance is a change of mind, not reformation; and it is included in "believe."

Now I am for living right. I am for getting better. But you don't get better to get saved. You trust Christ to get saved, then He helps you to get better.

What about confession? Doesn't the Bible teach that in order for a man to be saved, he must confess his sins? No, that is not in the Bible. When the jailer asked Paul and Silas, "Sirs, what must I do to be saved?" they replied in Acts 16:31, "Believe on the Lord Jesus Christ, and thou shalt be saved." A man cannot be saved without realizing that he is a sinner, but confessing that you are a sinner and confessing sins are two different things.

Suppose a seventy-year-old man came to trust Christ as Saviour. If I say to him, "Confess your sins and you may be saved," the poor man would be in trouble. He can't remember all the sins he has committed, so how can he confess them? He may confess that he is a sinner. He may say, "Dear Lord, I know I'm a sinner. I do believe You died for me. I trust You as my Saviour." But confessing that he is a sinner and confessing his sins are not the same.

The Bible does say in I John 1:9, "If we confess our sins, he is faithful and just to forgive us our sins, and to cleanse us from all unrighteousness." But note here the word "we" which refers to

Christians. All five chapters and all 105 verses in this epistle are written to believers.

First John 5:13 states, "These things have I written unto you that believe on the name of the Son of God. . . ." If the Christian sins, the way to obtain forgiveness and cleansing is by confession. The promise to believers is, "If we confess our sins, he is faithful and just to forgive us our sins, and to cleanse us from all unrighteousness."

Salvation is by grace alone, through faith alone. One must trust Jesus Christ completely in order to be saved. You cannot trust Jesus Christ 95% and something else 5%. You must trust Jesus Christ and Him alone 100%.

Will You Trust Christ Now?

If you will trust Him as your Saviour and write to tell me so, I have some free literature I want to send that will help you as you set out to live the Christian life. All you need do to receive your free literature is mail a letter to me:

Dr. Curtis Hutson
Sword of the Lord Foundation
P. O. Box 1099
Murfreesboro, Tennessee 37133

In your letter say, "I have read your sermon, 'By Grace Alone, Through Faith Alone.' I know that I'm a sinner and do believe that Jesus Christ died for me. I realize I cannot earn salvation by anything that I do, so here and now I trust Him completely as my Saviour. I am fully relying on Him to take me to Heaven when I die. Please send me the free literature that will help me as I set out to live the Christian life."

Then be sure you give your name and full address.

Chapter 23

"Forgiveness...According to the Riches of His Grace"

"Paul, an apostle of Jesus Christ by the will of God, to the saints which are at Ephesus, and to the faithful in Christ Jesus: Grace be to you, and peace, from God our Father, and from the Lord Jesus Christ. Blessed be the God and Father of our Lord Jesus Christ, who hath blessed us with all spiritual blessings in heavenly places in Christ: According as he hath chosen us in him before the foundation of the world, that we should be holy and without blame before him in love: Having predestinated us unto the adoption of children by Jesus Christ to himself, according to the good pleasure of his will, To the praise of the glory of his grace, wherein he hath made us accepted in the beloved. In whom we have redemption through his blood, the forgiveness of sins, according to the riches of his grace; Wherein he hath abounded toward us in all wisdom and prudence; Having made known unto us the mystery of his will, according to his good pleasure which he hath purposed in himself: That in the dispensation of the fullness of times he might gather together in one all things in Christ, both which are in heaven, and which are on earth; even in him: In whom also we have obtained an inheritance, being predestinated according to the purpose of him who worketh all things after the counsel of his own will: That we should be to the praise of his glory, who first trusted in Christ. In whom ye also trusted, after that ye heard the word of truth, the

gospel of your salvation: in whom also after that ye believed, ye were sealed with that holy Spirit of promise, Which is the earnest of our inheritance until the redemption of the purchased possession, unto the praise of his glory. —Eph. 1:1-14.

I call your attention to an expression in verse 7: "In whom we have redemption through his blood, the forgiveness of sins, *according to the riches of his grace.*"

I think sometimes we read verses over and over, yet fail to grasp the real meaning. They sound good to us, but if we are asked to explain them, we can't.

Martin Luther was walking the floor, greatly distressed over his sins. A godly old man asked him, "Didst thou not say in the creed this morning, 'I believe in the forgiveness of sins'?"

"Yes," answered Martin Luther.

But Mr. Luther, though he said every morning, *I believe in the forgiveness of sins,* had not grasped the meaning of the statement.

There is not a person who does not need to have his sins forgiven. Even after we are saved, we need continual forgiveness and cleansing.

I have sinned since I have been saved. I wish I hadn't. God knows I wish I were perfect, but I sure find comfort in I John 1:9, "If we confess our sins, he is faithful and just to forgive us our sins, and to cleanse us from all unrighteousness."

A man in New York was a wicked sinner, but before he died he trusted Jesus Christ as Saviour. On his tombstone, along with his name, the date of his birth, and the date of his death, is one word, "FORGIVEN."

I have read that the word "forgiveness" means "to bear the burden." If someone owed you $1,000 and you forgave the debt, it simply means you bore the burden of his debt. Jesus Christ can forgive because He has borne the burden. He bore our sins in His own body. He died on a cross in our place. He suffered Hell; He paid the debt. And in Him "we have redemption through his blood, the forgiveness of sins, according to the riches of his grace."

Three things I would like to cover in this message. First,

I. THE MEASURE OF FORGIVENESS

The measure of forgiveness is found in the expression, "according to the riches of his grace."

We have our own ideas about the measure of forgiveness, but here the Bible says, "In whom we have redemption through his blood, the forgiveness of sins, according to the riches of his grace."

1. Not According to the Character of the Offender

Forgiveness is not according to the character of the offender, but according to the character of the offended one.

Many believe that forgiveness is based upon character, that one must live a moral life to obtain forgiveness. That is not true. Forgiveness is based upon the character of the one who is offended. Only the offended one can forgive. It is "according to the riches of his grace" that you have forgiveness, not according to your character.

God has forgiven some awfully bad characters. One example is the Apostle Paul. Before his conversion, he persecuted the church and was responsible for the death of many Christians.

If it is "according to the riches of his grace," then it is not how big or how little the sin may be. We talk of little sins and big sins, but, in reality, there are no such things. It is impossible to measure the wickedness of one single sin, no matter how small it is. The idea is not what you have done but what you have left undone. In the final analysis, people do not go to Hell because they live sinful lives but because they will not receive Jesus Christ as Saviour. The Holy Spirit convicts of sin, the Bible says, "because they believe not on me" (John 16:9).

Sin was settled at Calvary 2,000 years ago when Jesus died for our sins. No matter how deeply you have gone into sin, the measure of forgiveness is not according to how many sins you may or may not have committed but "according to the riches of his grace." It is not according to the character of the offender but according to the character of the One who has been offended.

Let me illustrate.

I have known people to ask forgiveness for what I thought was a slight offense, and the person offended puffed up and said, "Well, you shouldn't have done that. I guess I'll forgive you, but I want you to know I'll never forget it."

On the other hand, I have seen people terribly wronged but, when asked to forgive, their response was altogether different. They looked so tenderly and said, maybe with a tear rolling down their cheeks, "You are already forgiven. You didn't have to ask me to forgive you; you know I will." The difference was in the offended one. Our likelihood of being forgiven is not based upon our character but upon the character of the one offended.

Your offense is not against the preacher, not against the deacon board, not against the Baptist church, not against the neighbors, but against God. In Psalm 51:4 David said, "Against thee, thee only, have I sinned, and done this evil in thy sight." Your offense is against God, not against man. And the only One who can forgive and justify you is God Himself.

Let us look at the offended One.

The Bible says in Ephesians 2:4, "But God, who is rich in mercy, for his great love wherewith he loved us. . . ." Notice that expression, "God, who is rich in mercy." Now, the Bible could have said, "God, who is rich in real estate"—since He owns the whole world: "The earth is the Lord's, and the fulness thereof" (Ps. 24:1). It could have said, "God, who is rich in beefsteak"—the cattle on a thousand hills are His. It could have said, "God, who is rich in gold"—He knows where the yet undiscovered gold is. It all belongs to Him. God is rich in real estate and in wealth. He owns everything!

But the Holy Spirit chose to talk about His riches in another direction. The Bible doesn't say, "God, who is rich in real estate. . . beefsteak. . . gold. . . silver. . . precious stones"; it says, "God, who is rich in mercy." He has a wealth of mercy! And He is the One I have offended.

If our forgiveness depended upon human beings, we might never have been forgiven. God is the offended One, and the measure of forgiveness is "according to the riches of his grace." Psalm 103:8 says, "The Lord is merciful and gracious, slow to anger, and plenteous in mercy." Psalm 145:8 states, "The Lord is gracious, and full of compassion; slow to anger, and of great mercy." "Slow to anger."

He is not like some folks I know who fly off the handle at the drop of a hat! He is not standing over you with a big stick waiting for you to make one mistake so He can send you to Hell. God is slow to anger and plenteous in mercy. If He weren't, we would all be in Hell today.

Psalm 100:5 says, "The Lord is good; his mercy is everlasting."

He is not like the woman who befriended the tramp who came to her door and asked for something to eat. She gave him a biscuit and a piece of ham. The tramp got out to the road, opened the little bag, saw the biscuit and threw it into the ditch. The woman cursed and said, "I'll tell you one thing, I'll never give another tramp a crumb! He can starve to death." One moment she was kind; minutes later, her kindness was gone. God is not like that. His mercy is everlasting. If the pardon were according to our character, we would never be pardoned.

Spurgeon once said,

If it should come to pass
That sheep of God could fall away;
Alas, my fickle, feeble soul
Would fall ten thousand times a day!

If it is according to the riches of His grace, then the worst of sinners should be encouraged. It is not according to our concept of God's grace but according to God's grace itself. Some men have a poor concept of the grace of God.

I used to work for a loan company. If a bill weren't paid on the due date, there was a so-called five-day "grace" period. But it certainly wasn't grace, because they added a late charge for every day the payment was late. If the bill wasn't paid by the end of five days, they came to see you. And after a few more days, they would pick up the goods and haul them away. That is not grace. Grace is not limited to a period of time.

I'm afraid we are guilty of measuring God's corn in our bushel. We judge God to act like we would act in the same situation, but God's ways are as high above our ways as the heavens are above the earth. When our patience wears out, God is still patient and loving.

Do you know why Methuselah lived so long? You say, "He ate well." Maybe so, but that is not why he lived long. The name "Methuselah" means "when he is dead it shall be sent." The year Methuselah died the Flood came. God was not anxious to pour out wrath on Noah's world. He wasn't anxious to flood the world and destroy all mankind! God wanted to wait and wait and wait; and so He said, "When he is dead, it shall be sent."

God stretched out Methuselah's years to 969; and he lived to be the oldest man in the world—not because he was in good health, but because there is a longsuffering God who is extraordinarily patient and whose grace far exceeds most ideas about it!

We conceive hard things of God. Our ideas of God's mercy are narrow. We sometimes feel that extreme wickedness vanquishes God's grace. How many of you know someone who is very wicked and lives an awful life, yet you never think about witnessing to him? You think he is too mean to be saved! "We can win a little girl much easier than an old drunkard" is an indication of our concept of God's grace.

The Bible says in Romans 5:20, "Where sin abounded, grace did much more abound." "Abound" means more than enough. Where there was more than enough sin, there was more than enough grace.

G-R-A-C-E

God's
Riches
At
Christ's
Expense.

2. Not According to Sins Committed

If the measure of forgiveness is "according to the riches of his grace," then it is not according to the number of sins committed by the individual. God has no problem forgiving sin. He doesn't see a dope addict, a drunkard, a harlot, or somebody else who is down in the depths of sin and say, "I'll have to work on this one!" No! God can save the dirtiest sinner as easily as the moral, pure, innocent five-year-old child; because 2,000 years ago He took the sin of all the world—the sin of the liar, the drunkard, the harlot, the dope addict, etc.—and placed it on Jesus Christ, then punished Him in our place. "While we were yet sinners, Christ died for us" (Rom. 5:8).

There is no adjective before the noun in that verse. Jesus didn't come to save *good* sinners, *fair* sinners, *vile* sinners, or any other special group of sinners; He came to save *sinners*. If you are included in "sinners," you qualify for salvation.

If forgiveness is "according to the riches of his grace," then it is not according to the number of sins I have committed.

You say, "But, Dr. Hutson, you don't know what I have done!

You don't know the horribleness of my sins!" It makes no difference. I know the grace of the One you sinned against, and that is what determines your forgiveness.

If there is someone here this morning who thinks he has gone to such an extreme that God can't forgive him, then here is an encouragement: "...the forgiveness of sins, according to the riches of his grace." Never forget that. When you think of Dr. Hutson, I want you to think, "According to the riches of his grace"! Not my grace—His grace. You see, no matter how bad the sin, God will forgive you "according to the riches of his grace."

We read in Matthew 12:31, "Wherefore I say unto you, All manner of sin and blasphemy shall be forgiven unto men: but the blasphemy against the Holy Ghost shall not be forgiven unto men." God says, "All manner of sin...shall be forgiven." Why? Because it is "according to the riches of his grace."

You say, "But wait a minute. You said *except* the blasphemy against the Holy Spirit."

Yes, but the only reason He doesn't forgive that is because the person who commits it does not seek forgiveness.

That is the greatest thing I ever heard! "In whom we have redemption through his blood, the forgiveness of sins, according to the riches of his grace."

3. Not According to the Lapse of Time

You cannot bind the reach of grace with the lapse of years. The text does not say that forgiveness of sin is according to such and such a time of life but "according to the riches of his grace."

It is a blessed thing to come to Christ when one is young. I praise the living God I was saved when I was eleven years old! However, if you have waited until you are sixty or seventy years old; if gray hair covers your head and time has plowed furrows in your brow; if you walk now with a feeble limp, if your eyesight is dim, and you are going down the other side of the hill, still you are not beyond forgiveness. It is not according to the lapse of time but "according to the riches of his grace."

I received a call in the middle of the night, and a lady said, "My sister is dying. Please rush to the hospital and see if you can win her to Christ."

I dressed and rushed to the hospital. When I arrived, the woman was under an oxygen tent and looked to me as if she were already dead. Reaching under the tent I touched her arm. It was cold, and my fingers made a dent in her flesh. I said, "The lady is already dead." The nurse assured me she was still alive.

I tried to talk to her, but she could not speak. I prayed silently, "Dear God, this woman is dying and going to Hell! Her sister is out in the hall praying for her to be saved. At least let me communicate with her."

I said, "Mrs. ________, if you can hear me, wiggle your finger." She wiggled her index finger.

I went through the plan of salvation, explaining that we are all sinners. I asked if she understood what I was saying. Again she wiggled her finger to let me know she did.

I then explained that as sinners we owe a penalty and that penalty is the second death, the lake of fire. I asked her to wiggle her finger if she understood that. She did.

I told her that Jesus Christ died on the cross, bore our sins in His own body, suffered our Hell, and paid our sin debt. I told her to wiggle her finger if she understood that and believed it. Again she wiggled her finger.

After I had explained how we are saved by grace through faith in the finished work of Jesus, I asked, "Will you trust Jesus Christ as your Saviour and rely on Him to take you to Heaven?" She died, wiggling her finger as I held her hand.

The thief on the cross was not baptized, he never gave a tithe, he never dedicated his life to Christ, he never won a soul. He prayed, "Lord, remember me when thou comest into thy kingdom," and Jesus stopped dying long enough to say, "To day shalt thou be with me in paradise."

Forgiveness is not according to the lapse of time but "according to the riches of his grace."

4. Not According to Our Remorse

It is not according to the bitterness and sorrow we feel in our hearts.

When I was small, I thought I had to tender the heart of God with my tears. I thought if I wept enough, felt badly enough in my heart, and agonized over my sin, God would forgive me. But God had already sent His Son to die on the cross for my sins. He is not a hardhearted bully, and our salty tears cannot soften His already tender heart. Forgiveness is not according to our bitterness, remorse, agony, and sorrow of heart; it is "according to the riches of his grace."

I know a boy eleven years old who prayed three hours before he was saved, but he didn't need to; because when he finished praying, he was saved by grace through faith in the finished work of Jesus.

It is not necessary to talk God into doing something He has already done. He wants to forgive me more than I want forgiveness. He showed the initiative, not me. He sent His Son before I was born. God wants me in Heaven more than I want to go to Heaven.

When Adam sinned, it was God who came to the Garden and said, "Adam...where art thou?" God didn't hide and say, "Find Me, Adam, if you can." Adam didn't beg, "O God, please, where are You!" No, it was God who came and said, "Adam, where are you?"

If it had not been for God's sending His Son to die on the cross, I would be in Hell—and so would you. It is not necessary to have heart failure before God will forgive you. He has already paid the sin debt. It is a gift. You either receive a gift or reject it. Everything you have you got one of three ways: you stole it, you earned it, or somebody gave it to you.

That is true of Heaven: you can't earn it. If you worked ten billion years, you couldn't buy one doorknob in Heaven, let alone one block of golden streets. If you could live 53,000 lifetimes, you couldn't buy one stone in the foundation. Jesus said, "It is finished." Why don't you believe Him and quit working for it and start trusting Him?

Forgiveness is "according to the riches of his grace." It is not according to how I feel in my heart, not according to my agonizing, nor how many tears I shed, but "according to the riches of his grace."

5. Not According to the Strength of One's Faith

If it is "according to the riches of his grace," it is not according to the strength of my faith. How many poor sinners have said to me, "I just don't think I have enough faith."

Tell me where the Bible says, "He that believeth MUCH on Jesus Christ shall be saved." The Scripture simply says, "Believe on the Lord Jesus Christ, and thou shalt be saved." Where does it say you have to have so much faith to be saved? It just says, "Believe."

When they placed the brazen serpent on the pole, Moses said, "Look and live." He didn't say, "If you have 20/20 vision, look and live." One could have said, "Well, turn my head toward it; I can't see very good!" and he would have been cured.

If you have very small faith and put it in Christ, you can get a great big salvation! It is not according to the strength of man's faith; it is "according to the riches of his grace."

A man was putting gasoline in an automobile while smoking a cigarette. A preacher was witnessing to him, trying to get him to trust Christ as Saviour. The man said, "Preacher, I would give the world if I had your faith." The preacher backed away and said, "I would give the world if I had yours!"

You see, he had more faith than the preacher, because the preacher was afraid to stand nearby as the man pumped gasoline while smoking a cigarette.

The question is not whether you have faith, but *where* is your faith? Jesus said to the disciples who thought the ship was going to sink, "Where is your faith?" It wasn't an absence of faith but a matter of misplaced faith. "In what are you trusting? Are you trusting this boat? Are you trusting your ability as sailors? What are you trusting? Where is your faith?"

So I ask you, "Where is your faith? What are you trusting to get you to Heaven?" If you put your faith in Jesus and what He did on the cross, you will go to Heaven when you die.

When you board a jet plane, you put your faith in the plane; they close the doors, and you are on your way. Even if you get up there and misbehave, you are still on your way. Salvation is not a matter of behaving; it is a matter of believing. Your testimony is a matter of behaving; salvation is a matter of believing.

You say, "Don't you believe in living right?"

I sure do, and I try to live right; but I would as soon trust my sins to get me to Heaven as to trust my righteousness. I would get there just as fast on my sins as I would on my righteousness, because all my righteousnesses are as filthy rags (Isa. 64:6).

A little faith will get you a big Saviour!

Forgiveness is not according to what I am or what I have done but "according to the riches of his grace."

Now, a brief word about

II. THE MANNER OF FORGIVENESS

It is absolutely F-R-E-E, "according to the riches of his grace." According to the riches of His free favor. It is free! Anybody can have it.

Forgiveness, like love, is unpurchasable. You can't buy love; you can't buy forgiveness. Then why should not everyone be forgiven? It is free. Why can't we go downtown and win the dope addicts, if everybody can be saved? Why don't we get the drunkards saved? We are all fallen creatures and everyone needs forgiveness.

A fellow was filling out his driver's license application. One of the questions was, "Have you ever been given a ticket?" He wrote, "No." The next question was, "Please explain." He wrote, "Nobody ever caught me."

The reason most of us have not been arrested is nobody ever caught us. We have certainly offended.

The manner of forgiveness—FREE. That suggests how easy it is for God to pardon. When you and I forgive, we have to pause and calculate to see if we can afford it. God doesn't have to do that. If He forgave nobody, He would be none the richer; and if He forgave everybody, He would be none the poorer.

We talk about God's being infinite. If I got ten billion dollars from God tomorrow, He wouldn't have any less than He did when He started giving. And if He forgave every sinner who ever lived for the most wicked sins ever committed, He would be none the poorer. He is infinite. His mercy is measureless. You can't say, *Well, He has forgiven so many, He is running out of mercy!* Oh, no! He is rich in mercy. You can't measure it. It is easy for God to forgive. You don't have to extract forgiveness from His clenched fist; God is more ready to forgive than we are to be forgiven.

When the prodigal son came home, who had the most joy? The father's joy was greater! It was he who stood on the front porch looking through binoculars of love to see the prodigal afar off. It was the father who anticipated the return by stalling that little calf and having it fattened. Every day he would go out and brush the calf, pour some corn into the trough and say, "My son is going to come home one of these days, and we are going to have a celebration!" And when the son came home, it was the father who called in the neighbors. Maybe the prodigal son was expecting to get a beating, but the father said, 'Go get the fatted calf and kill it. Get a robe and put it on him. Put a ring on his finger and shoes on his feet. Call in the musicians and let us have some music and dance and sing and be merry, because this my son was dead and is alive!'

God only kills the fatted calf one time for you; but every time you lead a sinner to Christ, He kills another fatted calf; and you can eat again. That is why I like soul winning; you can get in on the feast every time a sinner is saved.

Then, too, the manner, if it is "according to the riches of his grace," unquestionably means fullness. There is no limit.

Mercy there was great, and grace was free;
Pardon there was multiplied to me.

It also implies an irreversible certainty. If God forgave me, then condemned me afterwards, it would not be "according to the riches of his grace" but according to something I had done.

I believe in eternal security. It is an irreversible pardon. When you are forgiven, you are forgiven.

This fountain from guilt not only makes pure
And gives the believer an infallible cure,
But if guilt removed return and remain
Its pow'r must be proved again and again—

and again, and again, and again.

Now in closing, a word about

III. THE MEDIUM OF FORGIVENESS

"In *whom* we have. . .forgiveness of sins, according to the riches of his grace." The medium of forgiveness is Jesus Christ. There is no forgiveness outside of Him. Forgiveness of sin comes to us entirely through Christ. It is not through the church, not through the priest, not through ordinances, not through rituals.

Forgiveness comes only through Jesus Christ, and it is a present forgiveness.

The text says we *have* it: "In whom *we have*. . . ." It is not something we hope to get when we arrive in Heaven; we have it now! I am just as forgiven now as I will be when I get to Heaven. I could not be any more certain of Heaven if I were already in Heaven, because I already have forgiveness. "Being *now* justified by his blood. . ." (Rom. 5:8). "We have. . .forgiveness of sins. . . ." We are not going to get it, but we have it now. "In whom *we have* redemption through his blood, the forgiveness of sins, according to the riches of his grace." As many as come to Jesus Christ and trust Him, have it. It can be yours this moment, and you can know it.

In Pennsylvania in 1829, George Wilson was sentenced to die for robbing the mails and for murder. President Andrew Jackson issued a pardon for George Wilson. The pardon was taken to him, but he refused it. The court had to decide whether he was actually pardoned and could go free. The President issued the pardon, but George Wilson refused it. Was he pardoned or not?

Chief Justice John Marshall gave this ruling: a pardon is a piece of paper, the value of which depends upon the acceptance by the person implicated. If he does not accept the pardon, then he must be executed even though the President has given him a pardon.

I want to say to you that God's pardon is also a piece of paper (John 3:16; Eph. 1:7), the value of which depends upon its acceptance by the person implicated. The person implicated is "whosoever." Rejected, there is no pardon; accepted, there is pardon. "In whom we have. . .forgiveness. . .according to the riches of his grace."

Make Sure Today

You have just read my sermon, "Forgiveness. . .According to the Riches of His Grace." If you are not certain that you have trusted Christ as Saviour and are going to Heaven when you die, let me urge you to accept God's free pardon today. If you will admit that you are a sinner, and, believing that Jesus Christ died for you, trust Him completely for your salvation, God promises everlasting life. "For God so loved the world, that he gave his only begotten Son, that whosoever believeth in him should not perish, but have everlasting life" (John 3:16).

If you want forgiveness, then pray the following prayer:

> Dear Lord, I know I'm a sinner. I do believe that You died for me, and the best I know how I do trust You as my Saviour and depend on You for full forgiveness. From this moment on, I am trusting You to take me to Heaven when I die. Amen.

If you prayed that simple prayer, or prayed in your own words and told the Lord you would trust Him, then write to me so we may rejoice with you. I have some free literature I want to send that will help you as you set out to live the Christian life. All you need do to receive your free literature is write to me at the address below.

Dr. Curtis Hutson
Sword of the Lord Foundation
P. O. Box 1099
Murfreesboro, Tennessee 37133

In your letter say, "I have read your sermon, 'Forgiveness . . . According to the Riches of His Grace.' I do believe that Jesus Christ died for me, and here and now I trust Him for my forgiveness and salvation. Please send me the free literature that will help me as I set out to live the Christian life."

Be sure to include your name and address.

Chapter 24

Salvation for All Men

"For God so loved the world, that he gave his only begotten Son, that whosoever believeth in him should not perish, but have everlasting life. For God sent not his Son into the world to condemn the world; but that the world through him might be saved." —John 3:16,17.

"All we like sheep have gone astray; we have turned every one to his own way; and the Lord hath laid on him the iniquity of us all." —Isa. 53:6.

"He that spared not his own Son, but delivered him up for us all, how shall he not with him also freely give us all things?" —Rom. 8:32.

"Who will have all men to be saved, and to come unto the knowledge of the truth." —I Tim. 2:4.

"Nevertheless I tell you the truth; It is expedient for you that I go away: for if I go not away, the Comforter will not come unto you; but if I depart, I will send him unto you. And when he is come, he will reprove the world of sin, and of righteousness, and of judgment." —John 16:7,8.

The last invitation in the Bible:

"And the Spirit and the bride say, Come. And let him that heareth

say, Come. And let him that is athirst come. And whosoever will, let him take the water of life freely."—Rev. 22:17.

One of the most wonderful doctrines in the Bible is the doctrine of salvation—how men are to be saved. On any basic, fundamental teaching, Satan tries to get one to either go beyond the truth or stop short of it. To go beyond truth is just as much a lie as to stop short of truth.

I want to know exactly what the Bible teaches on every subject—not what someone thinks about it but what the Bible says.

It is reasonable to believe that in the matter of salvation Satan is more determined to confuse the minds of people than in any other matter, because salvation is the most important thing in a person's life. If you are not saved, nothing else really matters. No matter how many churches you join, no matter how good you live, no matter how healthy you are and how much money you have, if you are not saved, then nothing else really matters. The most important thing is knowing Jesus Christ as Saviour.

It is assumed by some that there are two basic beliefs concerning salvation: One is referred to as the Arminian belief and the other as the Calvinistic belief. When asked, "Are you an Arminian or a Calvinist?" I was very careful not to answer yes or no because I really wasn't sure, for I agreed with both some things taught by the people who held the Arminian view and some things taught by those who held the Calvinistic view.

The Calvinistic view has five basic points that I share with you by way of introduction before speaking on "Salvation for All Men." To help you remember the points, Bible teachers have used the word TULIP through the years. Each letter stands for one point of the Calvinistic doctrine.

T—total depravity. By total depravity, Calvin meant total inability. No man is able to be saved apart from Christ. But Calvin meant more than that. He meant no man is able to believe on Christ without God giving him that enablement: God enables some to believe and does not enable others to believe. He meant that God literally overpowers a man and makes him able or He does not overpower him and leaves him unable. That is what total inability means.

U—unconditional election. By this Calvin meant that God elects some to be saved and predestines others to be lost. Without taking into consideration the person, his will or anything else, God says, "I will elect that man to be saved and this man to be lost." That is unconditional election.

L—limited atonement. By this Calvin meant that Jesus Christ did not die for all men and His death on the cross did not atone for the sins of all the world. He meant that Christ's death on the cross atoned only for the sins of the so-called elect and that only the men whose sins were atoned for by the death of Christ would be saved.

I—irresistible grace. By this Calvin meant there is no need to encourage someone to believe on the Lord Jesus and be saved. There is no need for personal soul winning and an effort on our part to try to persuade men to trust Jesus as Saviour; because when God gets ready to save him, that irresistible grace will overpower him and he cannot resist being saved. A multiplicity of verses contradicts such teaching, such as:

"When I called, ye did not answer."—Isa. 65:12.

"How often would I have gathered thy children together, as a hen doth gather her brood under her wings, and ye would not!"—Luke 13:34.

"Ye will not come to me, that ye might have life."—John 5:40.

That doesn't sound like irresistible grace. It sounds like you can say no to the Lord or you can say yes.

P—perseverance of the saints. Here Calvin meant one must endure to the end to be saved and that those who are elected before the foundation of the world will endure until the end. They will persevere and finally be saved.

With that in mind, let us look briefly at what the Bible teaches on salvation for all men.

I. JESUS IS SAVIOUR OF THE WHOLE WORLD

In the first place, Jesus Christ is the Saviour of the whole world. John, chapter 4, records the story of Jesus' stopping by the well. A woman who had been married five times was there; and when Jesus asked her for a drink of water, she replied, "How is it that thou, being a Jew, askest drink of me, which am a woman of

Samaria? for the Jews have no dealings with the Samaritans."

The conversation continued, with Jesus telling her about the Living Water; if she would ask for it, she could have it. She did ask for and did receive the Living Water. She went into town and said, "Come, see a man, which told me all things that ever I did: is not this the Christ?" And when the Samaritans came out from town to see Christ, they said, "This is indeed the Christ, **the Saviour of the world"** (vs. 42).

In I John 4:14 the Bible says, "We have seen and do testify that the Father sent the Son to be the Saviour of the world." In I Timothy 4:10 we read that He "is the Saviour of all men, specially of those that believe." In John 3:16 and 17 the Bible says, "God so loved the world, that he gave his only begotten Son, that whosoever believeth in him should not perish, but have everlasting life. For God sent not his Son into the world to condemn the world; but that the world through him might be saved."

No way possible can one misunderstand what the Bible is saying in these passages, unless he has first adopted a philosophy not based on Scripture and is unwilling to admit what the Bible says about salvation for the world.

Jesus said in John 12:47, "I came not to judge the world, but to save the world." In I John 2:1,2 the Bible states,

"My little children, these things write I unto you, that ye sin not. And if any man sin, we have an advocate with the Father, Jesus Christ the righteous: And he is the propitiation for our sins: and not for our's only, but also for the sins of the whole world."

Ask any first grader what that means and he will tell you. If I say the whole world, any second grader knows what that means. What a pity that so-called Bible scholars cannot understand what first and second graders can!

II. JESUS CHRIST BORE THE SINS OF ALL THE WORLD

Not only is Jesus the Saviour of the whole world, but He bore the sins of all the world. In Isaiah 53:6 we read, "All we like sheep have gone astray; we have turned every one to his own way; and the Lord hath laid on him the iniquity of us all." That verse begins and ends with "all." I don't see how you can accept the first "all" and throw out the second. The first "all" says all have sinned, all have gone astray; and the second "all" says the Lord "hath laid on him the iniquity of us ALL." How many went astray? All. The same group included in the first "all" is included in the second. He bore the iniquity of how many? All. If He did not bear the sins of the man who never will receive Him as Saviour, then the man who never will receive Him as Saviour never could have received Him as Saviour.

An old English preacher had been in a meeting. He boarded the train and was about to leave. A young girl who was without the Saviour ran to the side of the train and yelled, "Please Sir, I want to be saved! Tell me how to be saved!" The train was beginning to leave the station, and looking out the window he said, "Young lady, go home and read Isaiah 53:6. Go in on the first 'all' and come out on the second 'all' and you will be all right!"

I could not give better advice to one wanting to be saved. If you are willing to come in on the first "all" and say, "Yes, I'm one of those sinners; I have gone astray; I have sinned; I have come short of God's glory," and willing to come out on the second "all" and say, "I'm one of the 'all' for whom Jesus Christ died; I'm one of the 'all' whose sins Jesus Christ bore in His own body on the tree," then you can be saved.

Not only is He the Saviour of the whole world, but He bore the iniquity of us all. Martin Luther said that Isaiah 53 is so precious it should be written on parchment of gold and lettered in diamonds. It has twelve verses and twelve mentions of the substitutionary death of Jesus.

Verse 5 says, "But he was wounded for our transgressions, he was bruised for our iniquities: the chastisement of our peace was upon him; and with his stripes we are healed." So you will not think His stripes were for the healing of some and His wounds were for the salvation of some, the next verse says He "laid on him the iniquity of US ALL."

You need not stop and watch and wait
And tarry long at Mercy's gate;
For Mercy's gate is opened free
And Christ has tarried long for thee.

The only men who are elected to be lost are those who themselves elect to be lost by refusing Jesus Christ as Saviour. He is the

Saviour of the whole world. He bore the sins of the whole world. He died for the whole world. Hebrews 2:9 says, "But we see Jesus, who was made a little lower than the angels for the suffering of death, crowned with glory and honour; that he by the grace of God should taste death for E-V-E-R-Y man." That doesn't sound like some are left out; it sounds like every man.

"For there is one God, and one mediator between God and men, the man Christ Jesus; Who gave himself a ransom for ALL" (I Tim. 2:5,6). His death on the cross was ransom for every person who has ever lived or ever will live! His death was ransom for every sinner who ever walked or will ever walk on God's earth. Jesus Christ gave Himself a ransom for ALL. "He that spared not his own Son, but delivered him up for us ALL, how shall he not with him also freely give us all things?" (Rom. 8:32). The only way you can misunderstand that is to want to misunderstand it.

III. THE ATONEMENT IS AS UNIVERSAL AS SIN

When the Bible speaks of ALL being sinners, it also tells how ALL may be saved. For instance, we read in Romans 3:22,23, ". . . for there is no difference: For all have sinned, and come short of the glory of God." Then in Romans 10:12,13 we find that expression again. This time it says, "For there is no difference . . . for the same Lord over ALL is rich unto ALL that call upon him. For whosoever shall call upon the name of the Lord shall be saved."

There is no difference in the fact that all have sinned. And there is no difference in the fact that Jesus Christ will save ALL who call on Him.

Again notice Isaiah 53:6, "All we like sheep have gone astray; we have turned every one to his own way; and the Lord hath laid on him the iniquity of us all." The first "all" shows the universal fact of sin: "All we like sheep have gone astray." The second "all" shows the universal fact of the atonement: ". . . and the Lord hath laid on him the iniquity of us all."

It is impossible to say this verse teaches the universal fact of sin without saying the same verse teaches the universal fact of the atonement. The same group, absolutely the same group, is referred to with both "alls." All have sinned: it is a fact. That Jesus Christ died for all is also a fact.

Some argue that if Jesus Christ died for all men, then all men are saved. That is not true. The death of Jesus Christ is sufficient for all, but it is efficient only to those who believe. The death of Jesus Christ on the cross makes it possible for everyone to be saved, but people are not saved until they trust Jesus Christ as Saviour.

IV. JESUS WANTS ALL PEOPLE SAVED

It is never right to base doctrine on human reasoning or logic, because in most cases what you think is right is usually wrong. Base doctrine on what the Bible says.

Some reason that God doesn't long to see all men saved, because all men are not saved. They reason that if God is omnipotent, if He can do anything and everything and He longs for everybody to be saved, then He could save everybody.

He could. It is not a matter of what God is able to do; it is a matter of what He will do. God is limited only by His own choice. He chooses not to save men who will not believe. He made man a free moral agent, and God never burglarizes the human will. He wanted man to choose to love Him. He wanted man to choose to serve Him. He wanted man to choose to come to Him. If He overpowered man's will and made man love Him, made man get saved against his will, that would not be much love. He wanted him to do it, but He wanted him to do it because he wanted to and willed to.

Second Peter 3:9 teaches that God longs for all men to be saved: "The Lord is not slack concerning his promise, as some men count slackness; but is longsuffering to us-ward, not willing that any should perish, but that ALL should come to repentance." The loving heart of God longs for the salvation of the man who rebels. The loving heart of God longs for the salvation of the sinner who curses and spits in His face. The loving heart of God longs for the salvation of the prostitute and the dope addict. The loving heart of God longs for, weeps for the salvation of the modernists, the liberals, and the communists. He "will have ALL men to be saved, and to come unto the knowledge of the truth" (I Tim. 2:4).

I know what you think. I know what I think. When I see some rebellious young person disobedient to his parents, spitting on the American flag, burning his draft card, I want to get him by the nape of the neck and work him over! Not so with God. When God sees him, He cries. Jesus looked out over the city of Jerusalem and while tears rolled down His cheeks, He cried, "Oh, Jerusalem, Jerusalem. . .how often would I have gathered thy children together, even as a hen gathereth her chickens under her wings, and ye would not!" The loving heart of God longs to see all people saved.

Acts 17:30 says, "And the times of this ignorance God winked at; but now commandeth ALL men every where to repent."

Salvation is for all men because Jesus is the Saviour of the whole world. Salvation is for all men because Jesus bore the sin of the whole world. Salvation is for all men because the atonement is as universal as our sinfulness. Salvation is for all men because the loving heart of God longs to see all men saved.

V. THE HOLY SPIRIT ENLIGHTENS AND DRAWS ALL MEN

The drawing of the Holy Spirit is as real to one as it is to the other.

In John 12:32 Jesus speaks of His death: "And I, if I be lifted up from the earth, will draw ALL men unto me." Again we read in John 1:4, "In him was life; and the life was the light of men." It didn't say that "the life was the light of some men," but "the light of men"—period. Verse 7 in the same chapter says, "The same came for a witness [speaking of John], to bear witness of the Light, that ALL men through him might believe." John said, "I am not the Light, but I came to bear witness of the Light." Why, John? ". . .that ALL men might believe." Verse 9 says, "That was the true Light, which lighteth EVERY MAN that cometh into the world." Every man is enlightened by the Holy Spirit.

Look at Psalm 19:1-3:

"The heavens declare the glory of God; and the firmament sheweth his handiwork. Day unto day uttereth speech, and night unto night sheweth knowledge. There is no speech nor language, where their voice is not heard."

John 16:8, speaking of the Holy Spirit, tells us, "And when he is come, he will reprove the world of sin, and of righteousness, and of judgment." It does not say He will reprove the elect, or that He will reprove a certain chosen group. It says He will "reprove the world of sin, and of righteousness, and of judgment."

Salvation is for all men because Jesus is the Saviour of the whole world. Salvation is for all because Jesus bore the sin of the whole world. Salvation is for all because atonement is as universal as our sinfulness. Salvation is for all because the loving heart of God longs for all to be saved. Salvation is for all because light has been given and the Holy Spirit convicts and draws everyone.

VI. ALL CAN BE SAVED

There is no such thing as a person who cannot be saved. Nothing could be clearer or plainer than John 5:40 where Jesus said, "Ye will not come to me, that ye might have life." It all hinges on one word: WILL. Human will—not God's will but our will. It does not say, "I will not save you," but, "Ye will not come to me."

Revelation 22:17, "The Spirit and the bride say, Come. And let him that heareth say, Come. And let him that is athirst come. And WHOSOEVER WILL, let him take the water of life freely." The only thing that stands between the sinner and salvation is the sinner's will.

D. L. Moody preached to agnostics and skeptics in a special meeting. After his wonderful sermon, Mr. Moody gave an invitation. "Who will come?"

One skeptic stood and said, "I can't."

D. L. Moody wept and said, "O Sir, it is not that you can't come, you can come."

Then with a hard face, the skeptic said, "I won't come."

Mr. Moody said, "That's it. It is not that you can't but that you won't come."

Then Moody continued asking, "Who will come?" One by one, man after man said, "I will," and a great host of those people got saved.

"How often would I have gathered thy children together, as a hen doth gather her brood under her wings, and ye would not." "Lord, do You mean You would have gathered that man who went to Hell?"

"Yes."

"You would have gathered that prostitute?"

"Yes."

"You would have gathered that dope addict, that drunkard?"

"Yes. How often would I have gathered you together, as a hen gathers her brood, but you would not."

"Whosoever heareth," shout, shout the sound!
Spread the blessed tidings all the world around;
Tell the joyful news wherever man is found:
"Whosoever will may come."

Whosoever cometh need not delay,
Now the door is open, enter while you may;
Jesus is the true, the only Living Way:
"Whosoever will may come."

"Whosoever will," the promise is secure;
"Whosoever will," forever must endure:
"Whosoever will," 'tis life forevermore;
"Whosoever will may come."

"Whosoever will, whosoever will!"
Send the proclamation over vale and hill;
'Tis a loving Father calls the wand'rer home:
"Whosoever will may come."

"Whosoever" is a broad word, isn't it?

When John 3:16 says, "For God so loved the world, that he gave his only begotten Son, that whosoever believeth..." has everlasting life, I would rather have the word "whosoever" in there than my own name. If I saw Curtis Hutson where "whosoever" is, I would wonder if there were not some other Curtis Hutsons. Then I would wonder if I were the right Curtis Hutson. But since He said "whosoever," I know that includes me.

All men can be saved.

VII. GOD INVITES ALL TO BE SAVED

I have one last thing to say—God invites all men to be saved. Salvation is for all men because Christ is the Saviour of the whole world. Salvation is for all men because Christ bore the sin of the whole world. Salvation is for all men because atonement is as universal as sin. Salvation is for all men because the loving heart of God longs for the salvation of all men. Salvation is for all men because all men can be saved. Salvation is for all men because God invites all men to come and be saved.

Isaiah 45:22 says, "Look unto me, and be ye saved, ALL THE ENDS OF THE EARTH: for I am God, and there is none else." O dear sinner friend, you are not left out! Neither is anybody else.

Isaiah 55:1, "Ho, every one that thirsteth, come ye to the waters, and he that hath no money; come ye, buy, and eat; yea, come, buy wine and milk without money and without price." Come, come, come, EVERYONE!

In Matthew 11:28,29, Jesus stretched His open arms and said, "Come unto me, ALL YE that labour and are heavy laden, and I will give you rest. Take my yoke upon you, and learn of me; for I am meek and lowly in heart: and ye shall find rest unto your souls."

But God gave you a human will, and your salvation hinges upon your will. God wills for you to be saved. God wants you to be saved. "Who will have all men to be saved" (I Tim. 2:4). But He won't burglarize your will. Don't foolishly think that God has irresistible grace and that someday He will overpower you and make you get saved. He will do no such thing. He has given you a clear presentation of the Gospel, but He will never force salvation on you.

Make Your Decision Now!

Do you know you are a sinner? Do you believe that Jesus Christ died on the cross? And don't you want to trust Him now as your Saviour? It is your decision. No one can make it for you. I urge you to trust Him now.

If you will trust Him and write to tell me so, I have some free literature I want to send that will help you as you set out to live the Christian life. All you need do to receive your free literature is write to me:

Dr. Curtis Hutson
Sword of the Lord Foundation
P. O. Box 1099
Murfreesboro, Tennessee 37133

In your letter say, "I have read your sermon, 'Salvation for All Men.' I believe that Jesus Christ died for me and that He will save me if I trust Him. Knowing that I am a sinner and being convinced that His death atoned for my sins, I here and now trust Him as my Saviour.

"I promise to attend a Bible-believing church and tell the

preacher that I have trusted Jesus Christ as my Saviour after having read your sermon. Please send me the free literature that will help me as I set out to live the Christian life."

Be sure you include your name and full address.

Chapter 25

"It Is Finished"!

"*When Jesus therefore had received the vinegar, he said, It is finished: and he bowed his head, and gave up the ghost.*"—John 19:30.

I am speaking this morning on the sixth cross utterance, "It is finished." Christ uttered seven things while hanging on the cross. Three came before the darkness, three after the darkness, and one utterance came during the darkness, "My God, my God, why hast thou forsaken me?" The fifth cross utterance was the cry of a victim—"I thirst." The sixth is the cry of a victor—"It is finished." "I thirst"; "It is finished." The "I" and the "It" refer to the person and work of our Lord Jesus Christ.

An equivalent statement appears at least two other times in the Scriptures. In Genesis, chapter 2, after the creation of the heavens and earth, we read, "Thus the heavens and the earth were finished, and all the host of them." Revelation 16:17 says, "The seventh angel poured out his vial into the air; and there came a great voice out of the temple of heaven, from the throne, saying, It is done," or, "It is finished."

The expression in Genesis 2:1 speaks of the finished work of creation. "It is done" in Revelation 16:17 speaks of the finished judgment of God upon the earth-dwellers after the rapture of the church and just before the millennial reign of Christ.

But the most important utterance came from Calvary 2,000 years ago when Jesus said, "It is finished."

Many wonderful words fell from the lips of our Saviour, things we ought to study and understand, but I believe His most important utterance was, "It is finished." And the most needful thing for man to understand is this expression, "It is finished"; because to misunderstand what He meant by these words could mean eternal ruin. Satan has done, and is doing, all in his power to keep men from understanding "It is finished."

Many churches do not understand it. They think the death of our Lord at Calvary made the down payment on salvation and that we must keep up the installments with our good works, good living and other things. A misunderstanding of this utterance could result in a man's dying and going to Hell without the Saviour.

Notice He did not say, "I am finished." I'm sure that some who stood by the cross that day thought He meant, "I'm finished; this is the end of Me." No, He wasn't finished. He was buried, and raised from the dead, and He now lives to make intercession for us. He is not finished!

I have read that "It is finished" is translated from only one Greek word. The Greeks prided themselves in the ability to say much with few words. The Greek word used here means it was finished and as a result it is forever done. It could be translated, "It stands finished." If you want to use only one word, you would translate it "done."

The songwriter expressed it,

'Tis done, the great transaction's done.
I am my Lord's and He is mine.

"It is finished."

In *A Handful of Stars*, F. W. Boreham catches the spirit of the word when he reminds us:

> It was a *farmer's* word. When, into his herd, there was born an animal so beautiful and shapely that it seemed absolutely destitute of faults and defects, the farmer gazed upon the creature with proud, delighted eyes and exclaimed, "Tetelestai! Tetelestai!"
>
> It was an *artist's* word. When the painter or the sculptor had put the finishing touches to the vivid landscape or the

> marble bust, he would stand back a few feet to admire his masterpiece and, seeing in it nothing that called for correction or improvement, would murmur fondly, "Tetelestai! Tetelestai!"
>
> It was a *priestly* word. When some devout worshiper, overflowing with gratitude for mercies shown him, brought to the Temple a lamb without spot or blemish, the pride of the whole flock, the priest, more accustomed to seeing the blind and defective animals led to the altar, would look admiringly at the pretty creature, "Tetelestai!" he would say, "Tetelestai!"
>
> And when, in the fullness of time, the Lamb of God offered Himself on the altar of the ages, He rejoiced with a joy so triumphant that it bore down all His anguish before it. The sacrifice was stainless, perfect, finished! He cried with a loud voice, "Tetelestai!" and gave up the ghost.

It is the word of the master workman looking with unashamed satisfaction at his finished task.

Someone has said the old Egyptians wrote over the portals of their palaces and temples, "We build like giants and we finish like jewelers." I don't know whether it was true of the Egyptian builders or not, but I do know that it was true of our Lord. Everything had to be perfect. Nothing could be left undone. "It is finished."

Now, there are four things that I see in this expression that I want to share with you today.

I. THE CONSUMMATION OF PROPHETIC SCRIPTURES

All the prophecies in the Old Testament that pointed forward to the coming of Christ and His dying at Calvary were fulfilled when Jesus uttered, "It is finished."

There are two types of prophecies in the Old Testament: the explicit verbal prophecies, then the prophecies in type.

God slew and skinned an innocent animal in order to clothe Adam and Eve in the Garden of Eden after they had fallen. That little animal was a picture of Jesus who was to come, who was to die and who was to shed His blood, that through His death the sinner could be clothed with the righteousness of God. Had we time, we could go through Genesis and Exodus, and all through the Old Testament, spending hours looking at the Old Testament types of Jesus who was to come and die for the sins of the whole world.

The ark that Noah built is one of the most complete and beautiful pictures of Jesus who was to come and be our Ark of safety. The judgment of God fell, but it did not fall upon those who were in the ark. It fell upon the ark itself. We who are in Christ are saved from the wrath of God, not because God withheld His wrath, but because God's wrath fell upon Jesus, our Substitute, 2,000 years ago at Calvary.

Type after type was fulfilled when Jesus said, "It is finished." It meant the consummation of prophetic Scriptures. Jesus saw to that. He looked back and saw the unfulfilled prophecy in Psalm 69:21 and said, "I thirst," that the Scripture might be fulfilled.

II. THE CULMINATION OF PERSONAL SUFFERING

I wish I had the vocabulary and ability to paint for you the picture of the sufferings of Christ. I do not think one sinner would stay away from the Saviour a moment longer if I could paint for him how much Christ suffered in order for us to be saved.

Somebody suggested that He suffered from three directions—from the hands of men, from the hands of Satan, and from the hands of God. Men plucked His beard; men scourged Him and left furrows across His back; men plunged the spear into His side; men plaited the crown of thorns, placed it upon His brow and pressed it down until the blood ran down His face. Men blindfolded Him; men smote Him with a reed and said, "Prophesy who smote you." Men mocked Him, and men spat upon Him. He suffered untold agony at the hands of men. Nobody ever suffered like Jesus. It meant the culmination of personal suffering at the hands of men.

But He also suffered at the hands of Satan. There's a prophecy that says Jesus would bruise the serpent's head and the serpent would bruise the Saviour's heel. Now the serpent, Satan, was bruising the heel of our Lord.

But not only was He suffering at the hands of men and the hands of Satan, He was suffering also at the hands of God.

Who was responsible for the death of Jesus? Was it the Roman soldiers? No. Was it the Jews? No. Was it sinners like us? In a sense, yes, because He was bearing our sin. But in the final analysis it was God who gave His Son in our place to pay our sin debt so we could go to Heaven when we die.

Isaiah 53:10 tells us who was responsible: "Yet it pleased the Lord to bruise him; he hath put him to grief: when thou shalt make his soul an offering for sin, he shall see his seed, he shall prolong his days, and the pleasure of the Lord shall prosper in his hand." God did it.

The Bible said, "For God so loved the world, that he gave his only begotten Son. . . ." The Romans didn't take Him. The Jews didn't take Him. He didn't go involuntarily, but He freely, willingly, gave His life a ransom that we might be saved.

God so loved the dope addict, God so loved the alcoholic, God so loved the adulterer, God so loved the murderer, God so loved the thief, that He gave His only begotten Son. Romans 8:32 says, "He that spared not his own Son, but delivered him up for us all, how shall he not with him also freely give us all things?"

You know something? When Jesus said, "It is finished," it meant no more scourgings, no more spittle in His face, no more crown of thorns, no more nails. It meant His sufferings were over. It meant that God would no longer turn His back on His own Son. It was the culmination of personal suffering.

III. THE CONQUEST OF SATAN

The Bible says in John 16:11, "Of judgment, because the prince of this world is judged." The prince of this world is judged and sentence has already been passed upon him.

One evangelist said when he reads in the Bible where it looks as if Satan is going to be the conqueror, he always turns to the last part of the Book and reads:

"And I saw an angel come down from heaven, having the key of the bottomless pit and a great chain in his hand. And he laid hold on the dragon, that old serpent, which is the Devil, and Satan, and bound him a thousand years."

He said, "When I was a boy, I read Western novels, and it often looked as if the villain was about to get the hero. Finally I'd finish the old Western book and learn in the last chapter that the hero came out on top."

Then he said, "I got to the place where when I'd buy a new book, I would read the last chapter first to make sure the hero was going to be all right. Then I'd turn back to the first chapter and read the book. When I read where the villain had the hero over the cliff, and it looked as if the hero was going to be killed, I would laugh inside, for I'd read the last chapter and I knew how it was all coming out."

Thank God, I've read the last chapter and I know that Satan has been conquered! When Jesus died, He conquered the power of Satan.

An old preacher used to go about preaching in the streets. One day he stopped in front of a saloon and asked if he could preach there. The saloonkeeper laughed and said, "Yes, you can preach here, if you'll stand on this keg of beer and preach."

"Okay," he said.

The old-fashioned preacher stood on the keg of beer, opened his Bible and said, "Friends, I'm preaching today where I've always wanted to preach—with the Devil under my feet!" And he let loose and preached.

Jesus has conquered the power of Satan. Someday Satan will be chained and bound in the bottomless pit. Somebody said, "He's chained now!" and another said, "If he's chained, he's chained to me." Someone else said, "He's chained now!" and another fellow said, "If he's chained, he's on an awfully long chain."

No, Satan is not chained today. That's the reason you have sin and trouble. The Devil is not bound, but when Jesus died He conquered him 2,000 years ago. And I can hardly wait until the angel says, "Okay, I've come to execute the sentence," then lays hold on the Devil and starts wrapping him with a chain. We'll all laugh, and the Devil will be embarrassed. Then I think I'll join the little children in singing,

The Devil is a sly old fox.
If I could catch him I'd put him in a box.
I'd lock the box and throw away the key,
For all the tricks he's played on me.
I'm glad I got converted.
I'm glad I got converted!
I'm glad I got converted by trusting in the Lord.

"It is finished" means the consummation of prophetic Scriptures, the culmination of personal suffering. It means the conquest of the power of Satan.

No Christian has any reason not to be victorious. I can think of reasons why I should fail as a businessman. I can think of reasons why I should fail as a salesman. I can think of reasons why I should fail as a politician. But I cannot think of one single reason why I should fail as a Christian. The power of Satan was conquered 2,000 years ago. And I John 4:4 says, ". . . greater is he that is in you, than he that is in the world."

There's no excuse for not being a successful Christian. "It is finished." Nothing can be added to improve it, and nothing can be taken away without marring it.

"It is finished" means:

IV. THE COMPLETION OF A PERFECT SALVATION

I wish I could get that truth over to you. Being a religious creature, man feels he must do something to help God with his salvation.

When Adam sinned, he hid himself in the Garden from the presence of God. Adam knew that he was wrong. He knew that he was naked. He knew that he had sinned. But Adam didn't know that he couldn't do anything about it. He made an effort to fix things up. He sewed fig leaves together and made an apron. Did you ever see an apron? You know an apron doesn't cover up much. That's man. He wants just a little bit of religion, just enough to be innoculated from the real thing.

Adam and Eve made aprons of fig leaves to cover their nakedness. And they were satisfied until they had to face God. God came walking in the cool of the day and calling, "Adam! Where art thou?" Suddenly Adam felt uncomfortable with his fig-leaf apron.

What was all right in front of Eve wasn't all right in front of God. What Eve had accepted, God would not accept. Adam knew it, so he hid himself in the Garden. God called until Adam spoke out and said, "I heard thy voice in the Garden, and I was afraid, because I was naked; and I hid myself."

God took away their fig-leaf religion and clothed them all the way down to their feet with coats of skin.

When Jesus Christ died on the cross, He said, "It is finished." That means your salvation is complete. You don't need to add anything to it. Simply trust Jesus Christ. He is enough!

I have tried to live a good, moral life, but I would not trust my good life to get me to Heaven. I'd go to Hell trusting my good life, just like I'd go to Hell trusting my sin. I would just as soon trust my sin to get me to Heaven as my righteousness. Isaiah 64:6 tells us, "But we are all as an unclean thing, and all our righteousnesses are as filthy rags; and we all do fade as a leaf; and our iniquities, like the wind, have taken us away."

When Jesus said, "It is finished," it meant that everything necessary to get you to Heaven was done. He died on the cross. He paid your sin debt. He suffered your Hell. Now you can go to Heaven by trusting Him as your personal Saviour.

Salvation is a gift. Trying to add to the finished work of Christ is like trying to paint a lily. Trying to add to the finished work of Christ is like trying to perfume a rose. It is like trying to smooth down ice or trying to add another hue to the rainbow. It is absolutely foolish. Salvation is complete!

I was painting the inside of our home when one of my girls, just a little tot, came and said, "Daddy, I want to help you."

I said, "No, don't help me."

"I want to help you."

"No, don't help me. You go play with your doll. I'll do this."

"I want to help!" And she helped! But I had to do it over after she helped.

When you come to God and say, "I want to help You get me to Heaven," you remind me of some child trying to help his father paint the wall. You mess the whole thing up. Keep your hands off! Believe that He died for you. Trust it! Stand on it! And Jesus said he that believeth on Him hath everlasting life.

"It is finished" was the consummation of prophetic Scriptures, the culmination of personal suffering, the conquest over the power of Satan and the completion of a perfect salvation. "It is finished"!

Nothing to pay, no, not a whit;
Nothing to do, no, not a bit.
All that was needed to do or to pay,
Jesus has done in His own blessed way.

Nothing to do, no, not a stroke;
Gone is the captor; gone is the yoke.
Jesus at Calvary severed the chain,
And none can imprison His free man again.

**Nothing to fear, no, not a jot;
Nothing unclean, no, not a spot.
Christ is my peace, and I've nothing at stake;
Satan can neither harass nor shake.**

**Nothing to settle; all has been paid;
Nothing of anger; peace has been made.
Jesus alone is the sinner's resource;
Peace He has made by the blood of His cross.**

**What about judgment? Ah, I'm thankful to say,
Jesus has met it and borne it away.
Drank it all up when He hung on the tree
Leaving a cup full of blessing for me.**

**What about terror? It hasn't a place
In a heart that is filled with a sense of His grace.
My peace is divine, and it never can cloy;
And that makes my heart overbubble with joy.**

**Nothing of guilt, no, not a stain;
How could the blood let any remain?
My conscience is purged, and my spirit is free;
Precious that blood to God and to me.**

**What of the law? Ah, there I rejoice.
Christ answered its claims and silenced its voice.
The law was fulfilled when the work was all done,
And it never can speak to a justified one.**

**What about death? It hasn't a sting;
The grave to a Christian no terror can bring;
For death has been conquered; the grave has been spoiled;
And every foe an enemy foiled.**

**What about feelings? Ah, trust not to them.
What of my standing? Who shall condemn?
Since God is for me, there's nothing so clear;
From Satan and man I have nothing to fear.**

**What of my body? Ah, that I may bring
To God as a holy, acceptable thing;
For that is the temple where Jesus abides;
The temple where God by His Spirit resides.**

**Nothing to pay, no, thanks be to God;
The matter is settled; the price was the blood.
The blood of the victim, a ransom divine.
Believe it, poor sinner, and peace shall be thine.**

—Author unknown.

Don't Delay!

You have read the sermon, "It Is Finished." You may never do anything about it, but 2,000 years ago Jesus Christ took every sin you ever have committed and all you ever will commit if you live to be a thousand years old. He bore those sins in His own body. When He died on the cross, He paid what you owe as a sinner.

If you will believe that you are a sinner and accept the fact that Jesus Christ did die to pay your sin debt, and if you will completely trust Him for salvation, you will have everlasting life. And when you die, you will go to Heaven. John 3:36 says, "He that believeth on the Son hath everlasting life." That is a promise of God. You can depend on it.

If you will trust Jesus Christ as your Saviour, I urge you to write and tell me of your decision. I have some free literature I would like to send to help you in your Christian life. Write to:

Dr. Curtis Hutson
THE SWORD OF THE LORD
P. O. Box 1099
Murfreesboro, Tennessee 37133

In your letter to me, say, "I have read your sermon, 'It Is Finished.' I do believe that Jesus Christ died for me. I believe that His death on the cross made full payment for my sins. And today the best I know how, I do trust Him as my Saviour. From this moment on, I am fully depending on Him to get me to Heaven. Please send me the free literature that will help me as I set out to live the Christian life."

Plainly write or print your name and address. God bless you!

Chapter 26

Lordship Salvation, a Perversion of the Gospel

"Paul, an apostle, (not of men, neither by man, but by Jesus Christ, and God the Father, who raised him from the dead;) And all the brethren which are with me, unto the churches of Galatia: Grace be to you and peace from God the Father, and from our Lord Jesus Christ, who gave himself for our sins, that he might deliver us from this present evil world, according to the will of God and our Father: To whom be glory for ever and ever. Amen. I marvel that ye are so soon removed from him that called you into the grace of Christ unto another gospel: Which is not another; but there be some that trouble you, and would pervert the gospel of Christ. But though we, or an angel from heaven, preach any other gospel unto you than that which we have preached unto you, let him be accursed. As we said before, so say I now again, If any man preach any other gospel unto you than that ye have received, let him be accursed [let him be "damned"]."—Gal. 1:1-9.

Lordship salvation is an unscriptural teaching regarding the doctrine of salvation and is confusing to Christians. Those who teach it claim that one must make Jesus Lord of his life in order to be saved. They use such expressions as, "You cannot receive Jesus Christ as Saviour without receiving Him as Lord," or, "If Jesus Christ is not Lord of your life, then you are not saved."

The Bible teaches salvation by grace through faith. Ephesians 2:8,9 says, "For by grace are ye saved through faith; and that not of yourselves: it is the gift of God: Not of works, lest any man should boast." But those who teach Lordship salvation say that it is not enough to trust Jesus Christ; you must also make Him Lord of your life in order to be saved. This kind of teaching frustrates the grace of God and is called in the Bible "another gospel."

Another Gospel Which Is Not Another

In verse 6, Paul said, "I marvel that ye are so soon removed from him that called you into the grace of Christ unto another gospel." Paul contrasts the Gospel of the grace of God with "another gospel" which he does not define. In verse 7 he said, "Which is not another. . . ." That sounds like a contradiction, but the word "another" does not come from the same Greek word. In verse 6 it means "another—different from the one we preach." In verse 7 the Greek word means "another of the same kind." So we might paraphrase the verse, "I marvel that you are so soon removed from him who called you unto the grace of Christ unto a different gospel which is not like the one we preach."

He goes on to say, "There be some that trouble you." The preaching of another gospel troubles people. He also calls it a perversion of the Gospel of the grace of God.

Then he says something very strong in verse 8: "But though we, or an angel from heaven, preach any other gospel unto you than that which we have preached unto you, let him be accursed [or "let him be damned"]."

Then he emphasizes it again in verse 9: "As we said before, so say I now again, If any man preach any other gospel unto you than that ye have received, let him be accursed [damned]."

Paul said, "I am startled; I marvel; I can't believe that you are so soon removed from the Gospel of the grace of Christ unto another gospel." "Another gospel" is not defined, so I will define it based upon the implication of the text.

The Gospel of the grace of Christ is one thing. Another gospel would be anything that contradicts the teaching of salvation by grace through faith. If a man preaches that one is saved by the substitutionary death of Jesus, by trusting Christ, then adds some form of works, he contradicts the Gospel of the grace of God. I could not put it any better than Romans 11:6, "And if by grace, then is it no more of works: otherwise grace is no more grace. But if it be of works, then is it no more grace: otherwise work is no more work."

Salvation cannot be by grace *and* works. It has to be either grace *or* works.

Most people have a poor concept of grace. I used to work for a loan company. It would give what is called a "grace period." If you didn't pay your debt on time, you had five days "grace" before you got a notice and were tagged with a late charge. That is not grace; that is probation. Grace is the unmerited, undeserved favor of God toward Hell-deserving sinners.

There is much confusion over the doctrine of salvation. If you ask the next ten people you see, "How does a person get to Heaven?" you will probably get ten different answers. And it is very likely that none would be correct.

In the final analysis, there are only two schemes of salvation that are taught by all religions. One is that man saves himself; the other is that God saves a man. They may say that man saves himself by reforming or cleaning up his life before he is saved in order to merit salvation; or that man saves himself by promising to keep the Ten Commandments before he is saved; or man saves himself by receiving the seven sacraments; or man saves himself by obedience. Others teach that man saves himself by behaving. Those who teach Lordship salvation say that man saves himself by making Jesus Lord of his life.

Romans 1:16 says, "For I am not ashamed of the gospel of Christ: for it [the Gospel] is the power of God unto salvation to every one that *behaves*..."? No, "...to every one that *believeth*."

The only thing you can do with the Gospel is believe it. The Gospel is the good news of how Jesus came to this earth, how He died on a cross in our place for our sins, how He was buried and rose again the third day. That is the Gospel.

Don't confuse the truth with the Gospel. The Gospel is the truth, but all truth is not the Gospel. It is the truth that I wear a necktie to church, but that is not the Gospel. It is the truth that I brush my teeth every morning, but that is not the Gospel. All truth is not the Gospel, but the Gospel is the truth.

When I preach on Hell, I preach a Bible truth that ought to be preached and one that Jesus preached, but it is not the Gospel.

Hell is not good news; Hell is bad news. If I preach on judgment, I preach the truth but not the Gospel. But when I preach that Jesus loved sinners, that He died in the sinner's place to pay the sinner's debt, that He was buried and after three days God raised Him from the dead to show His satisfaction with that payment, then I preach the Gospel.

An old preacher spoke to a large crowd of young preachers. Before leaving the platform, one young pastor said to him, "Sir, before you leave, give us a word of advice." The old preacher thought a moment, then said, "My preacher brethren, make it plain to men how they are to be saved."

Far too many preachers are muddying the Gospel. The waters of the grace of God must be kept crystal clear. It disturbs me when preachers scramble the grace of God with works. Paul said, "Though we, or an angel from heaven, preach any other gospel unto you. . . LET HIM BE DAMNED!" Strong language, but that is how God feels about preachers who pervert the Gospel. Paul says that even an angel is to be damned for preaching another gospel.

Something about us religious humans makes us want to add to the Gospel. We want to help God with our salvation. If we can't help Him save us, we want to help keep ourselves saved.

Adam and Eve gathered fig leaves and sewed them together to make aprons to cover their nakedness. They knew something was wrong and tried to right it before God came to visit. They were happy and well pleased with their fig-leaf religion until God came, then they were embarrassed with their fig-leaf covering and ran and hid themselves. God called them unto Himself, killed an innocent animal (a picture of the substitutionary death of Jesus), took the skin from the animal and made coats for Adam and Eve. He didn't let them keep one single fig leaf of their own making. Salvation is of the Lord.

Adam and Eve were satisfied to face each other with their fig leaves, but they were not satisfied to face God.

You may be satisfied to stand before men with your religion, but are you going to be satisfied when you stand before God Almighty? Remember, God put His Son on a cross, loaded Him down with your sin, and poured out His wrath on His own Son so He could save you from the penalty of sin, which is Hell!

Are you going to be satisfied to stand before God with your fig-leaf religion? There is no promise in the Bible to those who partially believe on Christ; one must trust Him alone and nothing else.

Those who teach Lordship salvation say, "If you do not give over the control of your life to Christ at the moment of salvation, you are not saved."

Must There Be a Commitment to Christ as the Lord of One's Life in Order to Be Saved?

Those who teach Lordship salvation say that you cannot divorce His Saviourhood from His Lordship; that you can't accept Him as Saviour without accepting Him as the Lord of your life also; that unless Jesus Christ is Lord of your life, you are not saved. But when you question these same people, you discover that Jesus is not Lord of their lives.

I asked one who taught Lordship salvation, "Has Jesus been Lord of your life since the day you trusted Him as Saviour? Has there ever been a time since you were saved when Christ has not been the absolute Lord of your life?" He hesitated a moment, then said, "Well, He has always been Lord, but there have been times when I didn't obey Him."

When we don't obey Him, He is not Lord or Boss. When we are in control, Jesus cannot be in control. In Luke 6:46 Jesus said, "And why call ye me, Lord, Lord, and do not the things which I say?" It is inconsistent to call Him "Lord, Lord," and not do what He says. When this man I mentioned realized that Jesus had not been Lord of his life, he rephrased his statement: "Well, I am not saying that you must absolutely make Him Lord of your life in order to be saved, but there must be a willingness to be controlled by the Lord at the time of salvation in order to be saved."

If there must be a willingness for Jesus to have the absolute control over one's life in order to be saved, how long can he wait before he becomes unwilling and disobeys again?

There are not two ways to be saved. One is either saved by grace through faith or saved by grace through faith plus surrender. The Bible says in Ephesians 2:8,9, "For by grace are ye saved through faith; and that not of yourselves: it is the gift of God: Not of works, lest any man should boast." If it is salvation by grace through faith, as this Scripture declares, then it is not salvation by grace through faith plus surrender, or plus anything else. It is salvation by grace through faith. PERIOD!

You say, "Dr. Hutson, don't you believe in surrender?" Absolutely! Wholeheartedly! But not to be saved. Surrender can be right or wrong, depending where you put it. A diamond ring is a beautiful thing on a lady's finger. It brings pleasure to the lady. But put that same ring in her high-heeled shoe, and it causes pain and discomfort.

The surrender of the life to the Lordship of Christ is a beautiful and wonderful thing; but when you make surrender a requirement for salvation, it becomes an ugly, dirty, wicked thing and frustrates the marvelous grace of God!

Bible Examples of Uncommitted Believers

Let me give you some Bible examples of uncommitted believers. *First, I will call your attention to some who had definite lapses from a fully surrendered life* after *they were saved.* Second, I will call attention to believers who did not commit their lives to Christ until long after they were saved. Third, we will call attention to one in the Bible who trusted Christ as Saviour but never surrendered to the Lordship of Christ.

David is an example of one who had a definite lapse in his surrender. Now David may or may not have surrendered his life to the Lordship of Christ at the moment of salvation, but Jesus dead sure wasn't Lord of David's life when he committed adultery with Bathsheba. David was lord at that time; David was running the show. David may or may not have surrendered to the Lordship of Christ at the moment of salvation, but Jesus Christ was not Lord of David's life when he sent Uriah into battle and had him killed. If Jesus was Lord of David's life, then it is certain that David had a lapse of his surrender. David's life was not committed to the Lordship of Christ when he committed adultery and murder! So if he had committed his life, he definitely had a lapse.

If total surrender to Christ is a prerequisite for salvation, then David lost his salvation until he totally surrendered again. But he didn't lose it! According to Psalm 51:12, all he lost was the joy of salvation. He prayed, "Restore unto me the joy of thy salvation." He didn't pray, "Lord, save me because You have not been the Lord of my life."

Noah is another example of one saved by the grace of God who, if ever committed to Christ, had a relapse. The Bible says in Genesis 6:8, "But Noah found grace in the eyes of the Lord." Noah was saved and may or may not have surrendered to the Lordship of Christ at the moment of salvation. But when the ark landed, Noah got drunk; and in a drunken stupor lay naked before his sons. If Noah had surrendered and committed his life to the Lordship of Christ when he was saved, he certainly had a lapse. You can't say Jesus Christ was controlling Noah's life when he got drunk! Noah was controlling his own life. You can't blame his immoral conduct on the Lord.

The Apostle Peter is another example of one who, if ever committed, had a relapse. Peter said, 'Though all men forsake thee, I will never forsake thee' (Matt. 26:33). But he followed the enemy and warmed himself by the Devil's fire.

One of the enemy came and said, "Hey! That fellow there is one of them; he's one of the Lord's boys."

Peter said, "Oh, no! I don't know Jesus."

Another one said, "Yes, Peter is one of Jesus' followers."

Peter insisted, "No, I don't know Christ. I'm not one of them!"

A woman said, "You are one of His disciples! Your speech betrays you."

And Peter began to curse. He said, "You blankety-blank-blank, low-down, sneakin' woman, I don't know Jesus Christ and never knew Him!"

If he surrendered to the Lordship of Christ in total commitment at the moment of salvation, he certainly had a lapse when he cursed and said, "I never knew Jesus Christ!"

In John 21, Peter quit the ministry. He said, "I go a fishing" (vs. 3). This was a public announcement that he never intended to preach again. "I am through preaching—I quit!" And six preachers went with him! When he got out on the lake in a boat, he took off his clothes and was out there naked in the middle of the night in a boat, fishing. It is all in John 21. If he was surrendered to Jesus Christ totally at the moment of salvation, he was not surrendered totally now. He quit the ministry and never intended to preach again! The Lord had to come and warm his backslidden heart by the fires in John, chapter 21, before he preached in Acts, chapter 2, and had 3,000 conversions.

There are other examples in the Bible of men who, if they were totally surrendered, had a lapse in their yieldedness or commitment after they were saved.

Now let me give you an example from the Bible of some believers who were saved and later made a commitment of their lives to Christ.

In Acts 19 we have the conversion of some people at Ephesus who had been worshiping the goddess Diana. An important part of that worship included the superstitious dependence on magical words and charms and sayings. Paul had been there two years preaching, and these people had believed on Christ. "And many that believed came, and confessed, and shewed their deeds" (vs. 18). Some of them had believed as much as two years earlier. Verse 19 says, "Many of them also which used curious [magical] arts brought their books together, and burned them before all men: and they counted the price of them, and found it fifty thousand pieces of silver"—$9,300.00 worth of books burned! They were just now burning their books of magic—two years after trusting Christ! These people were saved without surrendering to the Lordship of Christ at the moment of salvation.

We know many believers who trusted Christ as Saviour, then years later quit bad habits such as smoking. We even know some who, like Noah, got drunk after they were saved. Now we are not condoning sin; we are simply showing that Jesus was not Lord of these believers' lives.

I know some Christians who were saved and a year later quit some habits, while others waited several years. As a matter of fact, I don't know one Christian anywhere who surrendered to the absolute Lordship of Christ at the moment of conversion and has continued a life of complete surrender.

One dear man who teaches Lordship salvation told me that if Jesus was not Lord of an individual's life, then that individual was not saved. He also said that he had surrendered to the Lordship of Christ at the moment he was saved. Later this man was dismissed from a Christian organization because of conduct unbecoming of a Christian.

You don't get better to get saved; you get saved to get better.

You can't get better until you do get saved. You don't have anything to get better with. In Acts 19 we have people who were saved though they had not totally committed themselves to Christ at the moment of trusting Him as Saviour. *Two years later* they burned their magic books—two years later! These people certainly contradict the teaching of Lordship salvation.

The third example is one of a lifelong refusal to commit oneself to the Lordship of Christ. If you read only the Old Testament references to Lot, you wouldn't believe he was saved. But the Bible says in II Peter 2:7,8, "And delivered just Lot, vexed with the filthy conversation of the wicked. (For that righteous man dwelling among them, in seeing and hearing, vexed his righteous soul from day to day with their unlawful deeds)." Twice in verse 8 he is called "righteous," and verse 7 calls him "*just* Lot."

Now Lot was saved, justified. Second Peter 2:7,8 makes this amply clear. But when you read the Old Testament account of his life, it is plain to see that he was never surrendered to God before or after he was saved.

His Uncle Abraham set out on a journey, and Lot just followed his uncle! In the process, his herd of cattle grew; and his herdsmen began to fight with Abraham's herdsmen. Then they decided they had better separate. This little, puny, potato-string backboned nephew looked up at this giant of faith, Abraham, who said to Lot, "You choose either direction you want." Lot looked toward the mountains, then toward the well-watered plains of Jordan. If he had been surrendered, he would have said, "Uncle Abraham, I am not even supposed to be out here. I just followed you. You make the choice, and I'll take the one you don't want." But that little pipsqueak took the well-watered plains of Jordan. He wasn't surrendered.

When he went down to Sodom and called the Sodomites "brothers"—that is not being surrendered. If you call somebody who doesn't believe the Bible a "brother in Christ," you are not surrendered. It shows you don't know much about the Bible. The only man who is your brother is the one who has received Jesus Christ as Saviour. You become a son of God by faith (John 1:12). When he called those wicked Sodomites "brethren," do you think he was surrendered to Christ?

Two angels came down from Heaven, and Lot took them into

his house. The young and old men of the city of Sodom compassed about the house of Lot and clamored and cried, 'Send those men out to us that we may know them' (Gen. 19:5). They wanted to commit homosexuality with two angels who came from Heaven. That is where we get the word "sodomy." Do you know what Lot said? "I have two daughters which have not known man; let me, I pray you, bring them out unto you, and do ye to them as is good in your eyes: only unto these men do nothing; for therefore came they under the shadow of my roof." Does that sound like a committed Christian? It certainly doesn't!

When God sent an angel down to get Lot out of Sodom, Lot lingered. He didn't want to leave. Finally the angel had to get him by the arm and drag him out of Sodom before the fire and brimstone rained down from Heaven. He was so worldly and uncommitted and unsurrendered that his sons-in-law laughed at him when he tried to get them to leave. They laughed at his testimony.

But keep following him; his life gets worse. Before fire and brimstone rains down from God out of Heaven, they leave Sodom and Gomorrah. He takes with him his wife and two daughters. His wife looks back and turns into a pillar of salt. Lot goes into a cave with his two daughters and gets drunk. There was no liquor store in that cave, so Lot must have brought that wine with him when he left Sodom. While he was drunk, he committed incest with both his daughters; and both gave birth to babies.

Lot is a Bible example of one never surrendered to the Lordship of Christ, one who never made a total commitment to the Saviour. But we know he was saved because the Bible says so in II Peter 2:7,8.

So you have three Bible examples of uncommitted believers: those who trusted Christ and had lapses in their yieldedness or surrender after they trusted Christ as Saviour, those who trusted Christ as Saviour but did not surrender until some time later, and Lot who never did yield his life to the Lordship of Christ.

Scriptures That Clearly Refute Lordship Salvation

Not only do Bible examples refute Lordship salvation, but clear passages of Scripture refute it also. First Corinthians 12:3 says, ". . . no man can say that Jesus is the Lord, but by the Holy

Ghost." Now keep in mind that one does not have the presence of the Holy Spirit in his life until after he is saved. Romans 8:9 says, "Now if any man have not the Spirit of Christ, he is none of his." The Bible says in Galatians 4:6, "And because ye are sons, God hath sent forth the Spirit of his Son into your hearts, crying, Abba, Father." John 3:6 says believers are "born of the Spirit." They are sealed by the Spirit (Eph. 4:30). If you can't call Jesus Lord without the Holy Ghost, and you must call Him Lord to get saved, and you are not saved without the Holy Ghost, you have a problem!

Romans is a book about salvation. Romans, chapter 3, says that everybody needs to be saved. It describes humanity. It lays man out on God's examination table and gives him a divine diagnosis. God looks at man and says, "Their throat is an open sepulchre; with their tongues they have used deceit; the poison of asps is under their lips: Whose mouth is full of cursing and bitterness: Their feet are swift to shed blood: Destruction and misery are in their ways" (Rom. 3:13-16). He describes man from the crown of his head to the soles of his feet, and says that he is a totally depraved sinner. In Romans 3:10 God says, "There is none righteous, no, not one." In verse 23 He says, "For all have sinned, and come short of the glory of God." Romans 3 teaches that everybody needs to be saved!

Romans, chapter 4, gives three ways that you cannot be saved. Verses 1 to 4 teach that one cannot be saved by works. Verses 9 to 12 teach that one cannot be saved by the observance of ordinances. Verses 13 to 25 teach that one cannot be saved by keeping the law.

Romans, chapter 5, tells you the only way to be saved. Verse 1 says, "Therefore being justified by faith, we have peace with God through our Lord Jesus Christ." Justified by what? By surrender? By commitment? By making Jesus Lord of your life? No. "Justified by FAITH."

Romans, chapter 12, is written to those who are already saved, and verse 1 says, "I beseech you therefore, *brethren*, by the mercies of God, that ye present your bodies a living sacrifice, holy, acceptable unto God, which is your reasonable service."

Notice that Paul refers to them as "brethren," meaning they were saved. There is no such thing as the universal Fatherhood of God and the universal brotherhood of man. The only people who are our Christian brothers are those who have trusted Jesus Christ as Saviour. John 1:12 says, "But as many as received him, to them gave he power to become the sons of God, even to them that believe on his name." Everyone who has trusted Jesus or received Him as Saviour has become a son of God and is therefore a brother to all others who have trusted that same Saviour.

These people to whom Paul is writing are born-again believers but not committed, surrendered believers; and Paul is pleading with them, in view of all of God's mercies, to present their bodies as living sacrifices. They are saved but Jesus is not Lord of their lives.

Some say, "But the Bible says, 'If any man will come after me, let him deny himself, and take up his cross, and follow me' (Matt. 16:24). The Bible says if you don't love the Lord with all your heart, with all your soul, with all your strength, and hate your father and mother and all that, you can't be a disciple. The Bible says if you don't forsake all you have, you can't be a disciple (Luke 14:33)."

That is all true, but remember He is saying, "You cannot be my *disciple*." He doesn't say, "You can't go to Heaven." We must not confuse the requirements for discipleship with the requirements for salvation. Every disciple is a believer, but every believer is not a disciple. A disciple is a learner, a student.

God never says to the unsaved man, "Come after Me for salvation." He says, "Come unto me, all ye that labour and are heavy laden, and I will give you rest." But after one accepts Christ as Saviour, then He says in Matthew 4:19, "Follow me, and I will make you fishers of men." We come to Him for salvation and come after Him for service.

It is one thing to trust Jesus Christ as Saviour and quite another to surrender one's life to the Lord. There is such a thing as the dedicated Christian life. And there are carnal Christians, according to I Corinthians 3, who have never yielded their lives to Christ. The yielding of one's life or making Jesus Lord of one's life is not a requirement for salvation. That is Lordship salvation and a perversion of the Gospel.

Some Arguments of Those Who Try to Prove Lordship Salvation

Those who teach Lordship salvation say, "But the Bible says, 'Believe on the *Lord* Jesus Christ, and thou shalt be saved.' " Sure it does. But it does not say, "Obey the Lord Jesus Christ, and thou shalt be saved"; it does not say, "Make Jesus Lord of your life and thou shalt be saved." It simply says, "*Believe* on the Lord Jesus Christ, and thou shalt be saved." The thing the sinner is told to do is to believe. The Lord Jesus Christ is the Person in whom he is to believe. The Bible never says, "Believe and be saved"; it is always careful to identify the object of our faith. Our faith, our trust, our dependence must be in the Lord Jesus Christ.

We cannot trust our good works, our good life, our surrender, our baptism, our ordinances or anything else. We must trust Jesus Christ and Him alone for salvation. He plainly said, "I am THE way, THE truth, and THE life: no man cometh unto the Father, but by me" (John 14:6).

Why must we confuse the most important message in the world?

Suppose I am going to jump from a burning building into a net held by four men. A mechanic is holding one corner of the net, a dentist one corner, an airplane pilot one corner, and an insurance salesman the other corner. I am going to trust them to catch me. Someone could say, "Believe on Dr. Domansky, the dentist, and thou shalt be saved," but that doesn't mean I have to let him pull all my teeth in order to get saved. It simply means that I am going to have to trust him to catch me in that net. Someone else could say, "Believe on Mr. Smith, the insurance salesman, and thou shalt be saved." But that doesn't mean I have to buy my insurance from Mr. Smith to be saved. It simply means I must trust him to hold that net for me.

When the Bible says in Acts 16:31, "Believe on the Lord Jesus Christ, and thou shalt be saved," it doesn't mean you have to make Him Lord of your life. It simply means you must trust the Lord Jesus Christ for your salvation. Verse after verse in the Bible clearly says that salvation is simply by trusting Jesus Christ. John 3:36 says, "He that believeth on the Son hath everlasting life: and he that believeth not the Son shall not see life; but the wrath of God abideth on him."

The man who is trusting anything other than Jesus Christ is

not saved. That is the plain teaching of the Bible. The man who claims he is trusting Jesus Christ—plus his ability to yield to the Lordship of Christ, is not fully trusting the Saviour; and there is no promise to those who trust Jesus Christ plus something else, no matter how good the other thing may be.

When we get to Heaven, we are going to sing: "*Thou* art worthy to take the book, and to open the seals thereof: for thou wast slain, and hast redeemed us to God by thy blood out of every kindred, and tongue, and people, and nation" (Rev. 5:9). We are not going to sing, "*We* are worthy for we have committed and surrendered to the Lordship of Christ." Now when you teach salvation by grace through faith, that one is saved simply by trusting Jesus Christ, some call that "easy believism." But you will not find that expression in the Bible. That is a manmade expression.

It is not easy to get one to trust Jesus Christ, Him alone, and nothing else for salvation. As a matter of fact, that may be the hardest thing in the world to do.

You are called upon to believe in Someone whom your eyes have never seen. You are called upon to believe in Someone, and you have never met an eyewitness who ever saw Him. You are called upon to believe on Someone whom the so-called scholarship of the day denies. You are called upon to believe in Someone who died on the cross two thousand years ago. You are called upon to believe in Someone of whom the only record you have of Him has been kept by His friends. You are called upon not only to believe in His existence, but to believe that by depending on Him you can be justified on the basis that He was made guilty for your sins.

Now that is not easy! It is hard enough to trust someone we see and know, someone we have shaken hands with and talked to. But to trust in Someone whom we have not seen is difficult. The fact that most religions teach works, ordinances, sacraments, baptism or something else for salvation shows how difficult it is to get a person to simply trust Jesus Christ as Saviour. Salvation by grace is "believism" all right, but it is certainly not "easy believism."

Now don't misunderstand me. I am not saying that you simply admit there is a Christ and thou shalt be saved; I am saying what the Bible says, "Believe on the Lord Jesus Christ, and thou shalt be saved."

The Bible word "believe" means to depend upon, to rely upon, to trust in. Some argue against this on the basis of James 2:19, ". . . the devils also believe, and tremble." But the devils do not trust Jesus Christ as Saviour; they simply admit His existence.

It is one thing to believe an airplane will fly; it is quite another to trust your physical life to the pilot and plane to take you across the nation. To be saved, one must trust Jesus Christ completely for salvation.

No Christian in the world can say that when he was saved he totally committed himself to Christ and has since then been absolutely surrendered. Not even those who teach Lordship salvation will say that. They will say, "Jesus has been my Lord, but many times I have disobeyed Him." Then when you disobeyed Him, He wasn't Lord of your life.

Those who teach Lordship salvation say, "He's always Lord." "Lord" comes from the Hebrew word *Adonai,* meaning "Master." It also comes from the word *Jehovah,* the personal name of God. There are several translations of the word. In that sense, He is everybody's Lord. He is the tadpole's Lord, the bumblebee's Lord, the bullfrog's Lord, the rattlesnake's Lord—but that doesn't mean they are saved. He is Master of the whole universe. He can do what He wants to do, when He wants to do it!

Philippians 2:10,11, declares, "That at the name of Jesus every knee should bow, of things in heaven, and things in earth, and things under the earth; And that every tongue should confess that Jesus Christ is Lord, to the glory of God the Father." Does that mean that everyone will be saved, since the day will come when every knee will bow and every tongue will confess that Jesus is Lord? Of course not. When we talk about Jesus being Lord of one's life, we mean yielding to Him for the control of the life.

Jesus is Lord over many things about every individual—the color of my eyes, my height, my parents, etc. The Lord determined what color my eyes would be. The Lord determined who my parents would be. He was the Boss; He was the Master. The Lord determined my height. He determined the size of my ears, nose, the texture of my skin.

But one important area of my life where He gives me control is my will. God made us free moral agents. We are creatures of choice. He wants to be Lord of our wills, but He doesn't want to force us. He wants us to yield to Him because we want to do so.

He was a willing Saviour, and He will have only willing servants. We trust Him for salvation, and we yield to Him for service.

The Teaching of Lordship Salvation Confuses Believers

I have often heard those who teach Lordship salvation brag that three or four preachers got saved in their service. Some have said, "The youth pastor and three deacons got saved!"

Now I am for people trusting Christ as Saviour who have not already done so, but I am against any teaching that confuses believers.

We heard of a youth director who was supposedly saved after hearing a sermon on Lordship salvation. Then many of the young people who trusted Christ under the youth director's ministry, deciding they must not be saved, went forward and, in the words of the evangelist, were "really saved."

There is no difference between being saved and "really saved." There is no such thing as degrees in salvation. No one is more saved than the other. The Bible says in John 3:36, "He that believeth on the Son hath everlasting life: and he that believeth not the Son shall not see life; but the wrath of God abideth on him." Nothing can be plainer: those who are trusting Jesus Christ are saved, and they have everlasting life. And those who are not trusting Him are not saved, but the wrath of God abideth on them.

Saying one is "really saved" is like going to a funeral home, pointing to a casket and saying, "The person in that casket is dead," then pointing to another casket and saying, "The one in that casket is really dead!" There is no such thing as being dead, deader, and deadest.

One is either dead or alive, saved or lost, guilty or justified, believing or not believing. There is no in between. Why do good Christians supposedly get "really saved" under the preaching of Lordship salvation? Because they believe the preacher. If I believed that one must make Jesus Lord of his life in order to be saved, then I would go forward every time I heard a sermon on the subject and get saved because there have been times when I have been a disobedient child, times when I have yielded to my old carnal nature.

The problem is, those who go forward and supposedly really get saved will have the same problem again later because they are not going to live a perfect life. There will be times when they will yield to the flesh; then when they hear a preacher say, "Unless you make Jesus Lord of your life, you are not saved," they will look back and see that Jesus has not been Lord of their lives and reason that if the preacher is correct, then they must not have been saved. So they will go forward again to trust Christ as Saviour, and make Him Lord of their lives so they can really be saved.

Lordship salvation confuses believers and makes them doubt their salvation. The Bible is very plain: the only way to be saved is by trusting Jesus Christ. In John 3:18 Jesus divides the whole world into two groups: "He that believeth on him is not condemned: but he that believeth not is condemned already, because he hath not believed in the name of the only begotten Son of God." The condemned criminal is the one who has been arrested, tried, found guilty, and sentenced. The Bible says the man who is trusting Jesus Christ is not under the sentence; he is not condemned. And he who is not trusting Jesus Christ is condemned. Why? Because he has "not believed in the name of the only begotten Son of God." He is not trusting Jesus Christ fully for salvation.

Decide Now!

If you are trusting anything other than Jesus Christ, we urge you to trust Jesus Christ today for salvation. If you will trust Him and write to tell me so, I have some free literature to send you that will help as you set out to live the Christian life. All you need do to receive your free literature is write

Dr. Curtis Hutson
Sword of the Lord Foundation
P. O. Box 1099
Murfreesboro, Tennessee 37133

and say, "I have read your sermon, 'Lordship Salvation, a Perversion of the Gospel.' I know that I'm a sinner and believe that Jesus Christ died to save me. Here and now I fully trust Him and Him alone for my salvation. Please send me the free literature that will help me as I set out to live the Christian life."

Chapter 27

Repentance: What Does the Bible Teach?

There is no doubt that all men from Adam on have had to repent in order to have a right relationship with God. The importance of repentance is demonstrated by the fact that men of every biblical age preached it.

John the Baptist preached it in Mark 1:15 when he said, "Repent ye, and believe the gospel."

Paul preached it in Acts 20:21, "Testifying both to the Jews, and also to the Greeks, repentance toward God, and faith toward our Lord Jesus Christ."

The Apostle John proclaimed its necessity in Revelation 2:5 when he exhorted the church at Ephesus, "Repent, and do the first works; or else I will come unto thee quickly, and will remove thy candlestick out of his place, except thou repent."

And the Lord Jesus Christ Himself emphasized its importance when He said in Luke 13:3, "Except ye repent, ye shall all likewise perish."

The problem is not preaching repentance; it is giving a wrong definition to the word. Down through the centuries "repent" has come to mean a far different thing than when it was spoken by John the Baptist, the Apostle Paul, the Apostle John, and Jesus Christ Himself. If you look up "repent" or "repentance" in a modern dictionary, you will find such definitions as "to feel sorry or self-reproachful," "to be conscience-stricken," "to turn from sin."

Using these definitions, some have preached reformation instead of repentance. If you look up the Greek word translated "repent" in the King James Bible and used by Jesus, Paul, John and others in the New Testament, you will find that the word *metanoeo* means to think differently or afterwards, that is, to change the mind.

In this message on repentance, I want to discuss three things. First, faulty ideas about repentance; second, facts about repentance; and finally, faith and repentance.

First, let's look at some

I. FAULTY IDEAS ABOUT REPENTANCE

We suppose there are many faulty ideas about repentance, but we will deal here with the more popular ones. Perhaps the most popular false idea is that repentance is turning from sin.

We have heard some well-known preachers say, "If you want to be saved, repent of your sins, turn from your sins." If turning from your sins means to stop sinning, then people can only be saved if they stop sinning. And it is unlikely that anyone has ever been saved, since we don't know anyone who has ever stopped sinning.

I recently asked a large congregation if there was anyone present who had not sinned in the last week to raise his hand, and not a single hand was lifted. I don't know of anyone who lives a single day without sinning. Now to be sure, you may not commit murder, adultery, or you may not rob a bank, but you sin nonetheless. Romans 14:23 says, "For whatsoever is not of faith is sin." That simply means that if we do anything without a conviction of God's approval, then it is sinful. And I suppose everyone is guilty of this every day of his life.

James 4:17 says, "Therefore to him that knoweth to do good, and doeth it not, to him it is sin."

When I was a small boy, I recall hearing an old preacher pray, "Lord, forgive us of the sins of omission as well as the sins of commission." There is such a thing as a sin of omission. The Bible says to leave undone something we know is good is a sin. And who hasn't sinned in this respect?

The book of I John is written to believers. And I John 1:10 says,

"If we say that we have not sinned, we make him a liar, and his word is not in us." The pronoun "we" in this verse refers to Christians, believers. For any believer to claim that he has not sinned is to make God a liar.

Several years ago I read a book by a professor at a fundamental university. Under the chapter on salvation, he said, "Quit your sinning, and God will give you a new heart." He presented repentance as turning from sin. I wrote this dear brother and expressed my concern, knowing that such teaching frustrates the unbeliever and makes him think that salvation is unattainable since he cannot live a sinless life. This professor wrote back that he had repented, that he had turned from his sins. When I wrote to ask if he had sinned after he was saved, he had to honestly answer the question and admit that he had. I explained that if he had sinned after he was saved, then he had not turned from his sins; he had only turned from part of them, that is, the ones he had not committed since he had been saved. He then agreed to change the statement in his book.

If repentance means turning from sin, and turning from sin means to stop sinning, then a person must live a sinless life in order to be saved. And if that is the case, then nobody could ever be saved, because there are no perfect people.

You don't get better to get saved; you get saved to get better. You can't get better until you do get saved. In reality, one can begin living better only after he is saved. When the individual trusts Christ as Saviour, he receives a new nature. Second Peter 1:4 says, "Whereby are given unto us exceeding great and precious promises: that by these ye might be partakers of the divine nature." With this new nature come new desires and new power to make the desires a reality.

We read in Philippians 2:13, "For it is God which worketh in you both to will and to do of his good pleasure." It is the presence of God in the believer that gives him both the desire and power to live a better life. And no man has the indwelling Christ in the person of the Holy Spirit until after he is saved.

The Christian life is not an imitation of the Christ life; it is Christ living His life over again in us as we yield ourselves to Him. That is what Paul meant in Galatians 2:20: "I am crucified with Christ; nevertheless I live; yet not I, but Christ liveth in me:

and the life which I now live in the flesh I live by the faith of the Son of God, who loved me, and gave himself for me."

Several years ago, after I finished preaching a Sunday morning service, several people trusted Christ as Saviour, including a lady and her five children. I noticed a man sitting on the same pew who did not respond. After the service, I spoke to him, while many of the members of the church were shaking hands with the lady, her children, and others who had trusted Christ that morning.

"Sir," I said, "is this your wife and children?"

"Yes," he replied.

I said, "Isn't it wonderful that they have trusted Christ as Saviour!"

"Yes," he replied.

Then I asked, "Have you trusted Christ as your Saviour?"

He dropped his head and said, "I'm afraid I haven't."

"May I ask why you haven't trusted Christ as Saviour?"

"Well," he said, "to be honest with you, I'm afraid I can't live it."

I suspected that this man had an idea that in order to be saved, he must promise God that he would never sin again, or he thought that repenting was turning from sin. So I pressed the issue. "What do you mean, you can't live it?"

"Well," he said, "I know that I will probably sin again."

I said, "Sir, if getting saved is promising Jesus you will never sin again, then I would never get saved, because I know I cannot live a sinless life." I explained that to be saved one simply had to trust Jesus as Saviour. I opened the Bible to John 3:36 and read, "He that believeth on the Son hath everlasting life." Then pointing to the verse, I asked, "Does the verse say, 'He that believeth on the Son and lives it has everlasting life'?"

"Oh, no," he replied.

"Then what does the verse say?"

"He that believeth on the Son hath everlasting life."

"Then must one believe on the Son and live it in order to be saved? Or must one simply believe on the Son, as the Bible says, to have everlasting life?"

"Well," he said, "I suppose that one must do what the Bible says—believe on the Son."

"Then will you trust Jesus Christ right now as your Saviour?"

With a smile on his face, he answered, "I certainly will."

In a moment he joined his wife and children as the church members came by and shook hands, rejoicing with them in their decision to trust Christ as Saviour.

A few weeks later I received a call from a pastor a few miles out of Atlanta, Georgia. He said that a man, his wife, and five children had joined the church for baptism and told him that they were saved at Forrest Hills Baptist Church in Decatur, Georgia. "Dr. Hutson," he said, "I thought you would like to know about it."

Of course I was happy to hear they had united with the church near where they lived. That family went on to become faithful workers in the church. They even bought their own bus and began a bus ministry, bringing scores of children and adults in to hear the Gospel.

I think there are many who would like to be saved but have been presented the faulty idea that repentance is turning from sin and therefore they are convinced that they cannot be saved. Oh, if we would only make salvation plain and explain to men that we are not saved by doing anything; rather we are saved by trusting in what Jesus has already done. He died two thousand years ago for our sins. He fully paid the sin debt, and the Bible says, "that whosoever believeth in him should not perish, but have everlasting life" (John 3:16).

Now don't misunderstand me. We do not want to treat sin lightly, but then, we must not demand of an unbeliever that which is impossible for him to perform, and we must not make unbelievers feel that salvation is a hopeless, unattainable thing.

A second faulty idea is that repentance is sorrow for sin. The Bible says in II Corinthians 7:10, "For godly sorrow worketh repentance to salvation not to be repented of. . . ." Though godly sorrow may bring about repentance, it is not the same as repentance.

I'm afraid we have been guilty of building Bible doctrines off our experience rather than the Bible. We must remember that the Bible is the principle, not man's experience.

We have heard well-meaning preachers tell of their experience of salvation and describe their weeping and sorrow and how miserable and low-down they felt before they were saved. In doing so, they suggest to the unbeliever that he must feel a certain amount of sorrow before he can be saved. If that is the case, then how much sorrow must a man feel and exactly how much must he weep and moan before God will save him? This kind of teaching suggests to us the false idea that God is basically unwilling to save sinners, and unless one softens the heart of God by his tears, then God will never accept him and grant forgiveness for sin.

The truth is, God is more willing and ready to save than we unbelievers are to simply trust Him to do it. As a matter of fact, God has done and is doing all He can to save men. Two thousand years ago He placed all our sins on His Son Jesus Christ and then punished Jesus in our place to pay the sin debt we owe so that when we die, we won't have to pay it. That is exactly what the Bible means in John 3:16, "For God so loved the world, that he gave his only begotten Son, that whosoever believeth in him should not perish, but have everlasting life." In the matter of salvation, no amount of weeping or sorrow will coax God into doing something that He has not already done.

Remember, when Jesus was on the cross, He cried, "It is finished"! (John 19:30), which means that the price for our salvation was paid in full. Nothing can be added to it and nothing can be taken from it. We don't need to weep, beg, or plead for God to do something He has already done. What we do is accept Him, trust Him.

The problem is not that God is adamant and unapproachable but that man will not respond.

The great evangelist D. L. Moody insisted that the inquirer was not to seek sorrow but the Saviour. The death of Jesus Christ on the cross and His shed blood is sufficient for the forgiveness of sins. Ephesians 1:7 says, "In whom we have redemption through his blood, the forgiveness of sins, according to the riches of his grace."

Notice that forgiveness of sins is through His blood. It is not the death of Christ—plus sorrow; the death of Christ—plus tears; the death of Christ—plus mourning; or even the death of Christ—plus pleading. No, no, no! It is the death of Christ—period. The Word of God makes it clear that salvation is based entirely upon the death of Christ and the believer's faith or trust in Him. Acts 16:31 plainly says, "Believe on the Lord Jesus Christ, and thou shalt be saved." Believe. Not believe and weep, not believe and pray, not believe and mourn, not believe and feel sorrow for your sins, but believe, only believe.

I am glad when I see someone troubled over his sins, but we must be very careful in presenting the plan of salvation not to insist that a person have a certain degree of sorrow before he can be saved. That is not repentance, and such a requirement for salvation is not found in the Bible.

A third faulty idea about repentance is that it is reformation. Nearly all the religions of the world teach the idea that man must *do* something or *be* something in order to be saved. Some say you must join a particular church. If you don't belong to their particular group, then you cannot be saved. Others teach you must be baptized in water, that the water actually washes away sin. Others teach you must be baptized in a certain way and by a certain preacher. Still others teach you must behave in a certain manner. They will often say, "If you don't straighten up, you are going to Hell!" Others teach that you must make certain resolutions or promises in order to be saved, and if you don't live up to those resolutions, then you are lost. If we could only understand the clear plan of salvation, it would surely help to clear up a lot of confusion.

Salvation is a gift and there is nothing we can do or be in order to earn it. All you can do with a gift is receive it. John 1:12 says, "But as many as received him, to them gave he power to become the sons of God, even to them that believe on his name."

My beloved predecessor, Dr. John R. Rice, used to say, "If you go to Hell, you pay your own way; but you go to Heaven on a free pass." He was certainly right. Romans 6:23 says, "The wages of sin is death; but the gift of God is eternal life through Jesus Christ our Lord." Salvation is a gift.

Reformation is good in its place, but when you make reformation repentance and a prerequisite for salvation, then it is wicked and evil. Salvation is of God, not of man. John 1:13 says, "Which were born, not of blood, nor of the will of the flesh, nor of the will of man, but of God." The expression, "not of blood," simply means that salvation is not inherited through the bloodline. No one is saved because his mother or father is a Christian. ". . . nor of the will of the flesh" means that there is nothing the flesh can do to earn salvation, including reformation. ". . . nor of the will of man" means there is nothing man can do to save himself. ". . . but of God" means that nothing of man enters into salvation.

If that be true, then man's behavior—good or bad—has nothing to do with obtaining salvation. Titus 3:5 says, "Not by works of righteousness which we have done, but according to his mercy he saved us. . . ." Ephesians 2:8, 9 tells us, "For by grace are ye saved through faith; and that not of yourselves: it is the gift of God: Not of works, lest any man should boast." It is impossible to mix grace and works. Salvation is either by grace or works; it cannot be a combination of the two.

Notice the words of Romans 11:6, "And if by grace, then is it no more of works: otherwise grace is no more grace. But if it be of works, then is it no more grace: otherwise work is no more work."

Reformation as an instrument of salvation is absolutely futile, and repentance is not reformation. Reformation is an effort on the part of the individual to establish his own righteousness, and the Bible clearly teaches that we are not saved by our own righteousness but by the imputed righteousness of God. Look at Romans 10:1-4:

"Brethren, my heart's desire and prayer to God for Israel is, that they might be saved. For I bear them record that they have a zeal of God, but not according to knowledge. For they being ignorant of God's righteousness, and going about to establish their own righteousness, have not submitted themselves unto the righteousness of God. For Christ is the end of the law for righteousness to every one that believeth."

If we could reform and establish our own righteousness, that would not be sufficient. Says Isaiah 64:6 regarding our righteousnesses, "All our righteousnesses are as filthy rags. . . ." The best we can do is like filthy rags in the sight of a holy God. The only righteousness God accepts is His own, which is imputed to us the moment we trust Christ as Saviour.

What a blessed promise is Romans 4:5, "But to him that worketh not, but believeth on him that justifieth the ungodly, his faith is counted for righteousness."

My hope is built on nothing less
Than Jesus' blood and righteousness;

I dare not trust the sweetest frame,
But wholly lean on Jesus' name.

Repentance is not reformation.

No one will ever go to Hell who has put his trust in Jesus Christ, but many will end up in torment who have trusted their own righteousness and reformation. Matthew 7:22, 23 says:

"Many will say to me in that day, Lord, Lord, have we not prophesied in thy name? and in thy name have cast out devils? and in thy name done many wonderful works? And then will I profess unto them, I never knew you: depart from me, ye that work iniquity."

The people referred to in these verses are those who are trusting their own works, their own righteousness, for salvation, when they ought to be trusting Jesus Christ completely.

A fourth faulty idea about repentance is that it is penance. Dr. Harry Ironside said:

> "Penance is not repentance. Penance is the effort in some way to atone for wrong done. This man can never do, nor does God, in His Word, lay it down as a condition for salvation that one first seek to make up to either God or his fellows for evil committed. . . . On the contrary, the call was to repent, but between repentance and doing penance there is a vast difference."

Penance is a sacrament of the Roman Catholic Church involving the confession of sin and submission to penalties imposed, followed by absolution by the priest.

There is a penalty for sin, but God has only one such penalty and that is death. Ezekiel 18:4 reads, "The soul that sinneth, it shall die." Romans 6:23 says, "The wages of sin is death." And James 1:15 tells us, "Sin, when it is finished, bringeth forth death."

God's penalty for sin is death, and this death is described in the Bible as the second death, the lake of fire–Revelation 20:14: "Death and hell were cast into the lake of fire. This is the second death." No amount of penance will pay for our sins.

The Bible teaches that Jesus Christ paid for our sins two thousand years ago. First Peter 3:18 says, "For Christ also hath once suffered for sins, the just for the unjust, that he might bring us to God. . . ." The word "once" here does not mean once upon a time but once for all. The payment for sin was made once for all two thousand years ago when Jesus died on the cross for our sins. The Bible states in I Peter 2:24, "Who his own self bare our sins in his own body on the tree. . . ." God imposed the penalty for our sins before Adam and Eve committed the first sin in the garden. In Genesis 2:17 He said, ". . . in the day that thou eatest thereof thou shalt surely die." And the penalty imposed by God before the fall was paid in full by Jesus Christ on the cross two thousand years ago. All that's left for us to do is accept what Jesus has done and trust Him completely for salvation.

Oh, why must we complicate the matter and confuse unbelievers as to how to be saved! "What must I do to be saved?" asked the Philippian jailor in Acts 16:30, and Paul replied in verse 31, "Believe on the Lord Jesus Christ, and thou shalt be saved."

Repentance is not penance.

II. FACTS ABOUT REPENTANCE

There is a vast difference between what men think the Bible says about repentance and what the Bible actually says. Here are a few facts about "repent" as it is found in its various forms in both the Old and New Testaments.

The word "repent" is found forty-five times in the King James Bible; "repentance," twenty-six times; "repented," thirty-two times; "repentest," one time; "repenteth," five times; "repenting," one time; and "repentings," one time—a total of 111 times in both the Old and New Testaments. The word in its various forms is found forty-six times in the Old Testament and sixty-five in the New. Of the forty-six times the word appears in the Old Testament, twenty-eight times God does the repenting, not man.

For instance, in Exodus 32:14 the Bible says, "And the Lord repented of the evil which he thought to do unto his people."

In addition to the twenty-eight times that God repents in the Old Testament, there are nine other passages that tell of things about which God does not or did not repent. Of the forty-six times a form of the word "repentance" appears in the Old Testament, only nine times is man doing the repenting. Thirty-seven times it has reference to God's repenting or telling us of things about which God did not or will not repent.

Now, if "repent" means to turn from sin, we have a problem. We have God turning from sin, and that is certainly inconsistent with Bible teaching. God is sinless and has no sin to turn from. But if "repentance" means a change of mind, then it is consistent. You have God changing His mind about some things, but you have at least nine things in the Old Testament about which God says He will not change His mind.

Now that makes sense. There are many things about which I would change my mind, but there are some things about which I will not change my mind. For instance, I will not "repent" or change my mind about the fact that the Bible is the Word of God. I will not "repent" or change my mind about the fact that Jesus is the virgin-born Son of God. I will not change my mind about the fact that salvation is by grace through faith. And there are other important matters about which I will not "repent" or change my mind.

On the other hand, there are some things about which I would "repent" or change my mind. I may plan a certain activity next week, but before the time arrives, I may change my mind and decide to do something else. As a matter of fact, my wife says I change my mind often; and she is probably right. I have said that I have a clean mind; I change it often. But there are some things about which I will not change my mind.

Now if I can change my mind about some things and not about others, then God can certainly do the same.

Sometimes in the Old Testament the word carries with it the idea of feeling sorry or regretful. Sometimes where the word is used, one is said to repent from what is wrong toward what is right. Other times it speaks of repenting from what is right toward that which is wrong. It is sometimes used in connection with sin, but the Word itself does not mean turning from sin; it means a change of mind. Another time "repentance" in the Old Testament is related to one's going back on his word. Numbers 23:19 says, "God is not a man, that he should lie; neither the son of man, that he should repent: hath he said, and shall he not do it? or hath he spoken, and shall he not make it good?"

We mentioned earlier that "repentance" in its various forms is found sixty-five times in the New Testament. Fifty-eight of those times it is translated from the Greek words *metanoia* and *metanoeo.* According to a Greek dictionary of New Testament words, *metanoia* is the noun of *metanoeo,* and both words mean identically the same thing. The basic definition of the two words is "to change one's mind." The definition from the *Strong's Concordance* of *metanoeo* is, "to think differently, or afterwards, that is, reconsider."

It is these two Greek words that are always used to relate to salvation. No other Greek word translated "repent" or "repentance" is used in relation to salvation. The problem and confusion is not preaching repentance but attaching the wrong definition to the word. For instance, to say that repentance means to turn from sin, or to say that repentance is a change of mind that leads to a change of action, is to give a wrong definition to the word. And to teach that man must turn from his sins to be saved, or change his actions to be saved, is in contradiction to the clear teaching of the Word of God that one is saved by grace through faith.

Though we often hear the expression, "Repent of your sins," it is not found in the Bible. What the repentance or change of mind is about is always determined by the context.

For instance, in Acts 17:30 we read, "And the times of this ignorance God winked at [overlooked]; but now commandeth all men every where to repent." What they were to repent or change their mind about is clear from verse 29. Here the Scripture says, ". . . we ought not to think that the Godhead is like unto gold or silver, or stone, graven by art and man's device." They needed to change their mind about God and see that He is not a graven image made of gold, silver, or stone but that He is a living God and is going to be their Judge. Verse 31, "Because he hath appointed a day, in the which he will judge the world in righteousness by that man whom he hath ordained; whereof he hath given assurance unto all men, in that he hath raised him from the dead."

In Luke 13:5 Jesus said, "I tell you, Nay: but, except ye repent, ye shall all likewise perish." The context of this verse shows that they needed to repent or change their mind regarding punishment and sin. In this passage, Christ was talking to good people who believed that people suffered only because of their sins, and they concluded that those in Galilee whose blood Pilate mingled with sacrifices and those on whom the tower of Siloam fell were greater sinners because they died such horrible deaths. Jesus contradicts the thinking of these self-righteous people and tells them that they need to repent or change their mind and see themselves as sinners, too, or they will perish in their own self-righteousness.

One does not have to know the Greek language to see that "repent" in this passage does not mean feeling sorry for or turning from sin.

Finally, let me say a word about

III. FAITH AND REPENTANCE

Not long ago I preached a simple sermon on salvation and invited sinners to trust Christ as Saviour. Over one hundred precious people trusted Christ in that particular Sunday morning service.

After the service, a well-meaning Christian said to me, "I enjoyed your sermon, but you didn't say anything about repentance. You should have told those people they needed to repent." He seemed to think that my telling those people to trust Christ as Saviour was not sufficient.

And he is not alone in his thinking. Unless you use the word "repent" in presenting the plan of salvation, some preachers foolishly accuse you of preaching "easy believism." Somehow they have gotten the idea that just to preach, "Believe on the Lord Jesus Christ, and thou shalt be saved," is not sufficient.

In an article in THE SWORD OF THE LORD, Dr. John R. Rice said:

> Sometimes the preacher himself does not fully understand the plan of salvation. He thinks of salvation as a process. First, there is a period of conviction, then a period of repentance, then an act of faith.

He went on to explain that when one trusts Christ as Saviour he also repents.

Dr. Rice is absolutely right. Faith and repentance are the same; they are not two separate decisions. One cannot trust Christ as Saviour without repenting or changing his mind. The very fact that he trusts Christ for salvation shows that he has changed his mind regarding sin, salvation, and God.

If one book of the Bible had to be considered "the salvation book," it would have to be the Gospel of John. The Gospel of John is printed and distributed more than any other book of the Bible. The purpose of this book is given in John 20:31, "But these are written, that ye might believe that Jesus is the Christ, the Son of God; and that believing ye might have life through his name."

According to this verse, the whole purpose of the Gospel of John is that men might believe that Jesus is the Christ and believing they might have life through His name. In other words, it is written that men might be saved. Yet "repent" or "repentance" is not used one single time in the Gospel of John. On the other hand, "believe" is used more than ninety times in the twenty-one chapters.

The book of Romans was written to show how men are justified. After explaining in Romans, chapter 4, how men are not justified, Romans 5:1 states, "Therefore being justified by faith, we have peace with God through our Lord Jesus Christ." "Repentance" is found only two times in the book of Romans and in only one case does it have reference to salvation.

Romans 11:29 says, "For the gifts and calling of God are without repentance." If you make "repentance" here mean turning from sin, it would cause the verse to read, "For the gifts and calling of God are without turning from sin," which doesn't make sense at all. The verse means that the gifts and callings of God are irrevocable, that when God calls a man to preach, He never changes His mind about it.

While "repentance" is found only twice in the book of Romans, "faith" is found thirty-nine times. Romans 3:28 states, ". . . a man is justified by faith without the deeds of the law." And Romans 5:1 says, "Therefore being justified by faith, we have peace with God. . . ."

Since the word "repent" is not found at all in the Gospel of John, and "repentance" is found only twice in the book of Romans, and only one time is it used in connection with salvation, are we then to conclude that repentance is not necessary to salvation? Absolutely not! We have already shown the importance of repentance and its necessity. Now, since repentance is not found in connection with salvation in the Gospel of John and only once in the book of Romans, are we to conclude that neither of these two books tells one how to be saved or justified? Certainly not.

Those who know the Bible best would have to agree that these two books of the Bible contain the clearest presentation of the Gospel and how one is to be saved.

Since repentance is necessary to salvation, and since the word is not used at all in the Gospel of John and only once as referring to salvation in the book of Romans, then we must conclude that the word "repentance" is included in the words "believe" and "faith" which are found repeatedly in these two books.

John, chapter 3, contains the heart of the Gospel. It is here we find that wonderful verse, "For God so loved the world, that he gave his only begotten Son, that whosoever believeth in him should not perish, but have everlasting life." That verse is used in the conversation between Jesus and Nicodemus in this chapter. Jesus says to Nicodemus, "Ye must be born again" (vs. 7). In verse 9, Nicodemus asks, "How can these things be?" And Jesus gave the answer in verses 14 through 16, "As Moses lifted up the serpent in the wilderness, even so must the Son of man be lifted up: That whosoever believeth in him should not perish, but have eternal life. For God so loved the world, that he gave his only begotten Son, that whosoever believeth in him should not perish, but have everlasting life."

Nowhere in this chapter does Jesus use the word "repent." He only tells Nicodemus to believe in Him. In verse 18 He said, "He that believeth on him is not condemned: but he that believeth not is condemned already, because he hath not believed in the name of the only begotten Son of God." And He closes the conversation in verse 36 by saying, "He that believeth on the Son hath everlasting life; and he that believeth not the Son shall not see life; but the wrath of God abideth on him."

"Believe" in these verses means to trust, to depend on, to rely on. Nothing could be plainer. All one has to do to have everlasting life is trust Jesus Christ. Jesus has already died for the sinner, and all we need do is depend on Him for salvation. But He warns in verse 36, "He that believeth not the Son [does not depend on the Son] shall not see life; but the wrath of God abideth on him."

There is no promise in the Bible to those who partially believe on Christ. The promise is to those who believe on Him. We cannot trust Jesus Christ 90% and something else 10%; we must fully trust Him, Him alone and nothing else, for salvation.

Since Jesus did not use the word "repent" in telling Nicodemus how to be born again, then we must reach one of three conclusions. First, repentance is not necessary to salvation; second, repentance is necessary for salvation and Jesus didn't tell Nicodemus how to be saved; third, repentance is necessary to salvation and is included in the word "believe" which Jesus did use time and time again in this chapter. The correct conclusion, of course, is that repentance is necessary to salvation and is included in "believe." A man cannot trust Christ without repenting.

If you have never trusted Christ as your Saviour, we urge you to do so today. If you will trust Him and write to tell me so, I have some free literature I want to send that will help you as you set out to live the Christian life. All you need do to receive your free literature is write to me at this address:

Dr. Curtis Hutson
Sword of the Lord Foundation
P. O. Box 1099
Murfreesboro, Tennessee 37133

In your letter say, "I have read your sermon, 'Repentance.' Realizing that I am a sinner and believing that Jesus Christ died for me, I do trust Him as my Saviour. I am fully depending on Him to take me to Heaven when I die. Please send me the free literature that will help me as I set out to live the Christian life."

Be sure to send your name and address.

What Great Preachers Say About This Book:

From the very day that this book of sermons was placed in my hands I have had a burning desire in my heart that it could be placed in the hands of every preacher in the world. Sometimes when I have finished my message, I have asked myself the question, "Did I make it clear?" That question need never be asked about these twenty-seven great gospel sermons. I would pray that thousands of unsaved people would read this book because surely they would have the clearest presentation of the Gospel that they have ever confronted. However, my special burden concerning *Salvation Crystal Clear* is that preachers have this book. Many of God's dear men who believe the Bible and believe the Gospel could receive more help from this book in preaching so as to get people saved.

Salvation Crystal Clear is a delight to my soul. I have often said that Dr. Curtis Hutson could give the clearest and most effective invitations of any man I have ever heard. It may be because he has the ability to make the Gospel so clear in his preaching. The book of sermons is truly a masterpiece.

May I suggest that you:

1. Get a copy for yourself. It will help you to be a more effective soul winner.
2. Get a copy for your pastor. He will be helped and blessed and will thank you.
3. Send a copy to a missionary. They will be greatly helped in getting people saved on the mission field.
4. Send a copy to an unsaved friend or loved one. It could really be the means of their getting saved.
5. Send a copy to a Bible school student. It will help them in getting grounded in the Gospel.

Dr. Tom Malone, Sr.
Pastor Emeritus, Emmanuel Baptist Church
Chancellor, Midwestern Baptist College
Pontiac, Michigan

In his book, *Salvation Crystal Clear,* Dr. Curtis Hutson brings the clarity and power of his preaching to the printed page. This book contains material that would benefit any pastor and, also, be a tremendous soul-winning impetus for the layman.

As the president of a Christian college, I was immediately struck by the valuable properties that this book presented for our students in pastoral theology.

At Hyles-Anderson College, we have decided this semester to require that each of our pastoral theology majors buy this book. We are also testing them over each of these chapters in our church education course. If there is ever an area to be neglected during the brief four years that we have the average pastoral theology student, we have determined that it will *not* be the subject of salvation. We also feel that a tremendous aid to this goal is the reading of Dr. Hutson's book, *Salvation Crystal Clear.*

Dr. Wendell Evans
President, Hyles-Anderson College
Crown Point, Indiana

The greatest confusion in this hour is the confusion about "the way of salvation." In every city, there are churches proclaiming their individual doctrines on how to be saved. Some say, "salvation by works"; others say, "salvation by baptism," or "salvation by keeping the law." The Bible declares that salvation is through faith in the Lord Jesus Christ!

I want to recommend the book, *Salvation Crystal Clear,* by Dr. Curtis Hutson. Here are sermons that proclaim Christ, the only Saviour. They are sermons that have been used to win hundreds, yes, even thousands to our Lord Jesus Christ. It is my prayer that these messages might help many come to the Saviour and might encourage all of us for a renewed proclamation of the great message of the Lord Jesus Christ.

Dr. Raymond W. Barber
Pastor, Worth Baptist Church
President, Independent Baptist Fellowship International
Forth Worth, Texas

In a day when there is an emphasis in publishing on almost everything but salvation I am delighted to see the Sword leading the way in publishing such an outstanding book. I doubt that there is another full-sized book in print today comparable to *Salvation Crystal Clear.*

Dr. Shelton Smith
Pastor, Church of the Open Door
Westminster, Maryland

I have just completed the reading of *Salvation Crystal Clear,* and to describe the book in one simple word, I would say "EXCELLENT!" Surely you have set forth the subject and doctrine of salvation in plain and simple terms, and have made the way of salvation CRYSTAL CLEAR! May the Lord bless the messages in this book, and the challenge to a simple, clear-cut presentation of the Gospel to warm the hearts of many. Every fundamental preacher should read and study these messages again and again for his own benefit.

Dr. Bruce Cummons
Pastor, Massillon Baptist Temple
President, Massillon Baptist College
Massillon, Ohio